# INGMAR BERGMAN

## INTERVIEWS

CONVERSATIONS WITH FILMMAKERS SERIES
PETER BRUNETTE, GENERAL EDITOR

Courtesy of Photofest

# INGMAR
# BERGMAN
## INTERVIEWS

EDITED BY RAPHAEL SHARGEL

UNIVERSITY PRESS OF MISSISSIPPI/JACKSON

www.upress.state.ms.us

The University Press of Mississippi is a member of the Association of American University Presses.

First edition 2007
⊗
Library of Congress Cataloging-in-Publication Data
Ingmar Bergman : interviews / edited by Raphael Shargel. — 1st ed.
    p. cm.
    Includes index.
    ISBN-13: 978-1-57806-217-1 (cloth : alk. paper)
    ISBN-10: 1-57806-217-9 (cloth : alk. paper)
    ISBN-13: 978-1-57806-218-8 (pbk. : alk. paper)
    ISBN-10: 1-57806-218-7 (pbk. : alk. paper) 1. Bergman, Ingmar,
1918——Interviews. 2. Motion picture producers and directors—Sweden—
Interviews. I. Shargel, Raphael, 1965–
    PN1998.3. B47A3 2007
    791.4302'33092—dc22
    [B]

                                                              2007011140

British Library Cataloging-in-Publication Data available

# CONTENTS

## INTRODUCTION

*Eventually, he came in, bareheaded, wearing a sweater, a tall man, economically, intimidatingly lean. He . . . [seemed] by no means an easy man to deal with, in any sense, any relationship whatever, there being about him the evangelical distance of someone possessed by a vision . . . I thought how there was something in the weird, mad, Northern Protestantism which reminded me of the visions of the black preachers of my childhood.* —James Baldwin, 1960

*When one first meets Bergman, the very first glance catches quite an ordinary looking fellow, medium-sized, hair thinning on top. But then he moves and speaks—and the vitality pours forth. He is the kind of man who grabs your heavy suitcase and carries it despite your protests—and the sort whose words come to you conducted by graceful hands always in motion . . . As one who has endlessly explored the complexities of life, he makes you feel with his tone of tolerance and sensibleness that he has found for everything the simple answers.* —Richard Meryman, 1971

*At sixty-four, Bergman possesses the face of a mandarin. Though his pale gray-green eyes can quickly turn cold and suspicious, there is a childlike brightness in his features and he is capable of expressing a warm bonhomie . . . Still, there is a calculated quality to his casualness. Although he says he hates meeting people he doesn't know, he immediately throws an arm over the shoulders of a visiting stranger, and he punctuates his conversation with declarations of his sincerity and good will. One has the sense that this is learned behavior of sorts—the gestures of a lonely and self-preoccupied man who wants very much to be liked, a man who has worked with actors all his life and who is keenly aware of the masks we put on in public life.* —Michiko Kakutani, 1983

These prose snapshots were taken over a twenty-three-year period, but it is nevertheless remarkable that they should apply to the same person. In them, Ingmar Bergman, the major filmmaker who is the subject of this volume, appears alternately tall, medium-sized, and childlike. The first writer calls him imposing, the second nondescript, and the third inscrutable. Then, after closer inspection, all three revise their original impression: he becomes respectively possessed, vitally earnest, and condescending. Perhaps these observers approached him with only partial understanding, Kakutani catching calculations that Meryman overlooked, Baldwin observing a genuine fervor that was hidden from Kakutani. The extraordinary differences in these assessments indicate that it was impossible to size up Bergman in just one or even a few meetings. He did, after all, produce a magnificent series of films which differ vastly from one another even as they reflect an array of distinctive obsessions, which include the play of light upon the earth and bodies of water, the inexplicably conflicted nature of character, the quest for salvation through contact with the divine and with other people. Should we expect him, in his interviews, to emerge as anything other than a man who can wear many masks, sometimes contradicting himself even as he remains consistently thoughtful and passionate?

The conversations collected here give us the opportunity to observe Bergman the social animal. Over the course of this volume, he repeatedly states his longing to create in a communal setting; he says he gravitated toward theater and film because they were collaborative arts. Interviewing too is a collaboration of sorts. And though Bergman often cajoles and teases his interlocutors, especially when speaking in English to Americans, he rarely evades their questions. Bergman, particularly in the latter half of his life, made a career out of explaining himself and his art to the public. In the late 1980s and early '90s, he wrote two autobiographies, one detailing his personal experiences, the other concerning his professional career. *Fanny and Alexander* (1982), advertised as his farewell to the cinema, in fact inaugurates a series of films that deal with episodes in his life or in the lives of his parents, all of them also describing the trials of artistic creation. But this book, rather than allowing him to reflect in repose, discovers the craftsman in a variety of moods, some of his aesthetic and personal theories in flux, others fixed. It captures forty-five of the almost sixty years in which Bergman worked actively in cinema, documenting his opinions and preoccupations from 1957, the year after the breakaway success of *The Seventh Seal*, to 2002, as he was preparing to shoot *Saraband*.

Questioning Bergman, who even by 1957 had become something of a legend, must have been a daunting task. Interviewers unavoidably interpreted the experience of meeting him through the scrim of conclusions they had previously drawn about his work and reputation. They could hardly help being influenced by the mountain of critical writing devoted to deciphering his mysteries. Bergman's reluctance to give interviews was well known. His interlocutors—following him around the set, penciled in for an hour at his office in the Royal Dramatic Theater, making the arduous journey to his house on the far off island of Fårö—understood that they were being granted a rare privilege. Since serious students of film would be evaluating their queries and conclusions, the stakes were high. Bergman himself must have appreciated their situation. Most of his responses sound quite definitive. He appears determined to give an accurate account of his experiences and motivations. Yet at the same time, as he sizes up his interviewers, this maker of notoriously demanding movies seems surprisingly eager to give them what they are looking for. Those seeking contention get it; those hoping for a kindred spirit find one. This book is as much about Bergman's craft and thought as it is about the art of the interview itself.

It also encounters him at every stage of the creative process. Despite his reclusiveness, Bergman, once he allowed writers to enter his world, gave them extraordinary opportunities to observe him at work. Vilgot Sjöman, who was to become an important director in his own right—he is best known to American audiences for 1967's *I Am Curious (Yellow)*—was invited in 1961–62 to play master's apprentice during the entire process of creating *Winter Light*, which was to become Bergman's favorite picture. The excerpts printed here from *L136*, the remarkable diary Sjöman kept during this process, cover Bergman's planning and composition of the film's script. In 1966, Annika Holm caught Bergman in a tempest of creativity. Preparing to leave Stockholm for Fårö, where he would shoot *Hour of the Wolf*, he had just resigned his post as the director of the Royal Dramatic Theater and was still in the midst of editing *Persona*. While making *Shame* in 1968, he permitted Britt Hamdi to observe a day on the set. In 1977, James Jacobs filmed him during the making of *The Serpent's Egg* and later shot Liv Ullmann commenting on her collaboration with her director. Then, in what might be called a meta-interview, he sat with Bergman in the editing room and screened this footage, inviting him to comment both on his working methods and on Ullmann's thoughts about them. These pieces, along with Meryman's collation of comments by the director and his actors, offer some of the best insights we have into Bergman's methods and his collaboration with the members of his stock company.

Other interviews are notable for the attention given to particular aspects of Bergman's thought. John Simon and Jan Aghed, both movie critics, ask Bergman to voice his opinions about other filmmakers. Kakutani and Alan Riding attempt, as the titles of their articles suggest, a comprehensive overview of Bergman's life in film. A. Alvarez encourages Bergman to discuss Swedish society and politics. Cynthia Grenier queries him about sexuality and love. These and others press him to comment upon the themes that haunt many of his films: isolation, marriage, nightmares, and the questions Bergman tells Baldwin, in an interview that marks a striking meeting of minds, that he wished his films to free him from: "God and the Devil. Life and Death. Good and Evil . . . *Those* questions."

Because Bergman's art changed so much over the course of his long career, it should come as no surprise that he revises and reverses many of his responses. Though their commercial and critical failure would lead him strenuously to change his opinion, he registers enthusiasm for *All These Women* (1964), *The Touch* (1971) and *The Serpent's Egg* at the time of their making. While Bergman is in his grittiest period, on the set of *Shame*, Hamdi recounts a fascinating evening where the director, along with his cast and crew, screened *Smiles of a Summer Night*, the romantic farce many of them worked on thirteen years earlier. Noting the contrast between the lavish costumes and settings of that film and the minimalism he is currently embracing, Bergman cries that "excess is evil." Around this same period, he suggests to Lars-Olof Löthwall that he is wary about making films in color, that he will no longer use music, and that he will never work from a literary source. Yet just a few years later, *Cries and Whispers* (1972) won an Oscar for its breathtaking color cinematography, and *The Magic Flute* (1975) was a successful adaptation of Mozart's opera. Music, and Bach in particular, plays a huge role in his late work. *Fanny and Alexander*'s opulent production design hearkens back to the days of *Smiles of a Summer Night*.

Bergman's tendency to make decisive statements could rebound with even greater irony. As late as 1975, responding to the oft-asked question about whether he would ever work outside his country, he was still saying, "I feel extremely Swedish. I live here and couldn't live anywhere else for any length of time." Less than a year later, after being arrested for tax fraud, Bergman moved to Munich, commencing a self-imposed exile that lasted for years and continued even after the Swedish government issued him a formal apology. The interviews from the period of *The Serpent's Egg*, which he shot in Germany, find him inveighing bitterly against Sweden and the Swedish, though his anger softens after his return home and the beginning of his nostalgic phase. After 1980, Bergman is forever predicting his retirement from both interviewing and filmmaking. One of the most amusing aspects of this volume's later pieces is their authors' eagerness to believe that they are conducting the last interview about Bergman's last movie, even though Bergman, always voluble, seems persistently at work on a new film project. Though he merely wrote the screenplay to some of his later works, his choice of Bille August, Ullmann, and son Daniel Bergman as directors ensured that the films would be made under his influence. And, as *In the Presence of a Clown* (1997) and *Saraband* prove, the octogenarian Bergman retained the desire and the talent to create ambitious masterpieces on par with his best work.

Sometimes, his statements appear contradictory even when close examination proves them consistent. It is entirely possible that when Bergman tells Jan Aghed in 2002 that he finds Michelangelo Antonioni's *L'Avventura* boring and technically poor, he has not revised his opinion. In the 1970s, he praised the film to Simon and an audience at the American Film Institute, but if we study his careful words, it is clear that he lauded it not for its craftsmanship, which he found unprofessional, but for Antonioni's maverick impulse to convey original ideas, which he admired in theory.

Thus, even though some questions pop up repeatedly in this collection, Bergman's responses are telling, both when they change and when they do not. When he holds fast to an answer over time, we get closer to the bedrock issues that guide his creativity. One idea to which

Bergman often returns is his fascination with the human face. Again and again he suggests that faces reveal a character's inner life. Bergman is fond of asserting his desire to shoot a two-hour movie that consists of a single uninterrupted close-up, a Warhol-esque exercise that, as far as we know, he never seriously attempted to execute. Still, his point is well taken. Bergman's films are notable for their lingering shots of faces, which register unexpected transformations when most other directors would long before have turned the camera away. I think of the scene in *The Touch* where Bibi Andersson, abandoned by her lover, paces about his empty apartment in agony. The camera stays riveted to her face until, through her misery, she cannot stifle a yawn. This is an incredibly eloquent moment, showing, in an instant, that grief cannot transcend Andersson's bodily needs any more than this destructive affair can redeem the housewife from her ennui. Just as resonant is the little sequence in *Cries and Whispers* where Kari Sylwan, a maid kept busy in a household of demanding women, awakens in the morning to utter a simple prayer near a table where a candle is lit. As the camera lingers upon her profile, cutting between it and a photograph of the daughter whose death she mourns even as she gives thanks to God, she blows out the candle, reaches for an apple, and takes big bites. Without a hint of guilt or irony, she has followed prayer with an action as profane as having a snack, bringing the very fruit that inaugurated the first sin to her lips. These pauses, innocently carnal, convey, through the face, complexities of character in purely cinematic terms.

If the face, especially during moments of solitude, provides information in a sheerly visual manner, Bergman's interest in its features is related to the idea, expressed throughout this book, that the power of film rests upon its capacity to transcend the limitations of its script. The first piece in this volume, by Sjöman, is entitled "The Tensions of Ingmar Bergman" for Bergman often used the word "tension" when describing his work. The final creative "tension" Sjöman identifies is that between Bergman the writer and Bergman the director. At the AFI, Bergman quips that a director filming his own screenplay enters into a Jekyll-Hyde relationship with himself. "If Dr. Jekyll has written the script Mr. Hyde has to direct it and I tell you they don't like each other very well." The struggle arises because movie scenarios are written in words and films are a series of images. "When I write," he tells

Löthwall, "I must try to capture something in words which for all useful purposes, can't be expressed in words." Indeed, Bergman wishes his
films not only to supersede the verbal but also to move beyond the logical progression, the rage for clear argumentation, that written expression demands. Time and again he asserts that the meanings he wishes
to convey are not intellectual. Filmmaking, he claims, is a "technical"
and "emotional" exercise. His primary aim is to appeal to the feelings of
his viewers. He tells Aghed and others that the art form most like cinema is not theater or literature but music, which "transcends the intellect and directly touches the emotions." Allied to the analogy of music
is his comparison of films to dreams, whose logic Bergman finds
equally nonlinear and emotional. To Meryman, he claims that "all my
films are dreams," a point he reiterates at several instances to explain
visionary pictures like *Fanny and Alexander, Cries and Whispers, Persona,
Sawdust and Tinsel* (1953), and *Wild Strawberries* (1957).

A lesser artist might employ such a philosophy to defend murky,
vague work. But while Bergman says he strives to make "difficult" films,
he also attends meticulously to detail. Even allegories like *The Seventh
Seal* and *The Silence* (1963) or descents into nightmare like *Hour of the
Wolf* and *From the Life of the Marionettes* (1980) are intensely tactile,
exploring the physical reality of the worlds they summon forth. The
same is true for the pictures in which he tries to re-create his past experiences. His 1995 interview with Riding, conducted in the midst of his
autobiographical stage, finds him talking of his ability to recollect
details in a manner that recalls Victor Sjöström's character in *Wild
Strawberries*: "The doors between the old man today and the child are
still open, wide open . . . I can stroll through my grandmother's house,
and know exactly where the pictures are, the furniture was, how it
looked, the voice, the smells. I can move from my bed at night today to
my childhood in less than a second. And it has exactly the same reality." Even in his most impressionistic films, Bergman attempts to capture just such precise, palpable reality.

At the same time, he often talks about the necessary distance artists
must have from their art in order for their work to be both objective
and real. When he speaks in Aristotelian terms of *mimesis*, he puts his
emphasis not upon the reality that film captures, but upon the fact that
it is an imitation. He declares that because art is at essence an imitation

of experience and not the real thing, the artist is therefore a player of games, no matter how desolate or serious his films. "The moment you lose the sense of play, you should quit," he tells Hamdi. "If you forget that it's a game, that as a filmmaker you are *imitating reality*, then you are headed toward a terrible self-deception."

This spirit of play is just one device Bergman employs to dampen his egotism, which, he argues, after so much success, can grow out of proportion, misdirecting and corrupting the artist. Bergman hints that when famous filmmakers become so self-confident that they deny their limitations, they inevitably produce bad work. He tells Meryman that "I felt megalomania waft about my brow, but I think I'm immune. I've only to consider the utter unimportance of art in the world of men—and I come back to earth with a bump." He is very quick to admit that his films are flawed. When interviewers point out shortcomings, he almost always agrees. Even his unconditional affection for *Winter Light* functions as a form of self-criticism. The exception that proves his dissatisfaction, he calls it the one film where everything went as planned, which implies that all the others fell short of their full potential. One of the reasons he loves living on Fårö is that it teaches him necessary humility. In later interviews, he often notes that if he throws a temper tantrum in the Royal Dramatic Theater, four hundred people run around whispering about his bad mood. But if he raves on Fårö, the only result is that a bird might fly away.

Related to the impulse toward humility and self-criticism are his declarations about the benefits of anonymity. In an oft-reprinted essay on filmmaking written in the late 1950s, Bergman said he wished he were an artist in the medieval period, a member of an obscure group, building one part of a great cathedral. Sjöman, recalling the essay and wryly noting that Bergman was anything but invisible on set, states that "the dream Bergman embraces is a dream of anonymity." Later Bergman tells Simon that his remarks were misinterpreted. He does not wish to become unknown, but rather to be freed from the psychological burdens that can hamper creative expression: "What I meant originally was that anonymous creation in art . . . was very unneurotic. And that is the best kind of all, creating unneurotically; which is why the nineteenth-century romantic notion of original genius strikes me as very silly, and as having nothing to do with real creation." This reflection brings us back to his love for communal work, which accounts for his suggesting to Meryman that "I and my crew, my eighteen friends" are the authors of his films. Alvarez's Bergman extrapolates his creative method from the inclinations of his native country. The Swedish "like to plan together, to discuss, to work things out. It is the same when I make my pictures . . . This is a lovely way of working, and for me, it's a way out of neurotic loneliness."

Bergman moreover argues that his collaborative impulses extend to his audiences. Kakutani documents that he initially entered the theater out of a desire to escape his cold Lutheran upbringing and "touch" other people. Bergman uses the word both in its physical sense—he loves film and theater because he can lay hands on his fellow workers—and for its symbolism: he wishes to touch the feelings of his audience. He expresses hope that spectators will find personal meanings of their own in his films. He tells Meryman and Aghed that he wants his pictures to be "useful" to others, like "cars or tables or parts of roads." Note what these items have in common: they are mass produced, put out into the world for consumers to use for years afterwards and for their own ends.

But despite this repeated declaration, Bergman elsewhere asserts that his films have definitive meanings and that it is possible to misunderstand them. He tells the AFI audience that movies only have value when their directors make them with particular and original ideas in mind that can be communicated clearly to spectators. Elsewhere, he declares that *The Serpent's Egg* was produced to reveal how "the events swirling around us [are] a real threat, very dangerous . . . If audience members are affected by the film, it is probably because they feel subconsciously what I am trying to say about the violence that awaits us, even though right now the peril manifests itself only through periodic expressions." The purpose of *Shame* was "to show how humiliation, the rape of human dignity, can lead to the loss of humanity on the part of those subjected to it." Audiences who focused exclusively upon lesbianism and scenes of masturbation in *The Silence* "lost sight of essentials in favor of inessentials."

These statements clearly show Bergman directing his listeners' attention toward interpretations he believes are valid. He furthermore refuses to allow them to reject these analyses, even if they find their divergent conclusions "useful." He also acknowledges that the meaning of his films becomes clearer when they are viewed as a series and understood as references to his own life and artistic development. He wants viewers to see *Through a Glass Darkly* (1961), *Winter Light*, and *The Silence* as a trilogy, involving characters in quest of faith, love, and redemption who come to very different ends. He seems to think that viewers' admiration of *Persona* will increase when they learn it was written after a long illness and that their appreciation of *Cries and Whispers* will grow when they hear it originated from a single mental image of three women, dressed in white, waiting in a red room. *Wild Strawberries* was "a rundown of my earlier life, a searching final test." The cruel pastor in *Fanny and Alexander* was modeled on Bergman's own father, a Lutheran minister. Bergman claims to have arrived at the sympathetic portrait of his mother that can be found in *The Best Intentions* (1991), *Private Confessions* (1996), and *In the Presence of a Clown* after studying a pile of photographs which helped him sort out her past. Intriguingly, *Saraband* begins with Ullmann sitting before a table of old pictures, going through a similar exercise as she tries to make sense of her life. Thus, a "tension" unmentioned by the interviewers but important to this volume exists between Bergman's desire for his films to stand on their own, anonymously free, and his investment in them as exercises in self-analysis that only a connoisseur of Bergman's *oeuvre* can fully appreciate.

Indeed, there are moments in this volume where Bergman seems to turn completely away from the social commitment of filmmaking, explaining it as a form of private psychotherapy. Given that Bergman's late pictures are at least as haunted by cruelty and fear as his earlier efforts, it is hard to take his statements about the personally healing power of artistic creation without a grain of salt. Still, he asserts that making *The Seventh Seal* liberated him from his fear of God. Experiencing the terror of the period just between dark and dawn, Bergman announces to Hamdi that "I made *Hour of the Wolf* and was freed of my own hour of the wolf." Shortly before the release of *The Best Intentions*, Bergman tells Lasse Bergström that "every feeling of reproach, blame, bitterness, or even vague feeling that [my parents] have messed up my life is gone forever from my mind . . . It is a blessing. My brother died unreconciled. My sister is still raging. I am privileged." Bergman informs Simon that his duties as a filmmaker begin and end with what he owes to himself. "I feel responsible only for the craftsmanship being good, for the thing having the moral qualities of my mind, and, if possible, for my not telling any lies." On the one hand, he seems to be contradicting the notion that he wants his films to be "useful" to others. On the other, the demands he makes upon himself sound like those of the talented artisan, that proud builder of roads, tables, and cathedrals. His creations satisfy him only when they are both well crafted and uniquely expressive of the ideals he holds dear.

Bergman's thorny commitment to self and public is a helpful index to the personality that created films where human interrelationships are fraught with passion and hope as well as selfishness and bitterness. Although the interviewers in this volume do not directly confront Bergman about his love life, many in their introductions and asides delve into his parents' difficult union, his five marriages, and his public affairs with actresses, three of whom—Harriet Anders-son, Bibi Andersson, and Ullmann—were indispensable members of his stock company and continued to work with him long after their romantic break. His relationships with his cast and crew seem quite complex. Both he and Ullmann speak of his loyalty to actors. When he knows them well, he communicates with them almost silently, as if they can read one another's minds. He says similar things about his bond with Sven Nykvist, who photographed all of his films from 1960 through 1984. Yet even as he talks of their intense fellow feeling, he seems proud that he and Nykvist meet only to work on a film and never socially. Intriguingly, when interviewers eavesdrop on conversations between Bergman and his collaborators, the waters seem turbulent. Making *Shame*, Bergman and regular performers Max von Sydow and Gunner Björnstrand heartily enjoy one another's company, but their conversation, at least the part of it that Hamdi conveys, consists entirely of insults and put-downs. Meryman's depiction of Bergman's relationship with Elliot Gould, with whom he worked on *The Touch*, takes a sour turn. While filming, Bergman treated him like a comrade, calling him an actor of Shakespearean talents. After the film opened, Gould couldn't get a meeting with him. Talking about actors at other points in the book, Bergman suggests that his favorites are necessary to his survival while others are mere tools that can be discarded when they don't function properly.

A "tension" Sjöman does name that haunts the conversations in this book is that between film and theater. Throughout his career, Bergman divided his time directing for the stage and the camera. His response when asked to compare the two media is so similar from interview to interview that it feels canned. (It's a fair assumption that he had to field this question more than any other.) Bergman says he relishes rehearsing for the stage. Over a twelve-week period, the production develops organically. And if every experiment conducted during the first week is a failure, there is still plenty of time to make amends before the public sees the finished product. Theater, where performances change every night, is fluid. But while Bergman seems to embrace the pressures of stage directing, he seems tormented by those of filmmaking. He never tires of mentioning that on the movie set, cast and crew work an eight-hour day to produce three minutes of screenable film, which, unlike a scene in a stage production, cannot be altered later on. Bergman believes he is capable of growing old in the theater but not in the studio because he cannot imagine his elderly self mustering the energy to work at a laborious ant-like pace in this "abnormal process." Of course, he did go on to do just that, perhaps because he always knew that in essence, theater is an actors' and a playwrights' medium, while cinema belongs to the director. "Film is personal," he tells Holm. "Theater is objective."

Bergman's influences are another frequent topic of conversation. His films are rife with references to the playwrights whose work he often directed in the theater—Shakespeare, Molière, Ibsen, Strindberg—even though he never attempted to adapt them for the big screen. (He did direct a number of television versions of his staged dramas.) As for the inspiration he drew from other filmmakers, Bergman is eager to assert himself as part of a "Swedish film tradition." He mentions the giants of his native cinema, particularly the silent masters Sjöström and Mauritz Stiller, as well as Alf Sjöberg, whose film *Torment* (1944) was Bergman's first screenwriting credit. As for international influences, Bergman explains to Aghed by way of a story about French critical snobbery that he is not nearly as indebted to the universally beloved Jean Renoir as he is to Julien Duvivier and Michel Carnè, who seem considered by all but him to be lesser figures. The Italian neorealists influenced some of his apprentice work, but not his mature films. He makes similarly grudging claims about the technical expertise of George Cukor and Alfred Hitchcock, and holds fascinating contempt for the films of Orson Welles. But just as viewers will be hard pressed to find allusions to or borrowings from international contemporaries in his films, readers will discover scarcely a complimentary word about directors whose obsessions or techniques could be considered analogous to his and from whom one could imagine he learned a thing or two. Robert Bresson (with the exception of *Mouchette* and *Diary of a Country Priest*) and Carl Theodor Dreyer, Akira Kurosawa after *Rashomon* and Luchino Visconti after *La Terra Trema* hold small place in his cosmology. He pays compliments to his Swedish contemporaries but says nothing very specific about their movies. He holds affection for François Truffaut and a hearty contempt for Jean-Luc Godard. He acknowledges the power of Antonioni and especially Andrei Tarkovsky, whose *Andrei Rublev* he calls "one of the best and most unforgettable experiences in my life and in cinema." But for each, he approves only a few of their films; most are tripe. The only directors of his generation or later with whom he admits strong affinity are those whose cinema is so radically different from his that they cannot bear comparison or be seen as a challenge to his originality. He loves Federico Fellini and claims that he can watch Jacques Tati's *Mr. Hulot's Holiday* again and again without growing weary. To Löthwall, he asserts that "I am influenced by the culture around me, but mostly by media other than film." He tells Grenier that "I am by nature an autodidact." In sum, Bergman puts himself across as one who stands on the shoulders of giants but has no contemporary peer, a maverick who learned his craft from earlier masters but after his apprenticeship struck out entirely on his own. In this context, it becomes clear why he feels comfortable making complimentary remarks about young filmmakers who are no threat to his originality. His insistence at the AFI that he and Nykvist "have no camera style" is another way of claiming independence from contemporary methods and complete inimitability.

In this book, Bergman emerges as mischievous, adamantly self-correcting, self-effacing, territorial, jovial, sarcastic, and magnetic, qualities which, as I have suggested, are also reflected in the characters and tone of his films. For those whose small acquaintance with the director is through an enforced viewing of *The Seventh Seal* in a high school or college class, the adjective "Bergmanesque," has become a synonym for "turgid." Despite the misleading imagery that might pop into the head when his work is mentioned—gloomy Nordic landscapes, long screamy

faces that look like something out of Munch, a lover brooding in a corner about betrayal, medieval knights bewailing the death of God—
Bergman's films range from lighthearted farce to apocalyptic tragedy,
poignant family drama to national epic. Collectively, the pieces in this
book serve as an introduction and companion piece to the director's
pleasures as well as his profundities.

It is necessary to note that because some of these interviews refer to
works in progress, errors creep in, particularly for writers who make pre-
dictions about the future. William Wolf, describing the upcoming *Fanny
and Alexander*, asserts that it will star Bergman regulars Ullmann,
Sydow, and Erland Josephson. Only the latter actually appears. *Good
Intentions*, the script Bergman was working on in 1989, is ultimately
released in English as *The Best Intentions*. Despite his own intentions
when speaking prematurely, Bergman continued to give interviews. As
late as 2004, he appeared in a feature-length documentary about his life
and work. The comment that he retired from filmmaking in 1982 must
be disregarded. It is true that Bergman never shot anything after *Fanny
and Alexander* on an equally lavish scale, but the same can also be said
for every picture that precedes it. As for the sense that Bergman's
movies of the last twenty years don't count as films because they were
made for television, readers should be reminded that *Scenes from a
Marriage* and *Face to Face* (1976) as well as *Fanny and Alexander* were originally made for Swedish TV. Indeed, the shorter theatrical versions
culled from them, when compared to the originals, look like neutered
adaptations. Of the later works, *In the Presence of a Clown*, with its vast
cast, bears favorable comparison with his large-scale masterpieces.
Unavailable, as of this writing, on video, it is his most unjustly neglected picture. *Faithless* (2000), written by Bergman, directed by
Ullmann, and starring Josephson, is about a writer who makes a fiction
out of an incident in his life, re-imagining a love triangle from the perspective of the woman who left him. This return to storylines from *A
Passion* (1970) and *The Touch* is perhaps Bergman's frankest artistic statement about the culling of fiction from autobiography. And *Saraband*, a
sequel to *Scenes from a Marriage*, returns, with striking success, both to
the genre of the chamber film, whose most famous examples are
*Through a Glass Darkly* and *Cries and Whispers*, and to dream narratives
like *Persona* and *Hour of the Wolf*.

As this book goes to press, Bergman has passed his eighty-eighth birthday and has again stated that his career as a director is over. He has completed a series of video introductions to his best loved films. He is donating his papers to museums and web sites. Having ceased staging plays in Stockholm, he has disappeared from the public view. If he looked back on what he said in the pieces collected herein, he might be as disheartened by them as he is by some of his early films and essays. But that would be just another indication that he has always been a constantly restless filmmaker, ever revising his relationship to his art and its meaning.

As in other volumes in the Conversations with Filmmakers series, typographical and spelling errors have been silently corrected, but the interviews have not been substantially edited for republication.

I am deeply grateful to those who helped me complete this book. Peter Brunette, the editor of this series, tapped me to write it after a wonderful conversation at the Virginia Film Festival. Seetha Srinivasan, Anne Stascavage, and Walter Biggins, editors at the University Press of Mississippi, saw it through. Annika Hipple produced the translations of those Swedish interviews that had not before appeared in English; Brigitte Sion did the same for the French. Cynthia Grenier graciously helped me secure the rights to her interview. I had the honor of communicating with Vilgot Sjöman, who not only granted permission to translate and reprint his writings, but also told spellbinding anecdotes about his own experiences as well as those of Bergman and his company. My parents and sisters gave freely of their bottomless reserves of love and support. I dedicate this book to my greatest support, my dear wife Mia, who has made the first years of our marriage the happiest of my life.

RS

# CHRONOLOGY

1918    Ernst Ingmar Bergman born July 14 in Uppsala, Sweden, to
        Karin Bergman, nee Åkerblom, and pastor Erik Bergman.
        (Brother Dag born 1914, sister Margareta 1922.)
1934    A summer exchange student, he spends a month in
        Germany, and attends a Berlin rally at which Adolf Hitler
        makes an appearance.
1938    A brief stint of compulsory military service. Enters
        Stockholm University. Begins directing plays.
1940    Leaves university, but continues to stage plays.
1943    Begins working in the script department at Svensk
        Filmindustri. Marries Else Fisher. Daughter Lena born.
1944    *Torment*, directed by Alf Sjöberg, with a script by Bergman.
        Gunner Björnstrand, who would act in many of Bergman's
        major films through *Fanny and Alexander*, has a small role.
1945    Divorces Else Fisher. Marries Ellen Lundström. Daughter
        Eva born.
1946    *Crisis*, Bergman's first directorial effort. Son Jan born.
1946–50 Continues to work on screenplays for other filmmakers while
        directing a series of apprentice films, including *Night Is My
        Future*, *Port of Call*, *The Devil's Wanton*, *Three Strange Loves*, and
        *To Joy*, in which Victor Sjöström, the legendary Swedish director
        and one of Bergman's major influences, takes a supporting role.
        *It Rains on Our Love* has a bit part for Erland Josephson, who will
        star in many subsequent Bergman films and collaborate with
        him on two screenplays. In 1950, divorces Ellen Lundström.
1951    *Summer Interlude*. Directs commercials for Bris soap, one
        of which, "The Princess and the Swineherd," stars a fifteen-
        year-old Bibi Andersson. Marries Gun Grut.
1952    Becomes director at Malmö City Theater. *Secrets of Women*.

1953    *Summer with Monika*, Harriet Andersson's debut film with Bergman, reaps attention and shock for its revealing photography of the actress. *Sawdust and Tinsel*, which many cite as Bergman's first mature work. Divorces Gun Grunt.

1955    *Smiles of a Summer Night*, Bergman's sixteenth film.

1956    *Smiles of a Summer Night* wins an award at the Cannes Film Festival for "best poetic humor." Its success allows Bergman to exercise greater artistic freedom.

1957    Bergman cements his place in the international film scene with two masterpieces, *The Seventh Seal* (which wins a special Jury prize at Cannes) and *Wild Strawberries*. Both feature Max von Sydow, who will play major parts in Bergman films through 1970. The latter stars Sjöström, his last contribution to film before his death in 1960.

1958    *Wild Strawberries* wins the Golden Bear at the Venice Film Festival. *Brink of Life,* with a script by Ulla Isaksson, wins multiple prizes at Cannes. *The Magician.*

1959    Marries Käbi Laretei.

1960–61 *The Virgin Spring*, written by Ulla Isaksson and shot by Sven Nykvist, who will photograph all of Bergman's subsequent pictures through 1984. *Through a Glass Darkly*, a four-character chamber piece, the first of a trilogy and the first to be made on the island of Fårö. These win consecutive Academy Awards for Best Foreign Film.

1962    Son Daniel is born.

1963    *Winter Light* (*The Communicants*), which concerns a pastor undergoing spiritual crisis. Bergman later will cite it as his favorite picture. *The Silence*, the third film in the trilogy, which scandalizes many viewers, who consider it pornographic. Bergman is appointed head of the Royal Dramatic Theater, which takes him away from filmmaking for about two years.

1964    *Now About These Women* (*All These Women*), Bergman's last farce and first film in color.

1965    Early in the year, Bergman is ill with a viral infection whose disorienting side-effects keep him almost motionless for several months. Begins relationship with Liv Ullmann.

1966    *Persona*, his first film starring Ullmann, carries the dreamy, impressionistic, non-narrative, and self-referential quality of *The Silence* to even greater heights. Steps down from his post at the Royal Dramatic Theater, though he retains an office there. Builds a house on Fårö. Death of mother and divorce from Käbi Laretei. Daughter Linn born.

1968–69    Three major films in the wake of *Persona*, all shot, like it, on Fårö: *Hour of the Wolf, Shame*, and *A Passion (The Passion of Anna)*. The first of two documentaries about life on Fårö.

1970    Death of Bergman's father. End of relationship with Liv Ullmann.

1971    *The Touch*, Bergman's first English-language film. Marries Ingrid von Rosen.

1972–73    Bergman concludes the string of intense masterpieces inaugurated by *Persona* with *Cries and Whispers* and *Scenes from a Marriage*. The latter, shot in six episodes for Swedish television and released internationally to theaters in an abbreviated version, is hugely successful, credited for raising the divorce rates in several European countries and prompting people around the world to write to Bergman for advice on their marriages.

1975    *The Magic Flute*, a version of Mozart's opera, is broadcast on Swedish television and plays internationally in movie houses. Honorary doctorate from Stockholm University.

1976    *Face to Face*, a four-part television drama, which Bergman again cuts to theatrical length for international release. Arrested for tax fraud. Goes into self-imposed exile, taking up residence in Munich and directing plays and films there.

1977    *The Serpent's Egg*, shot in Munich, Bergman's second and last English-language film.

1978    *Autumn Sonata*, filmed in Oslo with Liv Ullmann and Ingrid Bergman, making her only appearance in an Ingmar Bergman picture.

1979    The Swedish government officially apologizes to Bergman for the tax arrest. The second Fårö documentary.

1980    *From the Life of the Marionetttes*, the last of the films to be shot in Germany.

1982    *Fanny and Alexander*, one of Bergman's most ambitious projects, is broadcast on Swedish television in four parts. It features Börje Ahlstedt and Pernilla August, who will play prominent roles in subsequent Bergman works. Bergman will later express dissatisfaction with the theatrical abbreviation of the film, which nevertheless wins tremendous acclaim and four academy awards upon its U.S. release (at the time a record for a non-English language film). Bergman announces his retirement from moviemaking, yet *Fanny and Alexander* marks the beginning of a series of fictionalized dramas about his personal and family history which he will write and sometimes direct for television over the next fifteen years.

1984    *After the Rehearsal*, a short film for television.

1986    Television film *The Blessed Ones*, written by Ulla Isaksson. *The Making of Fanny and Alexander*.

1987    Autobiography *The Magic Lantern* covers his personal life, with much material on his childhood and relationship with his parents.

1992    Release of two films with screenplays by Bergman, both adapted from memoirs dealing with his parents' marriage and his early childhood. Bille August directs *The Best Intentions*, a four-part television miniseries, while Bergman's son Daniel directs the feature *Sunday's Children*.

1993    A second autobiography, *Images: My Life in Film*, concerns his work in the cinema.

1995    *The Last Gasp (The Last Scream)*, for television. Death of wife Ingrid.

1996    Ullmann directs the television miniseries *Private Confessions*, whose script by Bergman picks up the story of his parents from *The Best Intentions*. Sven Nykvist is the cinematographer and Max von Sydow has a supporting role.

1997    *In the Presence of a Clown*, for television. It is the last and, with *Fanny and Alexander*, the finest of Bergman's fictionalized family dramas.

2000    *Faithless*, written by Bergman and directed by Ullmann.

2003    *Saraband*, directed for television in a new HDTV process. A sequel to *Scenes from a Marriage*, it stars Ullmann, Josephson, and Ahlstedt.

# FILMOGRAPHY

TELEVISION WORK is marked with an asterisk (*).

1944
HETS (*Torment; Frenzy*)
Producer: Harald Molander
Director: Alf Sjöberg
Screenplay: **Ingmar Bergman**
Cinematography: Martin Bodin
Music: Hilding Rosenberg
Art Direction: Arne Åkermark
Editing: Oscar Rosander
Cast: Stig Järrel (Caligula), Alf Kjellin (Jan-Erik Widgren), Mai Zetterling (Berta Olsson), Olof Winnerstrand (headmaster), Gösta Cederlund (Pippi), Hugo Björne (Dr. Nilsson), Stig Olin (Sandman), Olav Riego (Mr. Widgren), Märta Arbin (Mrs. Widgren), Jan Molander (Pettersson), Gunnar Björnstrand (teacher)
B&W, 101 minutes

1946
KRIS (*Crisis*)
Producer: Harald Molander
Director/screenplay: **Ingmar Bergman** (adapted from a radio play by Leck Fischer)
Cinematography: Gösta Roosling
Music: Erland von Koch
Art Direction: Arne Åkermark
Editor: Oscar Rosander
Cast: Inga Landgré (Nelly), Stig Olin (Jack), Marianne Löfgren (Jenny), Dagny Lind (Ingeborg), Allan Bohlin (Ulf), Ernst Eklund (Uncle Edvard), Signe Wirff (Aunt Jessie)
B&W, 93 minutes

DET REGNAR PÅ VÅR KÄRLEK (*It Rains on Our Love; Man with an Umbrella*)
Producer: Lorens Marmstedt
Director: **Ingmar Bergman**
Screenplay: **Ingmar Bergman** and Herbert Grevenius (adapted from a play by Oscar Braathen)
Cinematography: Hilding Bladh and Göran Strindberg
Music: Erland von Koch
Art Direction: P. A. Lundgren
Editor: Tage Holmberg
Cast: Barbro Kollberg (Maggi), Birger Malmsten (David), Gösta Cerderlund (Man with umbrella), Ludde Gentzel (Håkansson), Douglas Håge (Andersson), Hjördis Pettersson (Mrs. Andersson), Benkt-Åke Benktsson (prosecutor), Sture Ericson (Kängsnöret), Ulf Johansson (Stålvispen), Julia Caesar (Hanna Ledin), Gunnar Björnstrand (Mr. Purman), Åke Fridell (pastor), Erland Josephson (parish worker)
B&W, 95 minutes

1947
KVINNA UTAN ANSIKTE (*Woman without a Face*)
Producer: Harald Molander
Director: Gustaf Molander
Screenplay: **Ingmar Bergman** and Gustaf Molander
Cinematography: Åke Dahlqvist
Music: Erik Nordgren, Julius Jacobsen
Art Direction: Arne Åkermark, Nils Svenwall
Editor: Oscar Rosander
Cast: Alf Kjellin (Martin Grandé), Gunn Wållgren (Rut Köhler), Anita Björk (Frida Grandé), Stig Olin (Ragnar Ekberg), Olof Winnerstrand (Mr. Grandé), Marianne Löfgren (Mrs. Köhler), Georg Funkquist (Victor), Åke Grönberg (Sam Svensson), Linnéa Hillberg (Mrs. Grandé)
B&W, 102 minutes

SKEPP TILL INDIALAND (*A Ship Bound for India; Ship to India; Frustration; Land of Desire*)
Producer: Lorens Marmstedt
Director/Screenplay: **Ingmar Bergman** (based on a play by Martin Söderhjelm)

Cinematography: Gören Strindberg
Music: Erland von Koch
Art Direction: P. A. Lundgren
Editor: Tage Holmberg
Cast: Holger Löwenadler (Alexander Blom), Anna Lindahl (Alice Blom), Birger Malmsten (Johannes Blom), Gertrud Fridh (Sally), Naemi Briese (Selma), Hjördis Pettersson (Sofi), Lasse Krantz (Hans), Jan Molander (Bertil), Erik Hell (Pekka), Åke Fridell (Music hall director)
B&W, 98 minutes

1948
MUSIK I MÖRKER (*Night Is My Future; Music in Darkness*)
Producer: Lorens Marmstedt
Director: **Ingmar Bergman**
Screenplay: Dagmar Edqvist (based on her novel)
Cinematography: Gören Strindberg
Music: Erland von Koch
Art Direction: P. A. Lundgren
Editor: Lennart Wallén
Cast: Mai Zetterling (Ingrid), Birger Malmsten (Bengt), Bengt Eklund (Ebbe), Olof Winnerstrand (vicar), Naima Wifstrand (Mrs. Schröder), Hilda Borgström (Lovisa), Douglas Håge (Kruge), Gunnar Björnstrand (Klasson)
B&W, 87 minutes

HAMNSTAD (*Port of Call; Harbor City*)
Producer: Harald Molander
Director: **Ingmar Bergman**
Screenplay: Olle Länsberg and **Ingmar Bergman** (based on a story by Länsberg)
Cinematography: Gunnar Fischer
Music: Erland von Koch
Art Direction: Nils Svenwall
Editor: Oscar Rosander
Cast: Nine-Christine Jönsson (Berit), Bengt Eklund (Gösta), Mimi Nelson (Gertrud), Berta Hall (Berit's mother), Birgitta Valberg (Agnetta Vilander), Sif Ruud (Mrs. Krona), Erik Hell (Berit's father)
B&W, 97 minutes

EVA (*Eve*)
Producer: Harald Molander
Director: Gustaf Molander
Screenplay: **Ingmar Bergman** and Gustaf Molander
Cinematography: Åke Dahlqvist
Music: Erik Nordgren
Art Direction: Nils Svenwall
Editor: Oscar Rosander
Cast: Birger Malmsten (Bo Fredriksson), Eva Stiberg (Eva), Eva Dahlbeck
(Suzanne Boln), Åke Claesson (Erik Fredriksson), Wanda Rothgardt
(Anna Fredriksson), Stig Olin (Göran Bolin), Inga Landgré (Frida),
Erland Josephson (Karl)
B&W, 97 minutes

1949
FÄNGELSE (*The Devil's Wanton*; *Prison*)
Producer: Lorens Marmstedt
Director/Screenplay: **Ingmar Bergman**
Cinematography: Göran Strindberg
Music: Erland von Koch
Art Direction: P. A. Lundgren
Editor: Lennart Wallén
Cast: Doris Svedlund (Birgitta Carolina), Birger Malmsten (Tomas),
Eva Henning (Sofi), Hasse Ekman (Martin), Stig Olin (Peter), Irma
Christenson (Linnea), Anders Henrikson (Paul), Marianne Löfgren
(Signe Bohlin), Curt Masreliez (Alf)
B&W, 78 minutes

TÖRST (*Three Strange Loves*; *Thirst*)
Producer: Helge Hagerman
Director: **Ingmar Bergman**
Screenplay: Herbert Grevenius (adapted from the story by
Birgit Tengroth)
Cinematography: Gunnar Fischer
Music: Erik Nordgren
Art Direction: Nils Svenwall
Editor: Oscar Rosander

Cast: Eva Henning (Rut), Birger Malmsten (Bertil), Birgit Tengroth (Viola), Hasse Ekman (Doctor Rosengren), Mimmi Nelson (Valborg), Bengt Eklund (Raoul), Gaby Stenberg (Astrid), Naima Wifstrand (Miss Henriksson)
B&W, 84 minutes

1950
TILL GLÄDJE (*To Joy*)
Producer: Allan Ekelund
Director/Screenplay: **Ingmar Bergman**
Cinematography: Gunnar Fischer
Music: W. A. Mozart, F. Mendelsohn, B. Smetana, L. van Beethoven
Art Direction: Nils Svenwall
Editor: Oscar Rosander
Cast: Maj-Britt Nilsson (Marta), Stig Olin (Stig Eriksson), Birger Malmsten (Marcel), John Ekman (Mikael Bro), Margit Carlquist (Nelly Bro), Victor Sjöström (Sönderby), Sif Ruud (Stina), Erland Josephson (Bertil)
B&W, 99 minutes

MEDAN STADEN SOVER (*While the City Sleeps*)
Producer: Helge Hagerman
Director: Lars-Eric Kjellgren
Screenplay: Lars-Eric Kjellgren and Per Anders Fogelström, from an idea by **Ingmar Bergman**
Cinematography: Martin Bodin
Music: Stig Rybrant
Art Direction: Nils Svenwall
Editor: Oscar Rosander
Cast: Sven-Eric Gamble (Jompa), Inga Landgré (Iris), Adolf Jahr (Iris's father), Elof Ahrle (the boss), John Elfström (Jompa's father), Hilding Gavle (fence), Carl Ström (doorman), Ulf Palme (Kalle Lund), Barbro Hiort af Ornäs (Rutan)
B&W, 102 minutes

SÅNT HÄNDER INTE HÄR (*This Can't Happen Here*; *High Tension*)
Producer: Helge Hagerman
Director: **Ingmar Bergman**

Screenplay: Herbert Grevenius
Cinematography: Gunnar Fischer
Music: Erik Nordgren
Art Direction: Nils Svenwall
Editor: Lennart Wallén
Cast: Signe Hasso (Vera Irmelin), Alf Kjellin (Björn Almkvist), Ulf Palme
(Atkä Natas), Gösta Cederlund (doctor), Yngve Nordwall (Lindell),
Hannu Kompus (pastor), Sylvia Tael (Vanja), Stig Olin (young man)
B&W, 84 minutes

1951
SOMMARLEK (*Summer Interlude; Illicit Interlude*)
Producer: Allan Ekelund
Director: **Ingmar Bergman**
Screenplay: **Ingmar Bergman** and Herbert Grevenius (based on a story
by **Bergman**)
Cinematography: Gunnar Fischer
Music: Erik Nordgren
Art Direction: Nils Svenwall
Editor: Oscar Rosander
Cast: Maj-Britt Nilsson (Marie), Birger Malmsten (Henrik), Alf Kjellin
(David), Annalisa Ericson (Kaj), Georg Funkquist (Uncle Erland),
Stig Olin (ballet master), Renée Björling (Aunt Elisabet)
B&W, 96 minutes

FRÅNSKILD (*Divorced*)
Producer: Allan Ekelund
Director: Gustav Molander
Screenplay: **Ingmar Bergman** and Herbert Grevenius
Cinematography: Åke Dahlqvist
Music: Erik Nordgren, Bengt Wallerström
Art Direction: Nils Svenwall
Editor: Oscar Rosander
Cast: Inga Tidblad (Gertrud Holmgren), Alf Kjellin (Dr. Bertil Nordelius),
Doris Svedlund (Marianne Berg), Hjördis Petterson (Mrs. Nordelius),

Håkan Westergren (P. A. Beckman), Irma Christenson (Cecilia Lindeman), Holger Löwenadler (Tore Holmgren), Marianne Löfgren (Ingeborg), Stig Olin (Hans)
B&W, 103 minutes

In 1951, **Bergman** directed and Gunnar Fischer photographed nine television commercials for Bris ("Breeze") soap, one of which ("The Princess and the Swineherd") starred Bibi Andersson.

1952
KVINNORS VÄNTAN (*Secrets of Women*; *Waiting Women*)
Producer: Allan Ekelund
Director/Screenplay: **Ingmar Bergman**
Cinematography: Gunnar Fischer
Music: Erik Nordgren
Art Direction: Nils Svenwall
Editor: Oscar Rosander
Cast: Anita Björk (Rakel), Eva Dahlbeck (Karin), Maj-Britt Nilsson (Marta), Birger Malmsten (Martin Lobelius), Gunnar Björnstrand (Fredrik Lobelius), Karl-Arne Holmsten (Eugen Lobelius), Jarl Kulle (Kaj), Aino Taube (Annette), Håkan Westergren (Paul), Gerd Andersson (Maj), Björn Bjelvenstam (Henrik)
B&W, 107 minutes

1953
SOMMAREN MED MONIKA (*Summer with Monika*; *Monika*; *Monika: The Story of a Bad Girl*)
Producer: Allan Ekelund
Director: **Ingmar Bergman**
Screenplay: Per Anders Fogelström (and **Ingmar Bergman**, uncredited), based on Fogelström's novel
Cinematography: Gunnar Fischer
Music: Erik Nordgren
Art Direction: P. A. Lundgren
Editors: Tage Holmberg and Gösta Lewin
Cast: Harriet Andersson (Monika), Lars Ekborg (Harry), Dagmar Ebbesen (Harry's aunt), Åke Fridell (Monika's father), Naemi Briese (Monika's

mother), Åke Grönberg (Harry's boss), Sigge Fürst (Johan), John Harryson (Lelle)
B&W, 96 minutes


GYCKLARNAS AFTON (*Sawdust and Tinsel*; *Eve of the Clown*; *Eve of the Jesters*; *The Naked Night*)
Producer: Rune Waldekranz
Director/Screenplay: **Ingmar Bergman**
Cinematography: Sven Nykvist, Hilding Bladh
Music: Karl-Birger Blomdahl
Art Direction: Bibi Lindström
Editor: Carl-Olov Skeppstedt
Cast: Åke Grönberg (Albert Johansson), Harriet Andersson (Anne), Hasse Ekman (Frans), Anders Ek (Frost), Gudrun Brost (Alma Frost), Annika Tretow (Agda), Erik Strandmark (Jens), Gunnar Björnstrand (Sjuberg), Curt Löwgren (Blom), Åke Fridell (officer)
B&W, 86 minutes


1954
EN LEKTION I KÄRLEK (*A Lesson in Love*)
Producer: Allan Ekelund
Director/Screenplay: **Ingmar Bergman**
Cinematography: Martin Bodin
Music: Dag Wirén
Art Direction: P. A. Lundgren
Editor: Oscar Rosander
Cast: Eva Dahlbeck (Marianne Erneman), Gunnar Björnstrand (David Erneman), Yvonne Lombard (Suzanne), Harriet Andersson (Nix), Åke Grönberg (Carl-Adam), Olof Winnerstrand (Henrik Erneman), Birgitte Reimer (Lise), John Elfström (Sam), Renée Björling (Svea Erneman), Dagmar Ebbesen (nurse), Sigge Fürst (pastor)
B&W, 96 minutes


1955
KVINNODRÖM (*Dreams*; *Journey into Autumn*)
Producer: Rune Waldekranz
Director/Screenplay: **Ingmar Bergman**

Cinematography: Hilding Bladh
Art Direction: Gittan Gustafsson
Editor: Carl-Olov Skeppstedt
Cast: Eva Dahlbeck (Susanne), Harriet Andersson (Doris), Gunnar
Björnstrand (Sönderby), Ulf Palme (Lobelius), Inga Landgré (Marta
Lobelius), Bengt-Åke Benktsson (Magnus), Sven Lindberg (Palle), Kerstin
Hedeby-Pawlo (Marianne), Naima Wifstrand (Mrs. Arén)
B&W, 87 minutes

SOMMARNATTENS LEENDE (*Smiles of a Summer Night*)
Producer: Allan Ekelund
Director/Screenplay: **Ingmar Bergman**
Cinematography: Gunnar Fischer
Music: Erik Nordgren; R. Schumann, W. A. Mozart, F. Chopin, F. Liszt
Art Direction: P. A. Lundgren
Editor: Oscar Rosander
Cast: Ulla Jacobsson (Anne Egerman), Eva Dahlbeck (Desirée Armfeldt),
Harriet Andersson (Petra), Margit Carlquist (Charlotte Malcolm),
Gunnar Björnstrand (Fredrik Egerman), Jarl Kulle (Carl-Magnus
Malcolm), Åke Fridell (Frid), Björn Bjelvenstam (Henrik Egerman),
Naima Wifstrand (Mrs. Armfeldt), Jullan Kindahl (Beata), Gull Natorp
(Malla), Birgitta Valberg, Bibi Andersson (actresses)
B&W, 108 minutes

1956
SISTA PARET UT (*Last Couple Out; Last Pair Out; Tempest of Young Hearts*)
Producer: Allan Ekelund
Director: Alf Sjöberg
Screenplay: **Ingmar Bergman**
Cinematography: Martin Bodin
Music: Erik Nordgren, Charles Redland, Bengt Hallberg, Julius Jacobsen
Art Direction: Harald Garmland
Editor: Oscar Rosander
Cast: Eva Dahlbeck (Susanne Dahlin), Harriet Andersson (Anita), Bibi
Andersson (Kerstin), Björn Bjelvenstam (Bo Dahlin), Jarl Kulle (Ernst
Farell), Olof Widgren (Hans Dahlin), Aino Taube (Kerstin's mother)
B&W, 103 minutes

DET SJUNDE INSEGLET (*The Seventh Seal*)
Producer: Allan Ekelund
Director/Screenplay: **Ingmar Bergman** (based on **Bergman's** play
*Trämålning*)
Cinematography: Gunnar Fischer
Music: Erik Nordgren
Art Direction: P. A. Lundgren
Editor: Lennart Wallén
Cast: Gunnar Björnstrand (Jöns), Bengt Ekerot (Death), Nils Poppe (Jof),
Max von Sydow (Antonius Block), Bibi Andersson (Mia), Inga Gill
(Lisa), Maud Hansson (the witch), Inga Landgré (Karin), Gunnel
Lindblom (mute girl), Bertil Anderberg (Raval), Anders Ek (monk), Åke
Fridell (Plog), Gunnar Olsson (church painter), Erik Strandmark (Skat)
B&W, 96 minutes

1957
*HERR SLEEMAN KOMMER (*Sleeman's Coming; Mr. Sleeman Is Coming*)
Producer: Henrik Dyfverman
Director: **Ingmar Bergman**
Screenplay adapted from the play by Hjalmar Bergman
Production Design: Martin Ahlbom
Cast: Naima Wifstrand (Aunt Bina), Jullan Kindahl (Aunt Mina), Bibi
Andersson (Anne-Marie), Max von Sydow (Valter), Yngve Nordwall
(Sleeman)
B&W, 43 minutes

SMULTRONSTÄLLET (*Wild Strawberries*)
Producer: Allan Edelund
Director/Screenplay: **Ingmar Bergman**
Cinematography: Gunnar Fischer
Music: Erik Nordgren
Art Direction: Gittan Gustafsson
Editor: Oscar Rosander
Cast: Victor Sjöström (Isak Borg), Bibi Andersson (Sara), Ingrid Thulin
(Marianne), Gunnar Björnstrand (Evald Borg), Jullan Kindahl (Agda),
Folke Sundquist (Anders), Björn Bjelvenstam (Viktor), Naima Wifstrand
(Isak's mother), Gunnel Broström (Mrs. Alman), Gertrud Fridh (Karin),

Sif Ruud (Aunt Olga), Gunnar Sjöberg (Alman), Max von Sydow (Åker-
man), Åke Fridall (Karin's lover), Gunnel Lindblom (Charlotta)
B&W, 90 minutes

1958
*VENETIANSKAN (The Venetian)
Producer: Henrik Dyfverman
Director: **Ingmar Bergman**
Screenplay: Giacomo Oreglia, Bertil Bodén (translators of an anony-
mous sixteenth-century Italian play)
Art Direction: Härje Ekman
Cast: Folke Sundqvist (Julio), Maud Hansson (Nena), Eva Stiberg
(Angela), Gunnel Lindblom (Valeria), Helena Reuterblad (Oria), Sture
Lagerwall (Bernardo)
B&W, 56 minutes

NÄRA LIVET (*Brink of Life*; *So Close to Life*)
Producer: Gösta Hammarbäck
Director: **Ingmar Bergman**
Screenplay: Ulla Isaksson, based on her short story
Cinematography: Max Wilén
Art Direction: Bibi Lindström
Editor: Carl-Olov Skeppstedt
Cast: Eva Dahlbeck (Stina Andersson), Ingrid Thulin (Cecilia Ellius),
Bibi Andersson (Hjördis Petterson), Barbro Hiort af Ornäs (Brita), Erland
Josephson (Anders Ellius), Max von Sydow (Harry Andersson), Gunnar
Sjöberg (Dr. Nordlander), Ann-Marie Gyllenspetz (Gran), Inga Landgré
(Greta Ellius)
B&W, 84 minutes

*RABIES
Producer: Henrik Dyfverman
Director: **Ingmar Bergman**
Screenplay adapted from works by Olle Hedberg
Cast: Max von Sydow (Bo Stensson Svenningson), Gunnel Lindblom
(Jenny), Åke Fridell (Sixten Garberg), Bibi Andersson (Eivor), Folke
Sundqvist (Erik)
B&W, 89 minutes

ANSIKTET (*The Magician; The Face*)
Producer: Allan Ekelund
Director/Screenplay: **Ingmar Bergman**
Cinematography: Gunnar Fischer
Music: Erik Nordgren
Art Direction: P. A. Lundgren
Editor: Oscar Rosander
Cast: Max von Sydow (Albert Emanuel Vogler), Ingrid Thulin (Aman/
Manda), Gunnar Björnstrand (Vergerus), Naima Wifstrand (Vogler's
grandmother), Bengt Ekerot (Spegel), Bibi Andersson (Sara), Gertrud
Fridh (Ottilia), Lars Ekborg (Simson), Toivo Pawlo (Starbeck), Erland
Josephson (Egerman), Åke Fridell (Tubal), Sif Ruud (Sofia), Oscar Ljung
(Antonsson), Ulla Sjöblom (Henrietta), Axel Düberg (Rustan), Birgitta
Pettersson (Sanna) B&W, 102 minutes

1960
*OVÄDER (*Storm; Storm Weather*)
Producer: Henrik Dyfverman
Director: **Ingmar Bergman**
Screenplay adapted from the play by August Strindberg
Cinematography: Egon Blank, Sven-Eric Larson, Måns Reuterswärd,
Lars Swahn
Cast: Uno Henning (The Gentleman), Ingvar Kjellson (The Brother),
John Elfström (Strong), Birgitta Grönwald (Agnes), Mona Malm
(Louise), Gunnel Broström (Gerda), Curt Masreliez (Fischer)
B&W, 91 minutes

JUNGFRUKÄLLAN (*The Virgin Spring*)
Producer: Allan Ekelund
Director: **Ingmar Bergman**
Screenplay: Ulla Isaksson (adapted from a thirteenth-century ballad)
Cinematography: Sven Nykvist
Music: Erik Nordgren
Art Direction: P. A. Lundgren
Editor: Oscar Rosander
Cast: Max von Sydow (Töre), Birgitta Valberg (Märeta), Gunnel
Lindblom (Ingeri), Birgitta Pettersson (Karin), Axel Düberg (shepherd),

Tor Isedal (silent shepherd), Allan Edwall (beggar), Ove Porath (boy),
Axel Slangus (bridge guard), Gudrun Brost (Frida), Oscar Ljung (Simon)
B&W, 88 minutes

DJÄVULENS ÖGA (*The Devil's Eye*)
Producer: Allan Ekelund
Director/Screenplay: **Ingmar Bergman** (based on the radio play
*The Return of Don Juan* by Oluf Bang)
Cinematography: Gunnar Fischer
Music: Erik Nordgren
Art Direction: P. A. Lundgren
Editor: Oscar Rosander
Cast: Jarl Kulle (Don Juan), Bibi Andersson (Britt-Marie), Stig Järrel
(Satan), Nils Poppe (parson), Gertrud Fridh (Renata), Sture Lagerwall
(Pablo), Georg Funkquist (Rochefoucauld), Gunnar Sjöberg
(Macopanza), Torsten Winge (old man), Axel Düberg (Jonas), Kristina
Adolphson (woman with veil), Allan Edwall (demon), Gunnar
Björnstrand (narrator)
B&W, 86 minutes

1961
SÅSOM I EN SPEGEL (*Through a Glass Darkly*)
Producer: Allan Ekelund
Director/Screenplay: **Ingmar Bergman**
Cinematography: Sven Nykvist
Music: Erik Nordgren, J. S. Bach
Art Direction: P. A. Lundgren
Editor: Ulla Ryghe
Cast: Harriet Andersson (Karin), Gunnar Björnstrand (David), Max von
Sydow (Martin), Lars Passgård (Minus)
B&W, 89 minutes

LUSTGÅRDEN (*The Pleasure Garden*; *The Garden of Eden*)
Producer: Allan Ekelund
Director: Alf Kjellin
Screenplay: **Ingmar Bergman** and Erland Josephson, writing under the
pseudonym "Buntel Eriksson"

Cinematography: Gunnar Fischer
Music: Erik Nordgren
Art Direction: P. A. Lundgren
Editor: Ulla Ryghe
Cast: Sickan Carlsson (Fanny), Gunnar Björnstrand (David Franzén), Bibi Andersson (Anna), Per Myrberg (Emil), Kristina Adolphson (Astrid), Stig Järrel (Lundberg)
Color, 93 minutes

1963
NATTVARDSGÄSTERNA (*Winter Light; The Communicants*)
Producer: Allan Ekelund
Director/Screenplay: **Ingmar Bergman**
Cinematography: Sven Nykvist
Art Direction: P. A. Lundgren
Editor: Ulla Ryghe
Cast: Ingrid Thulin (Märta Lundberg), Gunnar Björnstrand (Tomas Ericsson), Gunnel Lindblom (Karin Persson), Max von Sydow (Jonas Persson), Allan Edwall (Frövik), Kolbjörn Knudsen (Aronsson), Olof Thunberg (Fredrik Blom), Elsa Ebbesen (Magdalena Lendfors)
B&W, 80 minutes

*TRÄMÅLNING (*Wood Painting*)
Producer: Henrik Dyfverman
Director: Lennart Olsson
Screenplay: **Ingmar Bergman** (from the play that formed the source material for *The Seventh Seal*)
Cast: Marianne Wesén (The Girl), Olof Bergström (Jöns), Oscar Ljung (The Knight), Ulla Akselson (The Witch), Åke Lindström (The Smith), Marianne Hedengrahn (Maria), Georg Årlin (The Actor), Gudrun Brost (Lisa), Margareta Bergfelt (Karin), Folke Sundquist (The Narrator)

*ETT DRÖMSPEL (*A Dream Play*)
Producer: Kåre Santesson
Director: **Ingmar Bergman**
Screenplay adapted from the play by August Strindberg
Cinematography: Bosse Larsson, Jan Wictorinus, Olle Mossberg, Per Olof Nordmark, Åke Dahlqvist, Albert Rudling

Music: Sven-Erik Bäck
Art Direction: Carl Cloffe
Editor: Monica Barthelsson
Cast: Ingrid Thulin (Agnes), Uno Henning (Officer), Allan Edwall
(Advocate), Olof Widgren (Poet), John Elfström (Glazier), Brita Öberg
(Mother), Ragnar Falck (Father), Eivor Landström (Lina)
B&W, 105 minutes


TYSTNADEN (*The Silence*)
Producer: Allan Ekelund
Director/Screenplay: **Ingmar Bergman**
Cinematography: Sven Nykvist
Music: Ivan Renliden
Art Direction: P. A. Lundgren
Editor: Ulla Ryghe
Cast: Ingrid Thulin (Ester), Gunnel Lindblom (Anna), Birger Malmsten
(waiter at bar), Håkan Jahnberg (waiter from room service), Jörgen
Lindström (Johan)
B&W, 96 minutes


1964
FÖR ATT INTE TALA OM ALLA DESSA KVINNOR (*All These Women;
Now About These Women*)
Producer: Allan Ekelund
Director: **Ingmar Bergman**
Screenplay: **Ingmar Bergman** and Erland Josephson
Cinematography: Sven Nykvist
Music: Erik Nordgren, Charles Redland
Art Direction: P. A. Lundgren
Editor: Ulla Ryghe
Cast: Bibi Andersson (Bumblebee), Harriet Andersson (Isolde), Eva
Dahlbeck (Adelaide), Karin Kavli (Madame Tussaud), Gertrud Fridh
(Traviata), Mona Malm (Cecilia), Barbro Hiort af Ornäs (Beatrice), Allan
Edwall (Jillker), Georg Funkquist (Tristan), Carl Billquist (young man),
Jarl Kulle (Cornelius)
Color, 80 minutes

1966
PERSONA
Producer: Lars-Owe Carlberg
Director/Screenplay: **Ingmar Bergman**
Cinematography: Sven Nykvist
Music: Lars Johan Werle
Art Direction: Bibi Lindström
Editor: Ulla Ryghe
Cast: Bibi Andersson (Alma), Liv Ullmann (Elisabet Vogler),
Margaretha Krook (doctor), Gunnar Björnstrand (Vogler), Jörgen
Lindström (boy)
B&W, 83 minutes

1967
DANIEL (segment from anthology film *Stimulantia*)
Producer: Olle Nordemar
Director/Screenplay/Cinematography: **Ingmar Bergman**
Music: W. A. Mozart
Editor: Ulla Ryghe
Cast: **Ingmar Bergman** (narrator), Käbi Laretei, Daniel Bergman
B&W, 15 minutes

1968
VARGTIMMEN (*Hour of the Wolf*)
Producer: Lars-Owe Carlberg
Director/Screenplay: **Ingmar Bergman**
Cinematography: Sven Nykvist
Music: Lars Johan Werle
Art Direction: Marik Vos
Editor: Ulla Ryghe
Cast: Max von Sydow (Johan Borg), Liv Ullmann (Alma Borg), Gertrud
Fridh (Corinne von Merkens), Georg Rydeberg (Lindhorst), Erland
Josephson (Baron von Merkens), Naima Wifstrand (old woman), Ulf
Johanson (Heerbrand), Gudrun Brost (Old Mrs. Von Merkens), Bertil
Anderberg (Ernst von Merkens), Ingrid Thulin (Veronica Vogler)
B&W, 88 minutes

SKAMMEN (*Shame; The Shame*)
Producer: Lars-Owe Carlberg
Director/Screenplay: **Ingmar Bergman**
Cinematography: Sven Nykvist
Art Direction: P. A. Lundgren
Editor: Ulla Ryghe
Cast: Liv Ullmann (Eva Rosenberg), Max von Sydow (Jan Rosenberg),
Sigge Fürst (Filip), Gunnar Björnstrand (Jakobi), Birgitta Valberg
(Mrs. Jakobi), Hans Alfredson (Lobelius), Ingvar Kjellson (Oswald),
Frank Sundström (Chief interrogator), Ulf Johansson (Doctor),
Vilgot Sjöman (Interviewer), Bengt Eklund (Guard), Gösta Prüzelius
(Vicar)
B&W, 103 minutes

1969
*RITEN (*The Rite; The Ritual*)
Producer: Lars-Owe Carlberg
Director/Screenplay: **Ingmar Bergman**
Cinematography: Sven Nykvist
Art Direction: Mago
Editor: Siv Kanälv
Cast: Ingrid Thulin (Thea Winkelmann), Gunnar Björnstrand
(Hans Winkelmann), Anders Ek (Sebastian Fischer), Erik Hell (Judge
Abrahamsson), **Ingmar Bergman** (priest)
B&W, 72 minutes

EN PASSION (*A Passion; The Passion of Anna*)
Producer: Lars-Owe Carlberg
Director/Screenplay: **Ingmar Bergman**
Cinematography: Sven Nykvist
Art Direction: P. A. Lundgren
Editor: Siv Kanälv
Cast: Max von Sydow (Andreas Winkelman), Liv Ullmann (Anna
Fromm), Bibi Andersson (Eva Vergérus), Erland Josephson (Elis
Vergérus), Erik Hell (Johan Andersson), Sigge Fürst (Verner)
Color, 101 minutes

1970

*FÅRÖ-DOKUMENT (*Fårö Dokument 1969; The Faro Documentary*)
Producer: Lars-Owe Carlberg
Director: **Ingmar Bergman**
Cinematography: Sven Nykvist
Editor: Siv Lundgren-Kanälv
B&W, 78 minutes

*RESERVATET (*The Reservation; The Sanctuary; The Lie*. The credits below refer to the Swedish rendition of **Bergman**'s screenplay. The script was also used for a 1973 TV film starring George Segal and Shirley Knight.)
Producer: Bernt Callenbo, Hans Sackemark
Director: Jan Molander
Screenplay: **Ingmar Bergman**
Cinematography: Jan Wictorinus, Per Olof Nordmark, Willy Thoreson
Art Direction: Bo Lindgren
Editor: Ronnie Årland
Cast: Gunnel Lindblom (Anna), Per Myrberg (Andreas), Pjer Nilsson (Henrik), Erland Josephson (Elis), Erik Hell (Georg), Toivo Pawlo (Albert), Georg Funkquist (Anna's father), Sif Ruud (Britt Prakt), Börje Ahlstedt (Feldt)
Color, 95 minutes

1971

BERÖRINGEN (English language version: *The Touch*)
Producer: Lars-Owe Carlberg
Director/Screenplay: **Ingmar Bergman**
Cinematography: Sven Nykvist (main title sequence by Gunnar Fischer)
Art Direction: P. A. Lundgren, Ann-Christin Lobråten
Editor: Siv Lundgren
Cast: Elliot Gould (David Kovac), Bibi Andersson (Karin Vergerus), Max von Sydow (Andreas Vergerus), Sheila Reid (Sara), Barbro Hiort af Ornäs (Karin's mother)
Color, 114 minutes

1972
VISKNINGAR OCH ROP (*Cries and Whispers*)
Producer: Lars-Owe Carlberg
Director/Screenplay: **Ingmar Bergman**
Cinematography: Sven Nykvist
Music: Frédéric Chopin (played by Käbi Laretei), J. S. Bach
Production Design: Marik Vos
Editor: Siv Lundgren
Cast: Harriet Andersson (Agnes), Kari Sylwan (Anna), Ingrid Thulin (Karin), Liv Ullmann (Maria/Maria's mother), Anders Ek (Pastor Isak), Inga Gill (storyteller), Erland Josephson (David), Henning Moritzen (Joakim), Georg Årlin (Fredrik), Linn Ullmann (Maria's daughter)
Color, 91 minutes

1973
*SCENER UR ETT ÄKTENSKAP (*Scenes from a Marriage*)
Producer: Lars-Owe Carlberg
Director/Screenplay: **Ingmar Bergman**
Cinematography: Sven Nykvist
Production Design: Björn Thulin
Editor: Siv Lundgren
Cast: Liv Ullmann (Marianne), Erland Josephson (Johan), Bibi Andersson (Katarina), Jan Malmsjö (Peter), Gunnel Lindblom (Eva), Barbro Hiort af Ornäs (Mrs. Jacobi), Anita Wall (Mrs. Palm)
Color, 299 minutes (TV version in six segments); 169 minutes (theatrical version)

1974
*MISANTROPEN (*The Misanthrope*)
Producer: Kjeld Larsen
Director: **Ingmar Bergman**
Screenplay adapted from Molière in a translation by Peter Hansen
Production Design: Kerstin Hedeby
Cast: Henning Moritzen (Alceste), Holger Juul Hansen (Philinte), Ebbe Rode (Oronte), Ghita Nørby (Célimène), Hanne Borchsenius (Éliante), Lise Ringheim (Arsinoe)
Color, 115 minutes

1975
*TROLLFLÖJTEN (*The Magic Flute*)
Producer: Måns Reuterswärd
Director: **Ingmar Bergman**
Screenplay adapted from the opera *Die Zauberflöte* by W. A. Mozart,
libretto by Emanuel Schikaneder
Cinematography: Sven Nykvist
Music: W. A. Mozart
Production Design: Henny Noremark
Editor: Siv Lundgren
Cast: Josef Köstlinger (Tamino), Irma Urrila (Pamina), Håkan Hagegård
(Papageno), Elisabeth Erikson (Papagena), Britt-Marie Aruhn (first
woman), Kirsten Vaupel (second woman), Birgitta Smiding (third
woman), Ulrik Cold (Sarastro), Birgit Nordin (Queen of the Night),
Ragnar Ulfung (Monostatos), Erik Saedén (speaker), Gösta Prüzelius
(first priest), Ulf Johansson (second priest)
Color, 135 minutes

1976
*ANSIKTE MOT ANSIKTE (*Face to Face*)
Producer: Lars-Owe Carlberg
Director/Screenplay: **Ingmar Bergman**
Cinematography: Sven Nykvist
Music: W. A. Mozart
Production Design: Anne Hagegård
Editor: Siv Lundgren
Cast: Liv Ullmann (Jenny Isaksson), Erland Josephson (Tomas Jacobi),
Aino Taube (grandmother), Gunnar Björnstrand (grandfather), Sif Ruud
(Elisabeth Wankel), Sven Lindberg (Erik Isaksson), Tore Segelcke (woman)
Kari Sylwan (Maria), Birger Malmsten, Gören Stangertz (rapists), Rebecca
Pawlo, Lena Olin (saleswomen), Bengt Eklund ("Ludde")
Color, 200 minutes (TV version in four 50 minute segments); 135 minutes
(theatrical version)

1977
THE SERPENT'S EGG (Swedish language version: *Ormens ägg*; German
language version: *Das schlangenei*)

Producer: Dino de Laurentiis
Director/Screenplay: **Ingmar Bergman**
Cinematography: Sven Nykvist
Music: Rolf Wilhelm
Production Design: Rolf Zehetbauer
Editor: Petra von Oelffen
Cast: Liv Ullmann (Manuela Rosenberg), David Carradine (Abel Rosenberg), Gert Froebe (Bauer), Heinz Bennent (Hans Vergerus)
Color, 119 minutes

1978
HÖSTSONATEN (*Herbstsonate*; *Autumn Sonata*)
Producer: Katinka Faragó
Director/Screenplay: **Ingmar Bergman**
Cinematography: Sven Nykvist
Music: Frédéric Chopin (played by Käbi Laretei), J. S. Bach, G. F. Handel
Production Design: Anna Asp
Editor: Sylvia Ingemarsson
Cast: Ingrid Bergman (Charlotte), Liv Ullmann (Eva), Lena Nyman (Helena), Halvar Björk (Viktor), Marianne Aminoff (Charlotte's secretary), Arne Bang-Hansen (Uncle Otto), Gunnar Björnstrand (Paul), Erland Josephson (Josef), Georg Løkkeberg (Leonardo), Mimi Pollak (piano teacher), Linn Ullmann (young Eva)
Color, 93 minutes

1979
*FÅRÖ-DOKUMENT 1979
Producer/Director/Screenplay: **Ingmar Bergman**
Cinematography: Arne Carlsson
Editor: Sylvia Ingemarsson
Color, 103 minutes

1980
*AUS DEM LEBEN DES MARIONETTEN (*Ur marionetternas liv*; *From the Life of the Marionettes*)
Producers: Horst Wendlandt, **Ingmar Bergman**
Director/Screenplay: **Ingmar Bergman**

Cinematography: Sven Nykvist
Music: Rolf Wilhelm
Production Design: Rolf Zehetbauer, Herbert Strabel
Editor: Petra von Oelffen
Cast: Robert Atzorn (Peter Egerman), Heinz Bennent (Brenner), Martin Benrath (Mogens Jensen), Toni Berger (guard), Christine Buchegger (Katarina Egerman), Gaby Dohm (secretary), Lola Müthel (Cordelia Egerman), Ruth Olafs (nurse), Karl-Heinz Pelser (interrogator), Rita Russek (Katarina), Walter Schmidinger (Tim)
Color/B&W, 104 minutes

1982
*FANNY OCH ALEXANDER (*Fanny and Alexander*)
Producer: Jörn Donner
Director/Screenplay: **Ingmar Bergman**
Cinematography: Sven Nykvist
Music: Daniel Bell
Production Design: Anna Asp
Editor: Sylvia Ingemarsson
Cast: Börje Ahlstedt (Carl Ekdahl), Pernilla Allwin (Fanny Ekdahl), Allan Edwall (Oscar Ekdahl), Ewa Fröling (Emilie Ekdahl), Bertil Guve (Alexander Ekdahl), Jarl Kulle (Gustav Adolf Ekdahl), Käbi Laretei (Aunt Anna), Mona Malm (Alma Ekdahl), Lena Olin (Rosa), Christina Schollin (Lydia Ekdahl), Pernilla Wallgren (Maj), Gunn Wållgren (Helena Ekdahl), Harriet Andersson (Justina), Jan Malmsjö (Bishop Edvard Vergérus), Gunnar Björnstrand (Filip Landahl), Erland Josephson (Isak Jacobi), Stina Ekblad (Ismael), Mats Bergman (Aron)
Color, 189 minutes (theatrical version); 312 minutes (TV version in four segments)

1983
*HUSTRUSKOLAN (*The School for Wives*)
Producer: Gerd Edwards
Director: **Ingmar Bergman** (based on a stage production by Alf Sjöberg)
Screenplay adapted from Molière in a translation by Lars Forssell
Cinematography: Jan Wictorinus, Per-Olof Runa, Lennart Söderberg

Production Design: John Virke
Editor: Jan Askelöf
Cast: Allan Edwall (Arnolphe), Lena Nyman (Agnès), Stellan Skarsgård (Horace), Björn Gustafson (Alain), Ulla Sjöblom (Georgette), Lasse Pöysti (Chrysalde), Oscar Ljung (Enrique), Olle Hilding (Oronte), Nils Eklund (Lawyer)

1984
*EFTER REPETITIONEN (*After the Rehearsal*)
Producer: Jörn Donner
Director/Screenplay: **Ingmar Bergman**
Cinematography: Sven Nykvist
Art Direction: Anna Asp
Editor: Sylvia Ingemarsson
Cast: Erland Josephson (Henrik Vogler), Ingrid Thulin (Rakel), Lena Olin (Anna)
Color, 72 minutes

1986
*DE TVÅ SALIGA (*The Blessed Ones*; *The Sign*)
Producers: Pia Ehrnvall, Katinka Faragó
Director: **Ingmar Bergman**
Screenplay: Ulla Isaksson (based on her novel)
Cinematography: Per Norén
Production Design: Birgitta Bensén
Cast: Harriet Andersson (Viveka Burman), Per Myrberg (Sune Burman), Christina Schollen (Annika), Lasse Pöysti (Dr. Dettow), Irma Christenson (Mrs. Storm), Björn Gustafson (neighbor)
Color, 81 minutes

1986
DOKUMENT FANNY OCH ALEXANDER (*The Making of Fanny and Alexander*)
Director/Screenplay: **Ingmar Bergman**
Cinematography: Arne Carlsson
Editor: Sylvia Ingemarsson
Color, 110 minutes

KARINS ANSIKTE (*Karin's Face*)
Director/Screenplay: **Ingmar Bergman**
Cinematography: Arne Carlsson
Editor: Sylvia Ingemarsson
Color, 14 minutes

1991
*DEN GODA VILJAN (*The Best Intentions*)
Producer: Ingrid Dahlberg
Director: Bille August
Screenplay: **Ingmar Bergman**
Cinematography: Jörgen Persson
Music: Stefan Nilsson
Production Design: Anna Asp
Editor: Janus Billeskov Jansen
Cast: Samuel Fröler (Henrik Bergman), Pernilla August (Anna Åkerblom),
Max von Sydow (Johan Åkerblom), Ghita Nørby (Karin Åkerblom),
Lennart Hjulström (Nordenson), Mona Malm (Alma Bergman), Lena
Endre (Frida Strandberg), Keve Hjelm (Fredrik Bergman), Björn Kjellman
(Ernst Åkerblom), Börje Ahlstedt (Carl Åkerblom), Hans Alfredson
(Gransjö), Lena T. Hansson (Magda), Anita Björk (Queen Victoria), Inga
Landgré (Magna Flink), Marie Richardson (Märta Werkelin)
Color, 325 minutes (television version in four segments); 181 minutes
(international television and theatrical release)

1992
*MARKISINNAN DE SADE (*Madame de Sade*)
Producers: Måns Reuterswärd, Katarina Sjöberg
Director: **Ingmar Bergman**
Screenplay adapted from a play by Yukio Mishima, translated by
Gunilla Lindberg-Wada and Per Erik Wahlund
Music: Ingrid Yoda
Production Design: Charles Koroly, Mette Möller
Editor: Sylvia Ingemarsson
Cast: Stina Ekblad (Renee), Anita Björk (Madame de Monteuil),
Marie Richardson (Anne), Margareta Byström (de Simiane),

Agneta Ekmanner (Countess de Saint-Fond), Helena Brodin
(Charlotte)
Color, 104 minutes

SÖNDAGSBARN (*Sunday's Children; Sunday's Child*)
Producer: Katinka Faragó
Director: Daniel Bergman
Screenplay: **Ingmar Bergman**
Cinematography: Tony Forsberg
Production Design: Sven Wichmann
Editor: Darek Hodor
Cast: Thommy Berggren (father), Henrik Linnros (Pu), Lena Endre
(mother), Jakob Leygraf (Dag), Anna Linnros (Lillan), Malin Ek (Märta),
Marie Richardson (Marianne), Irma Christenson (Aunt Emma), Birgitta
Valberg (Grandmother), Börje Ahlstedt (Uncle Carl), Maria Bolme
(Maj)
Color, 121 minutes


1993
*BACKANTERNA (*The Bacchae*)
Producer: Måns Reuterswärd
Director: **Ingmar Bergman**
Screenplay adapted from Euripides by Göran O. Eriksson and Jan Stolpe
Cinematography: Wulf Meseke, Per Norén, Sven-Åke Visén, Raymond
Wemmenlöv
Music: Daniel Börtz
Production Design: Mette Möller, Lennart Mörk
Editor: Sylvia Ingemarsson, Jan Askelöf
Cast: Sylvia Lindenstrand (Dionysos), Laila Andersson-Palme (Teiresias),
Sten Wahlund (Cadmus), Peter Mattei (Pentheus), Anita Soldh
(Agave)
Color, 131 minutes


1995
*SISTA SKRIKET (*The Last Gasp, The Last Scream*)
Producer: Måns Reuterswärd
Director/Screenplay: **Ingmar Bergman**

Cinematography: Per Norén, Sven-Åke Visén, Raymond Wemmenlöv
Music: Matti Bye
Production Design: Mette Möller
Editor: Sylvia Ingemarsson
Cast: Ingvar Kjellson (Charles Magnusson), Björn Granath (Georg af Klercker), Anna von Rosen (Elisabeth Holm)
B&W, 60 minutes

1996
*HARALD OCH HARALD (*Harald and Harald*)
Producer: Måns Reuterswärd
Director/Screenplay: **Ingmar Bergman**
Cinematography: Jan Wictorinus, Pär-Olof Rekola, Arne Halvarsson
Production Design: Göran Wassberg
Editor: Louise Brattberg
Cast: Björn Granath (Harald), Johan Rabaeus (Harald), Benny Haag (the white clown)
Color, 10 minutes

*ENSKILDA SAMTAL (*Private Confessions*)
Producer: Ingrid Dahlberg
Director: Liv Ullmann
Screenplay: **Ingmar Bergman**
Cinematography: Sven Nykvist
Production Design: Mette Möller
Editor: Michal Leszczylowski
Cast: Pernilla August (Anna Bergman), Samuel Fröler (Henrik Bergman), Thomas Hanzon (Tomas Egerman), Max von Sydow (Jacob), Anita Björk (Karin Åkerblom), Vibeke Falk (Mrs. Nylander), Kristina Adolphson (Maria), Gunnel Fred (Märta Gärdsjö)
Color, 195 minutes (TV version in two segments); 127 minutes (theatrical version)

1997
*LARMAR OCH GÖR SIG TILL (*In the Presence of a Clown*)
Producers: Pia Ehrnvall, Måns Reuterswärd
Director/Screenplay: **Ingmar Bergman**

Cinematography: Tony Forsberg, Per Norén, Sven-Åke Visén, Raymond
Wemmenlöv
Music: Franz Schubert
Production Design: Göran Wassberg
Editor: Sylvia Ingemarsson
Cast: Börje Ahlstedt (Carl Åkerblom), Marie Richardson (Pauline
Thibault), Erland Josephson (Osvald Vogler), Pernilla August (Karin
Bergman), Peter Storemare (Petrus Landahl), Anita Björk (Anna
Åkerblom), Lena Endre (Märta Lundberg), Agneta Ekmanner
(Rigmor), Gunnel Fred (Emma Vogler), Alma Berglund (Inga Landgré)
**Ingmar Bergman** (mental patient)
Color, 120 minutes


2000
TROLÖSA (*Faithless*)
Producer: Kaj Larsen
Director: Liv Ullmann
Screenplay: **Ingmar Bergman**
Cinematography: Jörgen Persson
Editor: Sylvia Ingemarsson
Production Design: Göran Wassberg
Cast: Lena Endre (Marianne) Erland Josephson (Bergman), Krister
Henriksson (David), Thomas Hanzon (Markus), Michelle Gylemo
(Isabelle), Juni Dahr (Margareta), Philip Zandén (Martin Goldman),
Thérèse Brunnander (Petra Holst), Marie Richardson (Anna Berg), Stina
Ekblad (Eva), Johan Rabaeus (Johan), Jan-Olof Strandberg (Axel), Björn
Granath (Gustav), Gertrud Stenung (Martha)
Color, 155 minutes


*BILDMAKARNA (*The Image Makers*)
Producer: Pia Ehrnvall
Director: **Ingmar Bergman**
Screenplay adapted from the play by Per Olov Enquist
Cinematography: Raymond Wemmenlöv
Production Design: Göran Wassberg
Editors: Sylvia Ingemarsson, Sofi Stridh, Sven-Åke Visén

Cast: Anita Björk (Selma Lagerlöf), Lennart Hjulström (Victor Sjöström), Carl Magnus Dellow (Julius Jaenzon), Elin Klinga (Tora Teje), Henry "Nypan" Nyberg (projectionist)
Color, 100 minutes

2003
*SARABAND
Producer: Pia Ehrnvall
Director/Screenplay: **Ingmar Bergman**
Cinematography: Stefan Eriksson, Jesper Holmström, Per-Olof Lantto, Sofi Stridh, Raymond Wemmenlöv
Music: J. S. Bach
Editor: Sylvia Ingemarsson
Production Design: Göran Wassberg
Cast: Liv Ullmann (Marianne), Erland Josephson (Johan), Börje Ahlstedt (Henrik), Julia Dufvenius (Karin), Gunnel Fred (Martha)
Color, 112 minutes

# INGMAR BERGMAN

## INTERVIEWS

# The Tensions of Ingmar Bergman

VILGOT SJÖMAN / 1957

FOR PEOPLE OF THE THEATER, this is the least romantic time of day. Looking through the windows, one can see that the sun is fading. The clock reads five-thirty in the evening. Rehearsals are finished and everyone has gone home to dinner. We are experiencing the great lull before the evening and the performance begin.

The cafeteria for employees is practically deserted. A single stage worker phones home to his wife. The sound of clinking glass can be heard from the window of the kitchen counter. Roast beef and potato salad are laid out. Naima Wifstrand is eating dinner at an empty table. Her poodle waits by her chair. The dusk deepens. Now Ingmar Bergman returns from visiting one of his actors, who is ailing. And Max von Sydow comes back from the dentist.

"What did the man do to you?"

"He drilled through the jacket crown and pulled up the nerve root. It smelled like Gorgonzola."

Knives scrape against china. It is dinnertime, a period of fatigue and emptiness before the great exertion. Von Sydow rises and goes out. In an hour he has to be made-up for Peer Gynt. Bergman remains seated in his chair. He feels the weariness of a long day's work.

The entire building seems gutted. The corridors, wainscoting, and walls are scratched and no longer welfare-state perfect. The whole theatre is beginning to feel like something *used*. Black boards cover the rounded proscenium. Behind a black drapery are Häggesta farm and

From *Vi*, no. 14 (April 5, 1957), 16–17, 38. Reprinted by permission of Vilgot Sjöman. Translated by Annika S. Hipple.

Mother Aase's cottage, where she will die in two hours. In the wings is the small fort of the lighting director, that breeding ground for ulcers. Forty-five minutes from now, he will arrive, the man who has the responsibility for five hours' uninterrupted light changes. In the great echoing studio, the Egyptian palms, smelling pungently of glue and turpentine, are waiting for Peer Gynt, the slave trader.

Now it is eleven o'clock in the evening. Von Sydow is at last making his way up through the darkness of the Norwegian fjords. Peer Gynt has by this time left the palms, the asylum in Cairo, and the giggling, pelvic-twisting Anitra, who has such dirty feet. Bergman, back in the theatre, wants to see how the new actor, replacing the one who is sick, is doing after the afternoon rehearsal. On the dark stage, the black-clad, aging, blind Solveig steps forward to meet the elderly Peer Gynt. The director observes the performers from somewhere in the dark performance hall.

"Malmö is a friendly city," Bergman says, even though he doesn't spend much time there. He practically lives at the theatre and is in agony when he has to be away from it. "I could manage without the film studio. But I wouldn't survive without the theatre."

For some, theatre is spectacle. For Bergman, it is home, daily bread, security. Here he feels that he is part of a collective.

No man has only one face. It is safe to assume that Bergman contains within him the opposite of what he appears to be. Like many celebrities—and more than most—Bergman has heard himself called an exhibitionist. Of course, this verdict is at least in part an empty accusation, for how could any artist *avoid* the urge for self-display? It is this impulse that motivates their work! But the dream Bergman embraces is a dream of artistic *anonymity*: "It is a pity that theatre ever separated itself from culture."

For as long as theatre was bound to the church, as in the Middle Ages in France, no one pondered whether or not it contained meaning. Its purpose was obvious: to serve God. When Bergman directed the Hälsingborgs City Theatre, he produced a modest mystery play about what happened when the Chartres cathedral was built. Carpenters, masons, artists labored for decades. Everyone had some duty, created something that meant more than they themselves did. Today, they are gone. Their names are gone. But the cathedral remains.

The dream of constructing an anonymous cathedral must mean a great deal if you sympathize with the knight in *The Seventh Seal*. His life had been full of comings and goings, but without goal or meaning. If theatre and film work could be like building a cathedral, then it would have a meaning that went beyond itself.

This dream of the cathedral must also have meaning for Bergman when he is most concerned about what critics and audiences will think of his work. When he made *The Seventh Seal*, he knew that it was a good film. For once, he believed, he could feel secure. Yet a week before the premiere, he suffered his usual torment. "If what I do means more than who I am—and in Chartres no one was even asked who they were; the important thing was their skill at their trade, that their hands were good at shaping what had to be shaped—then I could escape the emotional turmoil, the fear of criticism, the craving for prestige."

It seems that the many sides of Ingmar Bergman, his satisfactions and his dissatisfactions, resolve themselves through the longing to work anonymously. He feels satisfaction with what his hands are able to create: the professional's joy, the sense of truly knowing the craft of the film director. He also yearns to express a religious meaning in his work.

Bergman's professional skill is now greater than ever. He knows he can manipulate the light and the dark with equal success, producing *The Merry Widow* on the large stage and Kafka's *The Castle* on the smaller one. He can make serious films as well as comedies. "Theatre should be like the statue of Thalia out there in the hall. Look, how superbly she plows ahead! And look at her hand, in which she holds both masks, the comic and the tragic. It doesn't matter to her which one she wears. Both are equally important."

And on the way through the wings over the empty stage, he describes the security that the even pace of theatre always gives him. "In the film studio everything is hectic and flushed, for a short period. And everything circles around the director. In theatre the director is subordinate. Subordinate to the theatre. Dependent on everyone else."

In painting a portrait of Bergman, it is fitting to begin with this aspect of him, because from the outside he certainly doesn't seem like a dependent person. He seems like a confident leader as he takes long, heavy, and rapid strides through a corridor in Råsunda Film City or Malmö City Theatre, tossing his head suddenly, quickly, with eyes that are both unsuspicious and suspicious, hungry for knowledge, inquisitive and preoccupied. Those whom he passes cease to talk. Someone looks up from his newspaper. The initiative is with *him*, not with the others. For a moment the corridor is electrified. And then suddenly it is filled with a tremendous laugh, loud and booming, exaggerated as in a German expressionist play. The laugh may be at an anecdote or an idiotic review. It is always about something wonderful, funny, grotesque, or awful. Then the corridor is empty again, calm, no longer charged.

This is the external side of Ingmar Bergman, the one that stage workers, switchboard operators, and temporary visitors know well.

His actors know the internal side. Those who know it best are the ones he relies upon most heavily and believes in the most. They describe a tenderness, a calm and gentle way of dealing with intense talent. They note his efforts to give them a sense of freedom, a sense that this work is a fine game.

Bergman's method has developed over more than 20 years of theatre work, ever since the days he attended Martin Lamm's seminars in literary history and produced his first plays at Mäster Olofsgården. He has worked on every imaginable type of stage, the most dilapidated and the most professional. And he has worked with every sort of actor, amateurs and great artists. Everywhere he has searched for novelty, his sensibility fully charged. He has been proud to discover acting talent wherever it may be found: at the larval stage, in insecure theatre school students, or buried, doubted, and apparently nonexistent in established actors who have only partially succeeded.

He has written films for as long as he has worked in the theater. Stina Bergman in Svensk Filmindustri's screenplay division remembers how she humiliated the young director from Sagoteatern. She can describe how he came rushing down from the room above hers, irritated, upset, and disappointed over the comments and changes she made to his script about lonely youths in the fog of puberty. Out of this training *Torment* [Alf Sjöberg, 1944] grew.

Then there was another big step: getting into a studio, as a director.

In the thirteen years since *Torment* Ingmar Bergman has made film after film, one or two per year. To those who say he has made too many, he has several replies: you can't make films the way you make books, by sitting and waiting for a masterpiece to come; film is a product, a beautified everyday object, etc. Those who believe artists should work at a slow place would be horrified if they learned how many never-produced screenplays Bergman has composed.

His interior self reflects a different kind of anxiety from that which can be seen in his feverish activity, the anxiety at how quickly film directors get burned out, overwhelmed by highs and lows. One moment they are famous, incredibly gifted, prizewinning, and sought after. A year later, no one asks about them. What a balance beam filmmakers walk! If audiences don't go to see this one picture, then the producers won't dare to let me make another. Will audiences come? They *will!* Good, then I'll be allowed to make one more. At such moments the film director feels dependent upon his audiences. They reach deep below his skin in ways that novelists and literary critics cannot imagine.

When does he relax? His overseas trips almost always end in dissatisfaction and homesickness. After a couple of weeks, he is back, staying at a hotel, in Park Avenue or Siljansborg, planning his day and writing a new screenplay.

When it is ready, he goes down to Stockholm. If the producer okays it, the piles of paper start to grow around him. Production designer P. A. Lundgren and photographer Gunnar Fischer appear. They sketch. He explains. They create the picture bit by bit. Filming is underway.

"The magic of theatre? No, theatre has no magic left for me these days. It is manipulation, technique, and applied experience. But for me film still retains its magic."

In filming the unbelievable and the unexpected, the inexplicable can still occur.

"When the thief Raval died of the plague in *The Seventh Seal*, I did what I do usually and let the camera run for a while after his scene was through. Suddenly the sun appeared over the tops of the pine trees. Pale, but because the picture was underexposed, the effect was marvelous.

Instead of dying in darkness in a clearing in the woods, he died as sunlight broke over him."

Such things may or may not happen. The director has no control over them. This is the magic of film.

Bergman is also drawn to television. TV, like film, is an unexplored field.

A sketch of Ingmar Bergman would not be complete if it didn't address those aspects of his work that fill so many with irritation and fear.

There is the blend of theatre and faith, God and jesting. *Is that real?* people ask, meaning only that they are not comfortable with the mix. Yet the fascination with theatre and the fascination with faith are the most genuine aspects of Ingmar Bergman. You can't understand him completely without thinking of both.

Once he wrote a script about a girl named Birgitta Carolina. She went through the world as if living in a real-life morality play, encountering evil, oddity, degeneracy, poetry, and goodness. And the script ended with her finding salvation. In the final scene she stood singing in the uniform of the Salvation Army.

Even a reasonably sensible viewer must think that, as far as art is concerned, such a plot is rubbish. Herbert Grevenius called it "religious sentimentality," the worst criticism imaginable, when Bergman showed him the script. Bergman bowed to his judgment and let the film end with the girl's suicide.

No one who saw *Prison* could believe in the girl's death. It was rationalized into the film, unhinged from its emotional texture.

The fact that Bergman bowed to criticism and never made the childish and sentimental religious morality tale he originally imagined bears witness to his insecurity about both his faith and his doubt. That insecurity still remains. *The Seventh Seal* is a poem about it.

And his morbidity?

Bergman would of course not consistently compose his stories if he wasn't himself fascinated by cruelty and horror. Viewers may guess that his work is as cathartic for him as for others. If one could succeed in surgically removing his fascination, then much of the creative driving force which makes him such a splendid artist would disappear.

And those who think he delivers he morbid episodes unsuspectingly and irresponsibly know nothing about Bergman's own internal censor, his dialogue with himself. Think of the witch girl who is taken into the forest to be burned in *The Seventh Seal*. He knows that he has conveyed the scene in an austere and straightforward manner without adding anything extra to it. "You don't see the girl thrown onto the pyre. There is nothing irrelevant, nothing seductive." Still he himself is tormented by the scene without knowing why. Bergman, the minister's son, quotes his father, whom he has heard say: "I feel I can 'understand' the suffering of adults, but I can't 'understand' how God can permit the suffering of children." This is what the scene is about. Nevertheless, there is something unclear and unsettled in it, something that he doesn't feel he has covered properly.

But naturally the fascination with the horrifying can lead one astray, as I think it does in *Peer Gynt* when Bergman adds imbecilic, sick, mentally deficient people to the asylum scene in Cairo. Theatrically, the spectacle is overwhelming. But Ibsen's intent in the scene was only to make fun of pompous, hardened figures. To hear Bergman caustically mocking *truly* ill, mentally deficient people feels both incongruous with Ibsen's text and excessive, unintentionally cruel.

Right now Berman knows that the area he covers is not that of the social or the realistically psychological. His work follows, he says, "the natural structure of dreams." This is the type of film he wants to make right now, films that are dreams. And since so many have told him that he is pretentious, he plans to do the hardest thing there is: make art of the intentionally pretentious.

He consoles himself with the idea that he isn't alone as he digresses into the pretentious. He thinks *Peer Gynt* is magnificent theatre. Moreover he managed to find in it several of his own themes: buffoonery, flight, guilt. But the ending, with its eternally waiting Solveig, is hard to swallow. "In that Father Ibsen was as pretentious as I am."

Now and then Bergman is told that the should stick to directing and not write his own scripts. Such fruitless and meaningless recommendations are among a reviewer's worst weapons. For whatever points the critics wish to make, Bergman's need for expression is not just that of the director, but also the writer.

This is another tension under which Ingmar Bergman works.

# The Northern Protestant

## JAMES BALDWIN/1960

I ALREADY KNEW that Bergman had just completed one movie, was mixing the sound for it, and was scheduled to begin another almost at once. When I called the Filmstaden, he himself, incredibly enough, came to the phone. He sounded tired but very pleasant, and told me he could see me if I came at once.

The Filmstaden is in a suburb of Stockholm called Rasunda, and is the headquarters of the Svensk Filmindustri, which is one of the oldest movie companies in the world. It was here that Victor Sjöström made those remarkable movies which, eventually (under the name of Victor Seastrom) carried him—briefly—to the arid plains of Hollywood. Here Mauritz Stiller directed *The Legend of Gösta Berling*, after which he and the star thus discovered, Garbo, also took themselves west—a disastrous move for Stiller and not, as it was to turn out, altogether the most fruitful move, artistically anyway, that Garbo could have made. Ingrid Bergman left here in 1939. (She is not related to Ingmar Bergman.) The Svensk Filmindustri is proud of these alumni, but they are prouder of no one, at the moment, than they are of Ingmar Bergman, whose films have placed the Swedish film industry back on the international map. And yet, on the whole, they take a remarkably steady view of the Bergman vogue. They realize that it *is* a vogue, they are bracing themselves for the inevitable reaction, and they hope that Bergman is doing the same. He is neither as great nor as limited as the current hue and cry suggests. But he is one of the very few genuine artists now working in films.

He is also, beyond doubt, the freest. Not for him the necessity of working on a shoestring, with unpaid performers, as has been the case with many of the younger French directors. He is backed by a film company; Swedish film companies usually own their laboratories, studios, rental distribution services, and theaters. If they did not they could scarcely afford to make movies at all, movies being more highly taxed in this tiny country than anywhere else in the world—except Denmark—and 60 per cent of the playing time in these company-owned theaters being taken up by foreign films. Nor can the Swedish film industry possibly support anything resembling the American star system. This is healthy for the performers, who never have to sit idly by for a couple of years, waiting for a fat part, and who are able to develop a range and flexibility rarely permitted even to the most gifted of our stars. And, of course, it's fine for Bergman because he is absolutely free to choose his own performers: if he wishes to work, say, with Geraldine Page, studio pressure will not force him into extracting a performance from Kim Novak. If it were not for this freedom we would almost certainly never have heard of Ingmar Bergman. Most of his twenty-odd movies were not successful when they were made, nor are they today his company's biggest money-makers. (His vogue has changed this somewhat, but, as I say, no one expects this vogue to last.) "He wins the prizes and brings us the prestige," was the comment of one of his co-workers, "but it's So-and-So and So-and-So—" and here he named two very popular Swedish directors—"who can be counted on to bring in the money."

I arrived at the Filmstaden a little early; Bergman was still busy and would be a little late in meeting me, I was told. I was taken into his office to wait for him. I welcomed the opportunity of seeing the office without the man.

It is a very small office, most of it taken up by a desk. The desk is placed smack in front of the window—not that it could have been placed anywhere else; this window looks out on the daylight landscape of Bergman's movies. It was gray and glaring the first day I was there, dry and fiery. Leaves kept falling from the trees, each silent descent bringing a little closer the long, dark, Swedish winter. The forest Bergman's characters are always traversing is outside this window and the ominous carriage from which they have yet to escape is still among the properties. I realized, with a small shock, that the landscape of Bergman's mind was simply the landscape in which he had grown up.

On the desk were papers, folders, a few books, all very neatly arranged. Squeezed between the desk and the wall was a spartan cot; a brown leather jacket and a brown knitted cap were lying on it. The visitor's chair in which I sat was placed at an angle to the door, which proximity, each time that I was there, led to much bumping and scraping and smiling exchanges in Esperanto. On the wall were three photographs of Charlie Chaplin and one of Victor Sjöström.

Eventually, he came in, bareheaded, wearing a sweater, a tall man, economically, intimidatingly lean. He must have been the gawkiest of adolescents, his arms and legs still seeming to be very loosely anchored; something in his good-natured, self-possessed directness suggests that he would also have been among the most belligerently opinionated: by no means an easy man to deal with, in any sense, any relationship whatever, there being about him the evangelical distance of someone possessed by a vision. This extremely dangerous quality—authority— has never failed to incite the hostility of the many. And I got the impression that Bergman was in the habit of saying what he felt because he knew that scarcely anyone was listening.

He suggested tea, partly, I think, to give both of us time to become easier with each other, but also because he really needed a cup of tea before going back to work. We walked out of the office and down the road to the canteen.

I had arrived in Stockholm with what turned out to be the "flu" and I kept coughing and sneezing and wiping my eyes. After a while Bergman began to look at me worriedly and said that I sounded very ill.

I hadn't come there to talk about my health and I tried to change the subject. But I was shortly to learn that any subject changing to be done around Bergman is done by Bergman. He was not to be sidetracked.

"Can I do anything for you?" he persisted; and when I did not answer, being both touched and irritated by his question, he smiled and said, "You haven't to be shy. I know what it is like to be ill and alone in a strange city."

It was a hideously, an inevitably self-conscious gesture and yet it touched and disarmed me. I know that his concern, at bottom, had very little to do with me. It had to do with his memories of himself and it expressed his determination never to be guilty of the world's indifference.

He turned and looked out of the canteen window, at the brilliant October trees and the glaring sky, for a few seconds and then turned back to me.

"Well," he asked me, with a small laugh, "are you for me or against me?"

I did not know how to answer this question right away and he continued, "I don't care if you are or not. Well, that's not true. Naturally, I prefer—I would be happier—if you were *for* me. But I have to know."

I told him I was for him, which might, indeed, turn out to be my principal difficulty in writing about him. I had seen many of his movies—but did not intend to try to see them all—and I felt identified, in some way, with what I felt he was trying to do. What he saw when he looked at the world did not seem very different from what *I* saw. Some of his films seemed rather cold to me, somewhat too deliberate. For example, I had possibly heard too much about *The Seventh Seal* before seeing it, but it had impressed me less than some of the others.

"I cannot discuss that film," he said abruptly, and again turned to look out of the window. "I had to do it. I had to be free of that argument, those questions." He looked at me. "It's the same for you when you write a book? You just do it because you must and then, when you have done it, you are relieved, no?"

He laughed and poured some tea. He had made it sound as though we were two urchins playing a deadly and delightful game which must be kept a secret from our elders.

"Those questions?"

"Oh. God and the Devil. Life and Death. Good and Evil." He smiled. "*Those* questions."

I wanted to suggest that his being a pastor's son contributed not a little to his dark preoccupations. But I did not quite know how to go about digging into his private life. I hoped that we would be able to do it by way of the movies.

I began with: "The question of love seems to occupy you a great deal, too."

*I don't doubt that it occupies you, too,* was what he seemed to be thinking, but he only said, mildly, "Yes." Then, before I could put it another way, "You may find it a bit hard to talk to me. I really do not see much point in talking about my past work. And I cannot talk about work I haven't done yet."

I mentioned his great preoccupation with egotism, so many of his people being centered on themselves, necessarily, and disastrously: Vogler in *The Magician*, Isak Borg in *Wild Strawberries*, the ballerina in *Summer Interlude*.

"I am very fond of *Summer Interlude*," he said. "It is my favorite movie.

"I don't mean," he added, "that it's my best. I don't know which movie is my best."

*Summer Interlude* was made in 1950. It is probably not Bergman's best movie—I would give that place to the movie which has been shown in the States as *The Naked Night*—but it is certainly among the most moving. Its strength lies in its portrait of the ballerina, uncannily precise and truthful, and in its perception of the nature of first love, which first seems to open the universe to us and then seems to lock us out of it. It is one of the group of films—including *The Waiting Women, Smiles of a Summer Night*, and *Brink of Life*—which have a woman, or women, at their center and in which the men, generally, are rather shadowy. But all the Bergman themes are in it: his preoccupation with time and the inevitability of death, the comedy of human entanglements, the nature of illusion, the nature of egotism, the price of art. These themes also run through the movies which have at their center a man: *The Naked Night* (which should really be called *The Clown's Evening*), *Wild Strawberries, The Face, The Seventh Seal*. In only one of these movies—*The Face*—is the male-female relation affirmed from the male point of view; as being, that is, a source of strength for the man. In the movies concerned with women, the male-female relation succeeds only through the passion, wit, or patience of the woman and depends on how astutely she is able to manipulate the male conceit. *The Naked Night* is the most blackly ambivalent of Bergman's films—and surely one of the most brutally erotic movies ever made—but it is essentially a study of the masculine helplessness before the female force. *Wild Strawberries* is inferior to it, I think, being afflicted with a verbal and visual rhetoric which is Bergman's most annoying characteristic. But the terrible assessments that the old Professor is forced to make in it prove that he is not merely the victim of his women: he is responsible for what his women have become.

We soon switched from Bergman's movies to the subject of Stockholm.

"It is not a city at all," he said, with intensity. "It is ridiculous of it to think of itself as a city. It is simply a rather larger village, set in the middle of some forests and some lakes. You wonder what it thinks it is doing there, looking so important."

I was to encounter in many other people this curious resistance to the idea that Stockholm could possibly become a city. It certainly seemed to be trying to become a city as fast as it knew how, which is, indeed, the natural and inevitable fate of any nation's principal commercial and cultural clearing house. But for Bergman, who is forty-one, and for people who are considerably younger, Stockholm seems always to have had the aspect of a village. They do not look forward to seeing it change. Here, as in other European towns and cities, people can be heard bitterly complaining about the "Americanization" which is taking place.

This "Americanization," so far as I could learn, refers largely to the fact that more and more people are leaving the countryside and moving into Stockholm. Stockholm is not prepared to receive these people, and the inevitable social tensions result, from housing problems to juvenile delinquency. Of course, there are juke boxes grinding out the inevitable rock-and-roll tunes, and there are, too, a few jazz joints which fail, quite, to remind one of anything in the States. And the ghost—one is tempted to call it the effigy—of the late James Dean, complete with uniform, masochistic girl friend, motorcycle, or (hideously painted) car, has made its appearance on the streets of Stockholm. These do not frighten me nearly as much as do the originals in New York, since they have yet to achieve the authentic American bewilderment or the inimitable American snarl. I ought to add, perhaps, that the American Negro remains, for them, a kind of *monstre sacré*, which proves, if anything does, how little they know of the phenomena which they feel compelled to imitate. They are unlike their American models in many ways: for example, they are not suffering from a lack of order but from an excess of it. Sexually, they are not drowning in taboos; they are anxious, on the contrary, to establish one or two.

But the people in Stockholm are right to be frightened. It is not Stockholm's becoming a city which frightens them. What frightens them is that the pressures under which everyone in this century lives are destroying the old simplicities. This is almost always what people really mean when they speak of Americanization. It is an epithet which is used to mask the fact that the entire social and moral structure that they have built is proving to be absolutely inadequate to the demands now being placed on it. The old cannot imagine a new one, or create it. The young have no confidence in the old; lacking which, they cannot find any standards in themselves by which to live. The most serious result of such a chaos, though it may not seem to be, is the death of love. I do not mean merely the bankruptcy of the concept of romantic love—it is entirely possible that this concept has had its day—but the breakdown of communication between the sexes.

Bergman talked a little about the early stages of his career. He came to the Filmstaden in 1944, when he wrote the script for *Torment*. This was a very promising beginning. But promising beginnings do not mean much, especially in the movies. Promise, anyway, was never what Bergman lacked. He lacked flexibility. Neither he nor anyone else I talked to suggested that he has since acquired much of this quality; and since he was young and profoundly ambitious and thoroughly untried, he lacked confidence. This lack he disguised by tantrums so violent that they are still talked about at the Filmstaden today. His exasperating allergies extended to such things as refusing to work with a carpenter, say, to whom he had never spoken but whose face he disliked. He has been known, upon finding guests at his home, to hide himself in the bathroom until they left. Many of these people never returned and it is hard, of course, to blame them. Nor was he, at this time in his life, particularly respectful of the feelings of his friends.

"He's improved," said a woman who has been working with him for the last several years, "but he was impossible. He could say the most terrible things, he could make you wish you were dead. Especially if you were a woman."

She reflected. "Then, later, he would come and apologize. One just had to accept it, that's all."

He was referred to in those days, without affection, as "the young one" or "the kid" or "the demon director." An American property whose movies, in spite of all this temperament, made no money at the box office, would have suffered, at best, the fate of Orson Welles. But Bergman went on working, as screen writer and director in films and as a director on the stage.

"I was an actor for a while," he says, " a terribly bad actor. But it taught me much."

It probably taught him a great deal about how to handle actors, which is one of his great gifts.

He directed plays for the municipal theaters of Hälsingborg, Göteborg, and Malmö, and is now working—or will be as soon as he completes his present film schedule—for the Royal Dramatic Theatre of Stockholm.

Some of the people I met told me that his work on stage is even more exciting than his work in films. They were the same people, usually, who were most concerned for Bergman's future when his present vogue ends. It was as though they were giving him an ace in the hole.

I did not interrogate Bergman on this point, but his record suggests that he is more attracted to films than to the theater. It would seem, too, that the theater very often operates for him as a kind of prolonged rehearsal or preparation for a film already embryonic in his conscious-ness. This is almost certainly the case with at least two of his theatrical productions. In 1954, he directed, for the municipal theater of Malmö, Franz Lehár's *The Merry Widow*. The next year he wrote and directed the elaborate period comedy, *Smiles of a Summer Night*, which beautifully utilizes—for Bergman's rather savage purposes—the atmosphere of romantic light opera. In 1956, he published his play *A Medieval Fresco*. This play was not produced, but it forms the basis for *The Seventh Seal*, which he wrote and directed the same year. It is safe, I think, to assume that the play will now never be produced, at least not by Bergman.

He has had many offers, of course, to work in other countries. I asked him if he had considered taking any of them.

He looked out of the window again. "I am home here," he said. "It took me a long time, but now I have all my instruments—everything—where I want them. I know my crew, my crew knows me, I know my actors."

I watched him. Something in me, inevitably, envied him for being able to love his home so directly and for being able to stay at home and work. And, in another way, rather to my surprise, I envied him not at all. Everything in a life depends on how that life accepts its limits: it would have been like envying him his language.

"If I were a violinist," he said after a while, "and I were invited to play in Paris—well, if the condition was that I could not bring my own violin but would have to play a French one—well, then, I could not go." He made a quick gesture toward the window. "This is my violin."

It was getting late. I had the feeling that I should be leaving, though he had not made any such suggestion. We got around to talking about *The Magician.*

"It doesn't have anything to do with hypnotism, does it?" I asked him.

"No. No, of course not."

"Then it's a joke. A long, elaborate metaphor for the condition of the artist—I mean, any time, anywhere, all the time—"

He laughed in much the same conspiratorial way he had laughed when talking about his reasons for doing *The Seventh Seal.* "Well, yes. He is always on the very edge of disaster, he is always on the very edge of great things. Always. Isn't it so? It is his element, like water is the element for the fish."

People had been interrupting us from the moment we sat down, and now someone arrived who clearly intended to take Bergman away with him. We made a date to meet early in the coming week. Bergman stood with me until my cab came and told the driver where I lived. I watched him, tall, bare-headed, and fearfully determined, as he walked away. I thought how there was something in the weird, mad, Northern Protestantism which reminded me of the visions of the black preachers of my childhood.

One of the movies which has made the most profound impression on Bergman is Victor Sjöström's *The Phantom Carriage.* It is based on a novel by Selma Lagerlöf which I have not read—and which, as a novel, I cannot imagine. But it makes great sense as a Northern fable; it has the atmosphere of a tale which has been handed down, for generations, from father to son. The premise of the movie is that whoever dies, in his sins, on New Year's Eve must drive Death's chariot throughout the coming year. The story that the movie tells is how a sinner—beautifully played by Sjöström himself—outwits Death. He outwits Death by virtue, virtue in the biblical, or, rather, in the New Testament sense: he outwits Death by opposing to this anonymous force his weak and ineradicable humanity.

Now this is, of course, precisely the story that Bergman is telling in *The Seventh Seal*. He has managed to utilize the old framework, the old saga, to speak of our condition in the world today and the way in which this loveless and ominous condition can be transcended. This ancient saga is part of his personal past and one of the keys to the people who produced him.

Since I had been so struck by what seemed to be our similarities, I amused myself, on the ride back into town, by projecting a movie, which, if I were a moviemaker, would occupy, among my own productions, the place *The Seventh Seal* holds among Bergman's. I did not have, to hold my films together, the Northern sagas; but I had the Southern music. From the African tom-toms, to Congo Square, to New Orleans, to Harlem—and, finally, all the way to Stockholm, and the European sectors of African towns. My film would begin with slaves, boarding the good ship *Jesus*: a white ship, on a dark sea, with masters as white as the sails of their ships, and slaves as black as the ocean. There would be one intransigent slave, an eternal figure, destined to appear, and to be put to death in every generation. In the hold of the slave ship, he would be a witch-doctor or a chief or a prince or a singer; and he would die, be hurled into the ocean, for protecting a black woman. Who would bear his child, however, and this child would lead a slave insurrection; and be hanged. During the Reconstruction, he would be murdered upon leaving Congress. He would be a returning soldier during the first World War, and be buried alive; and then, during the Depression, he would become a jazz musician, and go mad. Which would bring him up to our own day—what would his fate be now? What would I entitle this grim and vengeful fantasy? What would be happening, during all this time, to the descendants of the masters? It did not seem likely, after all, that I would ever be able to make of my past, on film, what Bergman had been able to make of his. In some ways, his past is easier to deal with: it was, at once, more remote and more present. Perhaps what divided the black Protestant from the white one was the nature of my still unwieldy, unaccepted bitterness. My hero, now, my tragic hero, would probably be a junkie—which, certainly, in one way, suggested the distance covered by America's dark generations. But it was in only one way, it was not the whole story; and it then occurred to me that my bitterness might be turned to good account if I should dare to envision the tragic hero for whom I was searching—as myself. All art is a kind of confession, more or less oblique. All artists, if they are to survive, are forced, at last, to tell the whole story, to vomit the anguish up. All of it, the literal and the fanciful. Bergman's authority seemed, then, to come from the fact that he was reconciled to this arduous, delicate, and disciplined self-exposure.

Bergman and his father had not got on well when Bergman was young.

"But how do you get along now?" I had asked him.

"Oh, now," he said, "we get on very well. I go to see him often."

I told him that I envied him. He smiled and said, "Oh, it is always like that—when such a battle is over, fathers and sons can be friends."

I did not say that such a reconciliation had probably a great deal to do with one's attitude toward one's past, and the uses to which one could put it. But I now began to feel, as I saw my hotel glaring up out of the Stockholm gloom, that what was lacking in my movie was the American despair, the search, in our country for authority. The blue-jeaned boys on the Stockholm streets were really imitations, so far; but the streets of my native city were filled with youngsters searching desperately for the limits which would tell them who they were, and create for them a challenge to which they could rise. What would a Bergman make of the American confusion? How would he handle a love story occurring in New York?

# Excerpts from *L136: Diary with Ingmar Bergman*

## VILGOT SJÖMAN / 1963

### Between Christmas and New Year 1960

Dinner with Ulla Isaksson. Ingmar and Käbi come up for coffee. Artistic interpretation problems: Käbi talks about Hindemith; Ingmar about direction as interpretation—then he tells wild and funny stories about animals he has filmed: he snakes in *Thirst,* the squirrel in *The Seventh Seal,* and the cat in *The Devil's Eye.*

Suddenly the conversation switches to suffering. Ingmar tells of one of his co-workers out at the film studios who suffers from Bechterew's disease—his deformed back, his constant pains; the only thing that saves him is always being on the move. I have spoken to him out at the studios: a man of about forty; his name too is Bergman, Karl-Arne, always called just K. A. He has been property man for IB for many years now; he procures all the thousand and one props that are needed in the films; he puts all his emotional energy into work.

"K. A. is *impassioned*, I love him for that."

Ingmar speaks of K. A. with warmth and fascination, with an understanding of his suffering that is mixed with horror.

That was the first time I heard anything that had to do with *Winter Light*; but I didn't know that then.

(I recall the whole of this Christmas conversation six months later when I read the screenplay and meet the churchwarden Algot Frövik,

From Vilgot Sjöman, *L136: Diary with Ingmar Bergman*, trans. Alan Blair (Ann Arbor: Karoma Publishers, 1978). Reprinted by permission of Vilgot Sjöman.

former (retired) railroad clerk, thirty-nine years old; a very sick man who compares his own physical suffering with that of Christ:

*"Please excuse me, it sounds presumptuous of course, but physically I have, in all diffidence as it were, suffered just as much as Christ. His torment was fairly short, what is more. About four hours or so?")*

"I'm writing something else now. . . ."

## Undated, May 1961

What is it about? He doesn't tell Ulla I. either. Only his anxiety: "Guess how it feels: I'm to do a new film in the fall and I haven't written a line of it yet. The whole thing exists only in my head."

The only thing he reveals to Ulla is that it is to form the final phase of a trilogy:* *The Virgin Spring, Through a Glass Darkly*—plus the new one.

In that case it should have a religious theme.

## Undated

*An old wish*

In the fall of 1946 I began studying at the University of Stockholm: from the military service I came straight to Agne Beijer's lectures on Queen Christina's court ballets and encountered the extraordinary methods and problems of theatrical history. How can one reconstruct something so fleeting as the stage moment? Even the theatrical life we ourselves move in is gone tomorrow morning. Then why not try to capture it just now, when it is topical? In my spare time I wrote dramatic criticism, time and again aware of how little I knew about the director's and the actor's share in the whole. *That* was a brilliant detail—but who conceived it: the director or the actors? When was it born? Was it there from the start of the rehearsals? And I had a wild idea: day by day to

---

*He likes working with the idea of a trilogy; it is just that by degrees he moves the trilogy forward a step: the first part drops out when a new one appears. When we do the TV interview at Torö (8-12-61), *The Virgin Spring* has been omitted. Now *Through a Glass Darkly* is the first part of a trilogy.

describe how four different directors prepared a particular theatrical production—if they could think of letting a recorder into the very workshop.

I never got as far as daring to ask Olof Molander, Alf Sjöberg, Torsten Hammarén; I did however ask Ingmar Bergman once at the beginning of the 1950's when I had gone down to Malmö to write an article on Bengt-Åke Benktsson for the magazine *Vi*. Oh, no, he wouldn't mind. It was after lunch; I went with IB into the vast innards of the Malmö City Theater; in this dark forsakenness he was rehearsing the last act of Strindberg's *Ghost Sonata* with Gaby Stenberg and Folke Sundquist (". . . I love the first two acts as much as I loathe the last; but it's my blasted duty as director to give shape to it with just the same objectivity. . . ."); I felt the magic and the attraction, the desire to report what happened in the workshop, meticulously, factually, as vividly as possible.

## Thursday 1 June 1961

SF needs screenplays; Ingmar has commissioned one from me; when it is ready I am seized by the devil and ask to direct it myself. "You're crazy! If you had the faintest notion of all the work it takes to direct. . . ." He fires off a fifteen-minute sermon in his office today: a graphic horror picture of what can happen to a beginner in the film studio; then the agreement is fixed. (He is to check all my rushes; else he cannot accept responsibility to the board. Sensible condition.) I want to call the film *The Mistress*.

IB suggests that I prepare myself by following the shooting of his next film: a kind of course in direction.

All the better: then I can make my old dream come true at the same time. Does he agree? Oh yes. Will he really be able to stand having me in the studio every day—recording, making a note of every detail? Yes, it will be okay, he thinks. As long as I don't let him down. It has happened to him before, he says. Such and such a person let him down at such and such a time.

"In what way?"

"A stab in the back. He went around telling others what I was like. Others—but never a word to me. And when I found *that* out. . . ."

# Wednesday 14 June 1961

*The new idea for a film*
*Envy of Christ*

Lunch guest at Ingmar's table: a girl in a light kerchief, Inger Stevens who has come to see him. "Nice kid," he says (since she has confided to him that she is trying to get away from Hollywood). We see a test film of a young ballerina from the Opera, Kari Sylwan; then he tells me of an idea he has for a film:

"A parson shuts himself up in his church. And says to God: I'm going to wait here until you reveal yourself. Take all the time you want. I still won't leave here until you have revealed yourself.

"So the parson waits, day after day, week after week."

That was the original idea for the film, he says.

"Then I woke up one morning . . . well, you know the state when you wake up still grasping at a dream. I realized that the parson didn't have to wait as long as I had first thought. A lot can happen in an hour and a half—the time the film itself takes.

"So now I'm going to start, without beating around the bush, by showing a communion service. Only six communicants—one of them being the parson's wife. After the service the parson stays behind in the church. He is waiting for a man who has made an appointment with him. The man doesn't show up. The parson grows tired and irritated. But the man doesn't come because he has hanged himself."

"This film, too," he says, "is a chamber play, with only a few parts: the parson, his wife, one or two others—the chamber play has been neglected in films."*

He will depict the whole of the empty, dead, hollow routine in the communion service.

---

*I don't know when IB first began using the term "chamber play"; but having once discovered that films lend themselves so well to what Strindberg calls "the intimate procedure," "the strong important theme," he has been the most energetic follower of the Strindberg chamber play tradition. But it is not easy to define a "chamber play." Even Strindberg had difficulties—see "Open Letters to the Intimate Theater"—and IB maintains that two such structurally different films as *Wild Strawberries* and *Through a Glass Darkly* are both "chamber plays."

"How will you do it?"

"Oh, I've only to go to a country church north of Stockholm and show everything just as it is. I've driven around now the last few Sundays and had a look."

"With Käbi?"

"No, with my father." (Ingmar's father, the Rev. Erik Bergman.)

"Do you tell him about the ideas for your films?"

"No, never. But he helps me with practical details . . . It's awful being pressed for time: I must start shooting in September. And I don't want to rush a theme like this. It must take its time to be born, labor pains and all."

He tells me far too little for me to grasp what the film is really about. And I'm alarmed at the prospect of having to watch yet another film parson who succumbs under doubt and lack of faith—however many has one endured! Is Ingmar really capable of renewing that theme? Then he adds something that makes me prick up my ears:

"You see, this parson has a hatred of Christ that he won't admit to anyone. He is envious of Christ."

"*Envious*?"

"Yes, and jealous. He feels something akin to the elder son's hatred of the prodigal son, who gets all the attention when at last he comes home: fatted calf and all the rest. It simply occurred to me that I would make a clean breast of my own envy and jealousy of the Christ figure."

"Envious of Christ"—it calls to mind IB's childhood. What is it like being a small child in a clergyman's family, with father going off every Sunday to devote his time to someone else, an utter stranger called Jesus Christ?

A parson who is envious of Christ—what a fascinating theme! And how original—I imagine it has never been used in literature before.

"Hard to give shape to it, though. I'll just have to lift up what I have found in myself—as cleanly as I can."

He goes on to say how long it has taken him to interest himself in the Christ figure at all. And it can be seen from his films: whenever he touched on a religious theme, it has been about the God motif. So now, for the first time, he is going to penetrate in towards the Christ motif?

". . . because when the parson is waiting there in the church for the man who doesn't come, he understands for the first time how it must have been for Christ when he felt himself forsaken on the cross. It wasn't only that Judas betrayed him and that the disciples fell asleep at Gethsemane. But God forsook him when he hung on the cross. . . ."

"Who is to play the parson?"

"Gunnar Björnstrand. The very right one for the part, just now."

Talk of *The Face*, Tennessee Williams, Jean Anouilh; and then:

"When I've finished the script you can read it. And criticize it. I *want* criticism."

Pause. Swift, sensitive postscript:

"But you're not to criticize it in such a way that I lose my belief in this film and get scared of making it."

The fear of all writers that the theme will wither up, evaporate like fairy gold. And in the midst of this the literary inferiority complex.

"What the critics say about me as a director leaves me cold. They can say this and that is bad and this and that is brilliant—but when they say anything about me as a writer, I'm vulnerable."

On the bus going home from SF I notice that I am out of humor. I feel dogged by bad luck. Now that at last I can follow a film production—why did I have to strike one of his religious films, of all things! Now I shall be forced to try and record the innermost twists and turns of the religious themes—am I capable?

(A few years ago I wrote a religious settling of accounts with myself in the travel book *Flygblad*; I'll give it to him straight away, so that he knows where I stand.)

## Thursday 20 July 1961

*The second Thursday: The wife dead*
*Three sources for the new film*
*He settles accounts with* Through a Glass Darkly
*A mixture of religion and sexuality*

Last Thursday the parson still had a wife. Now she's dead.

"I woke up one morning and killed her off. It was a lovely feeling. And right." He gives a loud laugh as he tells me about it.

"The wife was to have played a big part, actually. But somehow I found it hard to write about her. Whenever I tried, nothing came."

These typical sudden changes in his ideas! Aversion mounts up: slug-
gishness, unwillingness to write; a sharp blow and his imagination is
flowing swiftly again, in new channels:

"Now the parson has a mistress instead. An hysterical, lonely, middle-
aged, flat-chested schoolteacher in the country. So now things are
moving."

"Who is to play that part?"

"Ingrid Thulin."

Pause: for my surprise. He laughs delightedly.

"So actually I'm writing a new *Fancy If I Married the Parson.*"

He's writing the script for the third time now. He is trying to apply
his usual industrious working schedule with fixed writing times and
relaxation in the evening. I can't grasp it. How can one avoid working
around the clock when one is right inside a work?!

"Can you really put the characters out of your mind when you've
finished writing for the day?"

"No, they're with me day and night. There is only one time when
they have vanished completely: eleven o'clock, when I sit down to
write. Then they're gone with the wind, like schoolchildren who don't
want to go inside to lessons."

Then the working moralist inside Ingmar shakes his finger and says
that it is *dangerous* to give in to one's disinclination.

"The remedy is to sit down pedantically every day at a definite time,
irrespective of whether you're in the mood or not. And then you get up
and prowl around the house, once an hour . . . until you start functioning."

Sighs, laughs, groans—I have never heard Ingmar speak of writing
other than as torment, resistance, a necessary evil. Never as enjoyment,
tingling desire.

"You see, this matter of working discipline. . . . It was when I was
directing down in Malmö. Paul Kletzki came and was to conduct a con-
cert. He was ill and wretched and rheumatic—sciatica, fever, the shivers—
in such a bad way that he had to keep one foot in a slipper while he
was rehearsing. And the Malmö orchestra has never played better in its
life! That's how little he allowed his body to stop him. For me it was a
damn good lesson—I was terribly down just then, for various reasons.
It looked as though I was not going to get Käbi, and I was rehearsing
*The Värmlanders* after *Faust* and it was a bit boring to work on. . . . But

Kletzki hadn't a *thought* of pampering himself as some artists do. I notice the same thing with Käbi: she can coddle herself and fuss over little things—but when it really comes to it, not a word out of her! She doesn't mind how hard she works."*

Today I find that the film didn't at all arise merely out of the theme that he first indicated, with the parson who waits for God to come. We talk for a long time; the literary historian in me begins looking for clues.

One thread-end is this:

"Käbi and I were married in Boda church in Dalarna on September 1st, 1959, nearly two years ago. The same fall we went to visit the parson who had married us; but we were still only in the village store when we met his wife and she was very grave; she was talking to a schoolgirl. When we got to the parsonage we were told that this girl's father had taken his life. The parson had had many talks with him, but it hadn't helped."

Another thread, joined to this one:

"This parson had the same difficulties as nearly all Swedish clergy-men: he found it heavy going when he tried to reach his parishioners. Hardly anyone came to church, and so on."

A third thread-end of an idea:

"I don't as a rule give a damn about foreign politics, but last spring I read in the papers about the Russians and the Chinese, and then I discovered that it's not the Americans the Russians are afraid of, it's the Chinese. The Chinese who are drilled so hard that they might very well start an atomic war. And reading all this put me in an awful state of mind."

"How does it come into the story?"

"I have a fisherman and his pregnant wife come to see the parson; they've made an appointment for a talk with him after the service. The fisherman has become introspective and brooding because he has read that the Chinese are going to destroy the whole world."

"Who will play the fisherman?"

"Max von Sydow."

---

* An old interest of Ingmar's, an old problem. Of the final episode in *Till Glädje* (1950): the young artist falters in the first big solo part in his life, but is forced to accommodate himself to humble, simple working discipline. Isn't there a thread leading from this to the parson in *Winter Light*, who holds the service *notwithstanding*? (The framework changes, that is all: artistic ambition in the first case; religious ambition in the new film.)

"And his wife?"

"Gunnel Lindblom, I think. If I can get her for the part. It would all fit in very well—she's expecting a baby herself."

The new film has been given a name now: *Nattvardsgästerna (Winter Light)*. I like it—it smacks of pure Swedish tradition, going right back to Tegnér's *The Communion Children* and Runeberg's *The Moose Hunters*. Apparently Ingmar has made good headway with writing, as he ventures to tell me a little about it:

"It's a counterpart to *Through a Glass Darkly*. An answer to it. When I wrote *The Glass* I thought I had found a real proof of God's existence: God is love. God is all kinds of love, even perverted forms—and the proof of God's existence gave me a great feeling of security . . . ."

*A great feeling of security*, he says literally.

". . . and I let the whole film work out into that proof, I let it form (he has recourse to a musical term) the actual *coda* in the last movement. But that lasted only until I started shooting the film."

(Then how is it he didn't alter the ending of the film? No, in his view that is one of the fundamental principles of work in the studio: don't leave your script in the lurch in the middle of shooting. Be faithful to what you wrote, even if now, here in the studio, you think it represents a bygone phase. Don't meddle with the unity it had *then*. That sort of thing is dangerous, from both an artistic and a practical production point of view. If you want to record new results, then wait until the next film.)

"That's why I break up that proof of God's existence in this new film. It's a settling-of-accounts film, more or less. I settle accounts with Daddy God, the god of auto-suggestion, the god of security."

IB is evidently in the habit of cutting up a tent into pedagogically clear sections so as to get order and a general picture of the whole. He divides the new film up into three parts:

1.   *The breaking up of the coda.* Squaring accounts with the god of auto-suggestion.
     "Hard to write that part?"
     "Not so hard."
2.   *The void after the break-up.*
"Not so hard to write either."
3.   *A new faith shows signs of life.*

"That's the hardest to write. I think I've found a solution. Have you ever head of 'duplication'? On certain Sundays the parson has to hold two services: one in the main parish and then one in the chapelry, the sub-parish in the next district. Now it is the custom in the Swedish church that if there are no more than three persons in the congregation, no service need be held. What I do is this: when Björnstrand comes to the district church, the church-warden comes up to him and says: 'There's only one churchgoer here.' Yet the parson holds the service all the same. That's all that is needed to indicate the new faith that is stirring inside the parson."

The opening of the film gives Ingmar the parson's son and moralist a few qualms of conscience. He searches his heart to see whether it is "only a gimmick," "a trick of the trade," to begin the film with the whole of the communion service. In that case he should refrain from it!

"But however much I turn it over in my mind, I still arrive at the thought that I *don't* do it just as a gimmick."

At times IB looks quite Asiatic. Eyes and lips gleam and he looks down on his co-workers from a height, conscious of position and psychological power. A smile like that on an Indian god's image. The sharp eye-teeth; the dark-green copper tints of the skin of his face.

At other times he is helplessly serious, as appealing as a child: with all his sensitivity laid bare. As now when he talks of religion, his face softens with seriousness. I catch a glimpse of both torment and the need of honesty.

On the few previous occasions when we have touched on religion, we have both been on our guard. Today too I am on the defensive, closed around my naturalism. Ingmar senses it and tries to bridge the gap between us by telling me his conception of the difference between "conviction" and "knowledge."

"I have the same conviction as you, if you know what I mean."

" 'Conviction' is naturalistic: don't count on anything other-worldly."*

---

* The naturalistic perspective can be found in Thomas's words to the fisherman in this finished film: "If it is so that God does not exist, what is the difference? Life becomes comprehensible. What a relief. Death becomes an extinguishing, a dissolution of body and soul. Etc."

"But I have a *knowledge* which says just the opposite. A knowledge which is at once distinct and evasive."

" 'Knowledge' says that God exists."

"You see, I believe that one can cut oneself off from God. Or one can say yes. I really think so."

(So may times he has returned to this theme. Now this parson who cuts himself off from God and love—in the shape of a woman, typically enough.)

"And intercession: I am convinced that it is a reality."

In *Through a Glass Darkly* Karin goes to pieces in the conflict between two powers. The good voices are behind the wall-paper.** Karin calls them mysteriously "the others"; Ingmar himself actually calls them "the saints." Opposed to them are the black voices, those who give fiendish promptings: when *they* get God into their hands, he becomes a repulsive and nightmarish spider-God.

As a young man he lived with a woman who from time to time was subjected to commands. Voices gave her orders; voices told her what to do—he drew on those memories for material for the character of Karin. And on one of his own most basic conflicts:

"There, in *Through a Glass Darkly*, there I really succeeded in expressing that mixture of religion and sexuality which I have always found so hard—so painfully hard—to sort out."

## Thursday 10 August 1961, Afternoon

*Four hours of rough treatment of the script*

He settles down in his little office at SF with a searching smile:

"Well? Do you think we should do this film?"

"Sure."

I myself can hear what that "sure" sounds like. This hedging, non-definite, unenthusiastic thing which is I; and which is the very opposite of his abrupt choice between cold and hot (either he is seized with enthusiasm or else he snaps and snarls). I brace myself and start according to

---

** The original title of that film was *The Wallpaper*.

plan reeling off everything I like about the script; but he waves all this aside impatiently, anxious about what is to come: the objections, the criticism.

"Why have you fought shy of the envy of Christ?"

"I haven't fought shy of it! It's there!"

"It's *talked* about, yes. In passing. But it's never dramatically formed, in picture and acting."

Ingmar gives a little smile.

"It *was* there, before, from the start. I even wrote it. . . ."

"How did you form it?"

"Oh, that's very simple: just by letting Thomas talk to the Christ image in the church. But I took it out."

"Why?"

"Because it didn't belong here, to *this* film. It belongs to the next film. You see, every object has its specific gravity, hasn't it? All that about the envy of Christ is too big to sort out this time, I felt very strongly that I must keep it till next time. This film is much simpler than that. I've had to begin at the beginning again, in fact, with a scraping bare of the God image."

(I seem to remember he sometimes spells it with a small "g" in the script = the old god image that is to be rejected?)

"You see, I feel that I can't run before I can walk. I've done it so many times before: tried to force myself to a result of faith. But you just can't *make* yourself believe. It must take its time: one year or two years or ten. Perhaps the whole problem disappears entirely, for all I know. I must also be prepared for that. At any rate for a time. That's how it was after *The Seventh Seal*."

Suddenly a timid and sensitive voice:

"What are you smiling at?"

Because I am touched, I want to answer; but I find it hard to explain myself. It has something to do at any rate with purity in an artistic striving. The will to listen carefully to a theme; and be loyal to it. Do one thing at a time. The insistence on work well done, the strict morality of the handicraftsman. All this ideal of patience in an explosively impatient man like Ingmar.

Lay building stone to building stone, so they form a life's work. This is Ingmar's twenty-fifth film. Not all of them belong to his life's work;

some are merely exercises. But even restricting oneself to ten. Ten well-made building blocks which together form a whole.

## Friday 11 August 1961

*After-thoughts*
So:

While working on the idea, Ingmar lifted the whole material *out of* a literary tradition (type: morality play, altar play) *into* another literary tradition (type: "Strindbergian penitent drama"). The movement went from the stylization of the church to everyday realism. From theater to film. (Check later to see if the finished film bears traces of this transition.)

It was lucky all the same that I bought out my suggestions for reconstruction; otherwise I would never have found out about this course of events, since Ingmar always throws away drafts and rough copies.

Why does he?

Is he ashamed of them? Does he think his problems of literary style will be exposed just there?

As it is now, one must trust his sudden explanation afterwards. Explanations that come by chance, *en passant*; like this one, for instance:

Once last summer he called *Through a Glass Darkly* a "romantic" film, particularly if one compared it with the bleakness of *Winter Light*. "Romance" as against all chill penury. Yesterday afternoon, tired after our discussion, he told me something of himself and Käbi, how they gradually discovered that they were "two badly injured people. I most, perhaps. She had her time as a refugee behind her. And I, I felt myself to be dying." With great tenderness:

"It all began very romantically between us, awfully romantically. Then we changed together. The romance passed; now it's something else that binds us together. Something else, something much more real."

And suddenly, the psychological key, tossed out in passing:

"That romantic first time corresponding to Thomas's marriage in the film."

*Through a Glass Darkly* was conceived during this first romantic phase—and was the only one of his films with a dedication: "To Käbi, my wife." Therefore this mysticism in the final coda: love exists. Love is real. Love is God. A mysticism which (so I guess) in a far too simple way soaked up the difficulties, the cruelties, the conflicts in life—therefore it must be contradicted and exploded, in expectation of a greater God image. The beautiful Karin mysticism in *The Glass* has to be succeeded by the harsh Märta Lundberg demand in *Winter Light*.

That must have been why Ingmar got nowhere as long as he tried to write about the parson and his wife.

Not until he broke the female image into two halves did the situation become fruitful for his imagination: on the one hand the dead wife, pallid, dreamy, marked by death, standing for the romantic "God is love" declaration. On the other hand the schoolteacher— strong, demanding, real.

# *Playboy* Interview: Ingmar Bergman

## CYNTHIA GRENIER / 1 9 6 4

IN THE MONTHS since Ingmar Bergman's *The Silence* world
premiered in Stockholm, moviegoers in a dozen countries have been
lining up around the block: some to see the final third of the Swedish
film maker's celebrated trilogy (following *Through a Glass Darkly* and
*Winter Light*) on the quest for love as a salvation from emotional death;
others to verify the judgment of some critics that this anatomy of lust
is the masterwork of Bergman's 20-year career. But most, quite
unabashedly, have come to ogle the most explicitly erotic movie scenes
on view this side of a stag smoker—even after the snipping of more
than a minute's film for the toned down U.S. version. The film has precipitated a rain of abuse on its 15-year-old creator—as a pornographer
(by members of the Swedish parliament), purveyor of obscenity (from
Lutheran pulpits all over Sweden) and corrupter of youth and decency
(via anonymous calls and letters). Outraged at the outcry, Bergman was
most offended by the accusation that he filmed the sex scenes merely to
shock and titillate his audiences. "I'm an artist," he told a reporter.
"Once I had the idea for *The Silence* in my mind, I had to make it—
that's all." The son of an Evangelical Lutheran parson who became the
chaplain to Sweden's royal family, Bergman remembers his years at
home "with bitterness," as a period of emotional sterility and rigid
moral rectitude from which he withdrew into the private world of fantasy. It was on his ninth birthday that he traded a set of tin soldiers for
a toy that was to become the catalyst of his creativity: a battered magic
lantern. A year later he was building scenery, fashioning marionettes,

From *Playboy*, vol. ii, no. 6 (June 1964), 61–68. Reprinted by permission of Cynthia Grenier.

working all the strings and speaking all the parts in his own puppet theater productions of Strindberg—foreshadowing his directorship of a youth-
club theater during his years at Stockholm University, where he produced
in 1940 an anti-Nazi version of *Macbeth* which became a minor cause
célèbre—and scandalized his family.

Fired with the zeal of social protest, Bergman quit school the next
year, moved into the city's bohemian quarter, began to dress and act
accordingly—and to germinate plot lines for satiric and irreverent plays
which he never got around to writing. He finally found steady employ-
ment as an assistant stage manager, rose swiftly to become a director,
and began to earn the reputation for dramatic genius, arrogance and
irresistibility to women (he's been married four times) that has become
part and parcel of the Bergman legend. Trying his hand at writing
a screenplay in 1944, he submitted the manuscript to Svensk Filmindustri, Sweden's largest movie company, which decided to film it.
Appropriately entitled *Torment*, it set the tone and theme for a new
career, and for the 25 films that followed. In the eight years since his
"discovery" abroad with the international release of *The Seventh Seal
Smiles of a Summer Night, Wild Strawberries, The Magician, Brink of Life*
and *The Virgin Spring*, he has become the acknowledged guru of the art-
film avant-garde, and many critics have joined fellow professionals in
hailing him as the world's first-ranking film maker.

An exacting taskmaster, he does not brook the slightest deviation
from the script in the course of shooting, nor countenance the presence
of outsiders anywhere in the studio—especially journalists, of whom he
has never been fond, on or off the set.

It was with some trepidation, therefore, that we approached the mer-
curial moviemaker with our request for an exclusive interview. But he
replied with a cordial invitation to visit him in Stockholm—which we
accepted, arriving late last February, in the middle of the somber Nordic
winter, for a week-long stay.

Our conversations took place in his small, sparsely furnished office
backstage at the Royal Dramatic Theater in downtown Stockholm,
where, as the newly appointed manager of the national theater, he was
devoting his directorial energies full time, on an extended sabbatical
from film making, to staging the works of such theatrical iconoclasts as
Brecht, Albee and Ionesco. Meeting with us for an hour or so each

morning ("when I'm most alive," he told us), he would arrive promptly at nine, dressed always, indoors and out, in heavy flannel slacks, polo shirt, wool cap and a tan windbreaker with a dry cleaner's tag still stapled to a cuff. Our interview began with a wry smile from our subject—and a disarming greeting in which he reversed roles by asking the first question.

BERGMAN:    Well, are you depressed yet?

PLAYBOY:    *Should we be?*

BERGMAN:    Perhaps you haven't been here long enough. But the depression will come. I don't know why anybody lives in Stockholm, so far away from everything. When you fly up here from the south, it's very odd. First there are houses and towns and villages; but farther on there are just woods and forests and more woods and a lake, perhaps, and then still more woods with, just once in a while, a long way off, a house. And then, suddenly, Stockholm. It's perverse to have a city way up here. And so here we sit, feeling lonely. We're such a huge country; yet we are so few, so thinly scattered across it. The people here spend their lives isolated on their farms—and isolated from one another in their homes. It's terribly difficult for them, even when they come to the cities and live close to other people; it's no help, really. They don't know how to get in touch, to communicate. They stay shut off. And our winters don't help.

PLAYBOY:    *How do you mean?*

BERGMAN:    Well, we have light in the winter only form maybe eight-thirty in the morning till two-thirty in the afternoon. Up north, just a few hours from here, they have darkness all day long. No daylight at all. I hate the winter. I hate Stockholm in the winter. When I wake up during the winter—I always get up at six, ever since I was a child—I look at the wall opposite my window. November, December, there is no light at all. Then, in January, comes a tiny thread of light. Every morning I watch that line of light getting a little bigger. This is what sustains me through the black and terrible winter: seeing that line of light growing as we get closer to spring.

PLAYBOY:    *If that's how you feel, why not leave Stockholm during the winter and work in the warmer climates of such film capitals as Rome or Hollywood?*

BERGMAN:    New cities arouse too many sensations in me. They give me too many impressions to experience at the same time: they all crowd in on me. Being in a new city overwhelms me, unsettles me.

PLAYBOY:    *There've been reports that you feel what you've called "the great fear" whenever you leave Sweden. Is that why you've never made a film outside the country?*
BERGMAN:    Not really; all that has very little to do with making movies. After all, actors and studios are basically the same all over the world. What worries me about making a film in another country is the loss of artistic control I might run into. When I make a film, I must control it from the beginning until it opens in the movie houses. I grew up in Sweden, I have my roots here, and I'm never frustrated professionally here—at least not by producers. I've been working with virtually the same people for nearly twenty years: they've watched me grow up. The technical demands of moviemaking are enslaving: but here everything runs smoothly in human terms: the cameraman, the operator, the head electrician. We all know and understand one another: I hardly need tell them what to do. This is ideal and it makes the creative task—always a difficult one—easier. The idea of making a film for an American company is very tempting, for obvious reasons. But its not one's first Hollywood film that's so difficult—its the second. Work in another country, with more modern equipment but with my same crew, with the same relationship to my producers, with the same control over the film as I have here? I don't think that's very likely.

PLAYBOY:    *You're said to be no less indisposed to come into contact with outsiders even on your own sets in Stockholm, from which all visitors are barred. Why?*
BERGMAN:    Do you know what moviemaking is? Eight hours of hard work each day to get three minutes of film. And during those eight hours there are maybe only ten or twelve minutes if you're lucky, of real creation. And maybe they don't come. Then you have to gear yourself for another eight hours and pray you're going to get your good ten minutes this time. Everything and everyone on a movie set must be attuned to finding those minutes of real creativity. You've got to keep the actors and yourself in a kind of enchanted cycle. An outside

presence, even a completely friendly one, is basically alien to the intimate process going on in front of him. Any time there's an outsider on
the set, we run the risk that part of the actors' absorption, or the technicians', or mine, is going to be impinged upon. It takes very little to
destroy the delicate mood of total immersion in our work. We can't risk
losing those vital minutes of real creation. The few times I've made
exceptions I've always regretted it.

PLAYBOY:     *You've been criticized not only for barring and even ejecting
intruders from your sets, but for outbursts of rage in which, reportedly, you've
ripped phones off walls and thrown chairs through glass control booths.
Is there any truth to these accounts?*
BERGMAN:     Yes, there is—or rather, *was*. When I was younger, much
younger, like so many young men I was unsure of myself. But I was
very ambitious. And when you're unsure, when you're insecure and
need to assert yourself, or think you do, you become aggressive in trying to get your own way. Well, that's what happened to me—in a
provincial theater where I was a new director. I couldn't behave that
way now and hope to keep the respect of my actors and my technicians. When I know the importance of every minute in a working day,
when I realize the supreme necessity of establishing a mood of calm
and security on the set, do you think I could, or would, have any right
to indulge myself that way? A director on a movie set is a little like the
captain of a ship: he must be respected in order to be obeyed. I haven't
behaved that way at work since I was maybe twenty-five or twenty-six.

PLAYBOY:     *Yet these stories of temper tantrums continue to circulate in print.*
BERGMAN:     Of course they do. Such stunts as ripping out telephones
and hurling chairs around make the sort of copy that journalists love
to give their editors and their readers. It's more colorful to read about
a violent temper than about someone instilling confidence in his actors
by talking quietly to them. It's to be expected that people will go on
writing—and reading—this sort of nonsense about a man year after
year. Do you begin to understand why I don't like to talk to the press?
You know people also say I don't like to see journalists, that I refuse to
talk to them anymore. For once they are right. When I am nice to
reporters, when I give them my time and I talk to them sincerely, they

go off and print a lot of old gossip, or their editors throw it in, because they think those old stories are more entertaining than the truth. Take that cover story done on me a few years ago by one of those American magazines of yours.

PLAYBOY:    Time *magazine?*
BERGMAN:    Yes, that's it. My wife read it to me when it came out here. The man they described sounds like someone I'd like to meet—perhaps a little difficult, not such a nice person, yet still an interesting fellow. But I didn't find myself in it. He was nobody I know.

PLAYBOY:    *It's been reported that you've had no less difficulty recognizing some of your own films when you read what the critics have to say about their merit and meaning. Is this true?*
BERGMAN:    I've given up reading what's written either about me or about my films. It's pointless to get annoyed. Most film critics know very little about how a film is made, have very little general film knowledge or culture. But we are beginning to get a new generation of film critics who are sincere and knowledgeable about the cinema. Like some of the young French critics—them I read. I don't always agree with what they have to say about my films, but at least they're sincere. Sincerity I like, even when it's unfavorable to me.

PLAYBOY:    *Well, your films have been unfavorably reviewed for, among other reasons, the private meanings and obscurity of many of their episodes and much of their symbolism. Do you think these accusations may have some validity?*
BERGMAN:    Possibly, but I hope not—because I think that making a film comprehensible to the audience is the most important duty of any moviemaker. It's also the most difficult. Private films are relatively easy to make: but I don't feel a director should make easy films. He should try to lead his audience a little further in each succeeding film. It's good for the public to work a little. But the director should never forget who it is he's making his film for. In any case, it's not as important that a person who sees one of my films understands it here, in the head, as it is that he understands it here, in the heart. This is what matters.

PLAYBOY:    *Whatever the nature of their understanding, a great many inter-*
*national critics concur in ranking you foremost among the world's film mak-*
*ers. How do you feel about this approbation?*
BERGMAN:    Success abroad has made my work much easier in Sweden.
I don't have to fight so much on matters really external to actual creative work. Thanks to success, I've earned the right to be left to my
work. But, of course, success is so transitory: it's such a flimsy thing to be
a la mode. Take Paris—a few years ago I was their favorite director. Then
came Antonioni. Who's the new one? Who knows? But you know, when
these young men of the *nouvelle vague* first started making films, I was
envious of them, envious of their having seen all the films at the *ciné-
mathèque* [film library], of their knowing all the techniques of moviemaking. Not anymore. On the technical side, I have become very sound. I
have acquired confidence in myself. Now I can see other directors' work
and no longer feel jealous or afraid. I know I don't have to.

PLAYBOY:    *Have their films influenced or instructed you in the development*
*of your own moviemaking style and skills?*
BERGMAN:    I've had to learn everything about movies by myself. For
the theater I studied with a wonderful old man in Göteborg, where I
spent four years. He was a hard, difficult man, but he knew the theater,
and I learned from him. For the movies, however, there was no one.
Before the War I was a school-boy, then during the War we got to see no
foreign films at all, and by the time it was over I was working hard to
support a wife and three children. But fortunately I am by nature an
autodidact, one who can teach himself—though it's an uncomfortable
thing to be at times. Self-taught people sometimes cling too much to the
technical side, the sure side, and place technical perfection too high.
I think what is important, most important, is having something to say.

PLAYBOY:    *Do you feel that America's New Wave directors have something*
*to say?*
BERGMAN:    Yes, I do. I have seen just a few examples of their work—
only *The Connection, Shadows* and *Pull My Daisy*: I should like very
much to see more. But from what I've seen, I like the American New
Wave much more than the French. They are so much more enthusiastic, idealistic, in a way—cruder, technically less perfect and less knowing

than the French film makers, but I think they have something to say, and that is good. That is important. I like them.

PLAYBOY:    *Have you enjoyed the Russian films you've seen?*
BERGMAN:    Very much. I think something very good will be coming from them soon. I don't know why, but I feel it. Did you see *Childhood of Ivan*? There are extraordinary things in it. Some of it's very bad, of course, but there is real talent and power.

PLAYBOY:    *How do you feel about the Italian directors?*
BERGMAN:    Fellini is wonderful. He is everything I'm not. I should like to be him. He is so baroque. His work is so generous, so warm, so easy, so unneurotic. I liked *La Dolce Vita* very much, particularly the scene with the father. That was good. And the end, with the giant fish. Visconti—I liked his first film, *La Terra Trema*: his best, I think, I liked Antonioni's *La Notte* a great deal, too.

PLAYBOY:    *Would you classify these among the best films you've ever seen?*
BERGMAN:    No, right now I think I have three favorite contemporary films: *The Lady with the Dog, Rashomon* and *Umberto D.* Oh, yes, and a fourth: *Mr. Hulot's Holiday.* I love that one.

PLAYBOY:    *Let's return to the subject of your own work, if we may. Where did you get the idea for your latest and most controversial film,* The Silence?
BERGMAN:    From a very big, fat old man. That's right. Four years ago, when I was visiting a friend in a hospital here, I noticed from his window a very old man, enormously fat and paralyzed, sitting in a chair under a tree in the park. As I watched, four jolly, good natured nurses came marching out, lifted him up, chair and all, and carried him back into the hospital. The image of him being carried away like a dummy stayed in my mind, although I didn't really know exactly why. It all grew from that seed, like most of my films have grown—from some small incident, a feeling I've had about something, an anecdote someone's told me, perhaps from a gesture or an expression on an actor's face. It sets off a very special sort of tension in me, immediately recognizable as such to me. On the deepest level, of course, the ideas for my films come out of the pressures of the spirit: and these pressures vary.

But most of my films begin with a specific image or feeling around which my imagination begins slowly to build an elaborate detail. I file each one away in my mind. Often I even write them down in note form. This way I have a whole series of handy files in my head. Of course, several years may go by before I get around to transforming these sensations into anything as concrete as a scenario. But when a project begins to take shape, then I dig into one of my mental files for a scene, into another for a character. Sometimes the character I pull out doesn't get on at all with the other ones in my script, so I have to send him back to his file and look elsewhere. My films grow like a snowball, very gradually from a single flake of snow. In the end, I often can't see the original flake that started it all.

PLAYBOY:    *In the case of* The Silence, *the "original flake"—that paralyzed old man—is certainly hard to discern in the explicit scenes of intercourse and masturbation that aroused such heated reactions, pro and con. What made you decide to depict sex so graphically on the screen?*
BERGMAN:    For many years I was timid and conventional in the expression of sex in my films. But the manifestation of sex is very important, and particularly to me, for above all, I don't want to make merely intellectual films. I want audiences to feel, to sense my films. This to me is much more important than their understanding them. There is much in common between a beautiful summer morning and the sexual act; but I feel I've found the cinematic means of expressing only the first, and not the other, as yet. What interests me more, however, is the interior anatomy of love. This strikes me as far more meaningful than the depiction of sexual gratification.

PLAYBOY:    *Do you agree with those who say that the American version of* The Silence *has been emasculated by the excision of almost two minutes of film from the erotic scenes?*
BERGMAN:    I'd rather not comment on that.

PLAYBOY:    *All right. But is it possible that this encounter with American censorship regulations will induce you to exercise a certain degree of self-censorship in future films?*
BERGMAN:    No. Never.

PLAYBOY:    *How did you persuade actresses Thulin and Lindblom to perform the actual acts depicted in the picture's controversial scenes?*

BERGMAN:    The exact same way I have gotten them, with all my other actors, to perform in any scene in any of my other films. We simply discuss quietly and easily what they must do. Some people claim I hypnotize my actors—that I use magic to bring the performances out of them that I get. What nonsense! All I do is try to give them the one thing everyone wants, the one thing an actor *must* have: confidence in himself. That's all any actor wants, you know. To feel sure enough of himself that he'll be able to give everything he's capable of when the director asks for it. So I surround my actors with an aura of confidence and trust. I talk with them, often not about the scene we're working on at all, but just to make them feel secure and at ease. If that's magic, then I am a sorcerer. Then, too, working with the same people—technicians and actors—in our own private world for so many years together has facilitated my task of creating the necessary mood of trust.

PLAYBOY:    *How do you reconcile this statement with the following declaration, which you made five or six years ago in discussing your film-making methods: "I'd prostitute my talents if it would further my cause, steal if there was no other way out, kill my friends or anyone else if it would help my art"?*

BERGMAN:    Let's say I was pretty defensive when I said that. When one is unsure of himself, when he's worried about his position, worried about being a creative artist, he feels the need, as I said before, to express himself very strongly, very assertively, in order to withstand any potential criticism. But once you've finally become successful, you feel freed from the imperatives of success. You stop worrying about striving, and can devote yourself to your work. Life becomes so much easier. You like yourself better. I find that I'm beginning to enjoy much that I never did before, to learn that there is much I haven't seen. I feel a little older—not much, but a little—and I like it.

You know, I used to think that compromise in life, as in art, was unthinkable, that the worst thing a man could do was make compromises. But of course I did make compromises. We all do. We have to. We couldn't live otherwise. But for a long time I wouldn't admit to myself—although, of course, at the same time I knew it—that I, too, was a man who compromised. I thought I could be above it all. I have learned that I can't. I have learned that what matters, really, is being alive. You're alive: you can't stand dead or half-dead people, can you? To me, what counts is being able to feel. That's what *Winter Light*—the film of mine that people seem to understand least—is trying to say. Now that you've been in Stockholm in midwinter for a few days, I think you can begin to understand, a little, what this film is about. What do you make of it?

PLAYBOY:     *We're more interested in learning what* you *make of it.*

BERGMAN:     Well, it was a difficult film, one of the hardest I've made so far. The audience has to work. It's a progression from *Through a Glass Darkly*, and it in turn is carried forward to *The Silence*. The three stand together. My basic concern in making them was to dramatize the all importance of communication, of the capacity for feeling. They are not concerned—as many critics have theorized—with God or His absence, but with the saving force of love. Most of the people in these three films are dead, completely dead. They don't know how to love or to feel any emotions. They are lost because they can't reach anyone outside of themselves.

The man in *Winter Light*, the pastor, is nothing. He's nearly dead, you understand. He's almost completely cut off from everyone. The central character is the woman. She doesn't believe in God, but she has strength: it's the women who are strong. She can love. She can save with her love. Her problem is that she doesn't know how to express this love. She's ugly, clumsy. She smothers him, and he hates her for it and for her ugliness. But she finally learns how to love. Only at the end, when they're in the empty church for the three o'clock service that has become perfectly meaningless for him, her prayer in a sense is answered: he responds to her love by going on with the service in that empty country church. It's his own first step toward feeling, toward learning how to love. We're saved not by God, but by love. That's the most we can hope for.

PLAYBOY:     *How is this theme carried out in the other two films of the trilogy?*

BERGMAN:     Each film, you see, has its moment of contact, of human communication: the line "Father spoke to me," at the end of *Through a Glass Darkly*; the pastor conducting the service in the empty church for Marta at the end of *Winter Light*; the little boy reading Ester's letter on the train at the end of *The Silence*. A tiny moment in each film—but the crucial one. What matters most of all in life is being able to make that contact with another human. Otherwise you are dead, like so many people today are dead. But if you can take that first step toward communication, toward understanding, toward love, then no matter how difficult the future may be—and have no illusions, even with all the love in the world, living can be hellishly difficult—then you are saved. This is all that really matters, isn't it?

PLAYBOY:    *Many reviewers felt that this same message—that of salvation from solitude through love—was also the theme of your best-known and most commercially successful film,* Wild Strawberries—*in which the old physician, as one critic wrote, "after a life of emotional detachment, learns the lesson of compassion, and is redeemed by this change of heart." Are they right?*

BERGMAN:    But he doesn't change. He can't. That's just it. I don't believe that people *can* change, not really, not fundamentally. Do you? They may have a moment of illumination, they may see themselves, have awareness of what they are, but that is the most they can hope for. In *Winter Light*, the woman, the strong one—she can see. She has her moment of awareness, but it won't change their lives. They will have a terrible life. I wouldn't make a film about what happens to them next for anything in the world. They'll have to get along without me.

PLAYBOY:    *Speaking of the character of Marta in* Winter Light, *you've been widely praised for your sympathetic depiction of, and insight into, the feminine protagonists in your films. How is it—*

BERGMAN:    You're going to ask how it is I understand women so well. Women used to interest me as subjects because they were so ridiculously treated and shown in movies. I simply showed them as they actually are—or at least closer to what they are than the silly representations of them in the movies of the thirties and forties. Any reasonably realistic treatment looked great by comparison with what was being done. In the past few years, however, I have begun to realize that women are essentially the same as men, that they both have the same problems. I don't think of there being women's problems or women's stories any more than I do of there being men's problems or men's stories. They are all human problems. It's people who interest me now.

PLAYBOY:    *Will your next film be in any way a continuation of the theme elaborated in your recent trilogy?*
BERGMAN:    No, my new film, and my last for a while, is a comedy, an erotic comedy, a ghost story—and my first film in color.

PLAYBOY:    *What's it called?*
BERGMAN:    *All the Women.* They may like it in America: the theme song is *Yes, We Have No Bananas.* It amuses *me*, anyway. I've already told one Swedish writer that I'm hoping it will start the Bergman Ballyhoo Era. It's not long since I finished the final cutting. You know, I don't at all mind editing or cutting my films. I don't have any of this love-hate feeling that some directors have toward cutting their own work. David Lean told me once that he can't bear the task of cutting, that it literally makes him sick. I don't feel that way at all. I'm completely unneurotic in that respect.

PLAYBOY:    *You said a moment ago that this will be your last film "for a while." How long is a while?*
BERGMAN:    Two years, probably. I want to immerse myself in my work as director at the Royal Dramatic Theater here. Theater fascinates me for several reasons: for one thing, it's so much less demanding on you than making films. You're less at the mercy of equipment and the demand for so many minutes of footage every day. You aren't nearly so alone. It's between you and the actors, and later on, the audience. It's wonderful—the sudden meeting of the actor's expression and the audience's response. It's all so direct and alive. A film, once completed, is inalterable: in the theater you can get a different response from every performance. There's constant change, always the chance to improve. I don't think I could live without it.

# Ingmar Bergman: "For Me, Film Is Face"

ANNIKA HOLM / 1966

EVEN BEFORE THE SEASON at the Royal Dramatic Theatre ended, Ingmar Bergman was working on his new movie, *Hour of the Wolf.*

Last Monday he experienced, for the first time in three and a half years, the joy of heading directly out to Film City without first having things to do at the theater. On that day, he labored over two films. He edited the last part of *Persona* and held a production meeting to prepare for the shoot of *Hour of the Wolf,* which began the next morning.

The two films maintain some similarities. Both emerged from a big project, *The People Eaters,* which Bergman was to have made last summer on the island of Väderö in Halland. That aborted project gave birth to these.

*Hour of the Wolf* takes place in and around an isolated cottage near Hovs Hallar. Liv Ullmann plays a pregnant woman. Max von Sydow is her husband. Other roles are played by Ulf Johansson, Gudrun Brost, Erland Josephson, and Naima Wifstrand.

After four days in a studio at Film City, the crew travels on Whitsunday Eve to Hovs Hallar for two weeks of exterior shooting. In anticipation of the new movie, Bergman provided some insight into his relationship with film and theatre.

For three years Bergman has devoted most of his time to theatre. Now he has returned to film. Has he tired of theatre? Or has the desire to make film overpowered him?

---

From *Dagens Nyheter,* May 28, 1966. Reprinted by permission of *Dagens Nyheter.* Translated by Annika S. Hipple.

"I took the job as theatre director because I thought theatre had a true significance, that I was there to manage something. I didn't do it primarily for my own sake, but because I felt that it had value in and of itself.

"The films I make are entirely for my own sake, in the same way that I think an artist paints a painting or an author writes a book for his own sake."

There is another difference between working with theatre and with film, namely between re-creation and creation. In films Ingmar Bergman works with his own material from start to finish. From idea to premiere he is driven by an inner need. Or, rather, the film drives him.

## Theatre—my career

"In the theatre I am first and foremost a professional. There I am not so much concerned with inspiration, because I do not need to feel an emotional affinity for the play. It is the professional execution that interests me.

"In the past I felt an urge to do certain plays, so I did them, and I felt less interest in other plays, and those I didn't do. Now I think that a good piece of theatre is always fun to produce, no matter what it is."

And if it were your own script?

"These days I would never be able to produce my own play. I would be too mortally embarrassed to work every day with my own text. In the theatre it is always an actor's creation that the director attends to. In film there is always a mixture of actors, director, camera, sound, the whole machine. For me that difference is now definitive. Film is personal. Theatre is objective."

But even film can become impersonal. Once it is completed, it is gone, says Bergman. A couple of years ago he said in an interview that for this very reason film is uninteresting. He can't oversee the effects; he can't be concerned about whether or not a thousand people on Formosa see his film. But it does matter to him, he said then, if twenty people from Farsta make the trip to the Dramaten.

"Of course . . . I am vain and want to be loved. It's great if a film does well and people like it. But the moment a film has gone far enough to reach another's consciousness, it becomes uninteresting."

It hasn't always been like this, but it has become more so over the course of 21 years in filmmaking.

"I think that the negative response to *Winter Light* was the first blow. I was very close to that film, but it was maligned and audiences turned away from it. That was the only time I felt that I had succeeded in making a film the way I truly wanted to make it.

"And then this loathsome fuss surrounding *The Silence*, where people lost sight of the essentials in favor of inessentials."

Now, in anticipation of the *Persona* premiere this fall, Bergman says he is less vulnerable. Not much is known yet about it, other than that it concerns a sick woman and her caregiver and that it is about identity and transformation. The Latin word "persona" refers to an actor's mask. "It's an exciting film," says Bergman hesitantly, "but you shouldn't ask me what it's about."

There are some clues in the word "cinematography." Bergman originally wanted to call the film simply *Cinematography*.

## The great fascination

"That's the way it is. It's my form of cinematography. For me cinematography is first and foremost close-ups. People's faces. I notice that this is what fascinates me more and more, and what I experience as unceasingly exciting. And it's not primarily just any faces, but those of the actors.

"Because as an actor deals with existing or agreed-upon material, he creates new dimensions and new secrets. And I feel that you get much further, the actor gets much further, when he deals with something concrete rather than with improvisation. As soon as he can work on a concrete idea, he moves from his own personality into a sort of anonymity. He hides himself behind a role and, in this way, can become much more naked, much more ruthless. An actor rarely wants to be private. Privacy makes him shy. But when he is given a 'yes' or a 'no' or three lines from the telephone book, he can be completely ruthless and give of himself in a way that he never can with something he himself has been a part of creating.

"I am fascinated by how, in a given moment, the blood may rush to an actor's face, or his gaze suddenly change—how he takes on an irrational, secretive tone of voice, whose source is completely mysterious. This, in the end, becomes what's essential.

"You can never force or entice or seduce actors. Their performances are a matter of a security and a freedom that can only come from the actors themselves."

Robert Bresson, the Frenchman, who has also been financed by Svensk Filmindustri, showed his film in Cannes a week or so ago and spoke about his film aesthetic. He believes in the necessity of using non-actors in film. Bresson, discussing his work, also used the word "cinematography."

"I think that Bresson is superb, even though his films don't mean anything to me. Nevertheless, I admire him as I admire any artist who carries out his vision without compromise and with passion. That's worthy of respect in today's international film market, with this *insane* commercialization. You see people get twisted. They become commercialized and afraid. I have felt that fear often. And deep inside me, there is probably some left . . . it would be terrible to be robbed of my livelihood. But then I have theatre, my profession. It is a great security, because—as I've said now and then—every film is my last film."

## Why do they whine?

In saying this, Bergman does not mean to attack the Swedish film climate. He gets almost angry when he hears words like "overproduction" and "uniformity." WE ARE DOING WELL in this complete freedom. Peter Kylberg makes a film according to his sensibilities and can have it shown at the city's quality cinema. Jörn Donner is permitted to carry stubbornly on. Bo Widerberg exists, with his streak of genius. We have a gold nugget like Jan Troell.

"As long as Sweden can afford to back us, we will continue. That's good, isn't it? It is in this sort of climate that talent can emerge. Then it's a matter of holding on. Making films is a matter of staying alive. And of never becoming afraid. The moment you become afraid, I think you're done for."

In this rich film climate we have a Film School, where Ingmar Bergman is supervisor.

"The whining from film school students surprises me enormously. There's probably no one who has had it as good as they do, with so many opportunities. They attend a school that isn't completed, that will be shaped almost more by the students than by the teachers. Such a school should be formed in a state of excitement, in a big scuffle, but not with whining."

## The adventure abroad

Ingmar Bergman has repeatedly turned down opportunities to work abroad. He says that his work environment is Sweden, that he has no need to look elsewhere. But in this era of co-productions, the plea will surely come again—Make a film abroad!

"But then I would want to bring with me my own coworkers. Without them I wouldn't want to make a film.

"It would perhaps be fun some day to make an English-language film, provided I can work under circumstances where I am allowed to make it as I want and not as others want.

"That's an adventure that maybe I should experience one day."

# Ingmar Bergman Is Making a Film on Fårö Again

## BRITT HAMDI/1967

INGMAR BERGMAN is making a film on Fårö again.

Svensk Filmindustri will spend a cool three million on it, the largest investment the company has ever made.

For the crew of forty, this means three months of hard work and almost uninterrupted isolation on Fårö—an island that is now quite different from the way it is in the summer, when it serves as a tourist spot.

For Ingmar Bergman, this means—as usual—that he must outdo himself.

On a gray morning, we come to Bergman's strictly guarded headquarters. The day seems to have difficulty deciding whether it will rain or be foggy. Right now the fog has prevailed, lying thickly over the marshes and throwing a gray net over an old farmhouse with chicken coops, rabbit pens, and a greenhouse that has seen better days. Cars emerge from the mist, as unreal as if they had come from Mars. They brake behind the latrine and deliver their cargo of actors, film technicians, and military advisors. The people move like a commando troop. They surround the cottage and disperse into small groups. Some of them, making a strategic advance, open the cottage door.

Bergman exclaims, "Do you know that every cold is a minor brain inflammation? That's what my doctor says, and he knows what he's talking about."

Now it starts to rain.

From *Vecko-Revyn*, December 6, 1967, 34–41. Reprinted by permission of *Vecko-Revyn*. Translated by Annika S. Hipple.

The director glares angrily at the weather, sinks deeper into his old leather jacket and mutters behind its top button. "Last night I decided to stop production on this movie."

Gunner Björnstrand interjects dryly, "This morning *I* felt that this was my best role!"

Max von Sydow is costumed in striped flannel pajamas with an undershirt showing at the neck. (Bergman: "It's supposed to be that way, the undershirt under the pajamas. That's how he's worn it since he was a child"). Von Sydow warms his soul by listening to Bach's Brandenburg Concertos on the record player, while at the same time massaging his thighs slowly and carefully. It seems rather absurd to imagine it at this moment, but in just a few months these same legs will strut on Broadway in a musical about the romance between Prince Albert and Queen Victoria. During yesterday's filming, von Sydow, in his role as Jan Rosenberg, was directed to throw himself headlong, again and again, onto a gravelly courtyard and to practice distance running by splashing through marshes. Bergman inquires how Max is feeling.

"Thanks. My hand, back, and legs hurt. But I'm sober!"

The Bach fades. Somewhere in the background a transistor radio can now be heard. A voice sings that "love should be tended, and lips meet in a green-painted boat." The director rises and gives Björnstrand a sympathetic pat. He wanders off with hunched shoulders, hands in his pants pockets. A sound technician comes up to him, concerned about some excess noise in yesterday's takes. The prop director checks on an interior set, a pantry. Someone else talks about a shipment of dynamite that is expected with the next ferry. The director listens and advises and feels cold.

"Film is a pest," he mumbles. "One big damned pest."

He remains in the courtyard, exchanging five words with the script girl Katinka and significantly more with cinematographer Sven Nykvist. Then he sees Liv Ullmann, fresh as a spring song, approaching through the steady rain. Approvingly, he says, "Liv is the only woman I know who is beautiful even when she is crying."

Fifteen minutes later things are underway.

Ingmar Bergman is making a film on Fårö again.

It is his third on this barren, singular island off Gotland, where the place names sound foreign. The screenplay is entitled *Shame*. But you can never tell if the film will be released with this title. It may be shortened before it's finished.

Initially, it was called *Dreams of Shame*. It is significant that Bergman peeled off the dreams. These days, he's not much in for miracles.

One evening at Sudersand's hotel, the headquarters for the SF team, there is a screening of his 1955 film *Smiles of a Summer Night*.

At that time, most of the people in the room already belonged to the Bergman group. Taking the film in, they all agree about one thing in particular. Its glitter, its whimsy, its dazzling array of gorgeous women and vital men, its tale of exuberant love expressed in a beautiful setting is clearly the work of the youthful Bergman. With reference to Bergman's career, the film recalls Picasso's early experiments in realistic painting, where everything was included, all the anatomical details. Today, Bergman, like Picasso, has developed a stern and ruthless craving for simplicity. At its core, his art follows the maxim, "excess is evil."

As the crew watch *Smiles of a Summer Night*, we can perhaps forgive the small sighs that are heard now and then from the Windsor chairs. Most come from Mago, the costume designer, who back then was permitted to indulge himself in tulle hats, plumes, and beautiful sweeping ballroom garb. Jarl Kulle, dressed elegantly and in lush mustachios, seemed to strut across the screen as a stately precursor to Danilo in *The Merry Widow*. This morning, by contrast, Mago ran about in the miserable rain and sprayed fake mud on a platoon of soldiers. It's not quite the same thing. But he consoles himself with the fact that Ullmann is wearing an old fur bequeathed by Marlene Dietrich after her latest attic cleaning and that a whiff of the Divine One's perfume can still be sensed in the lining.

In the darkness Gunnar Björnstrand tilts his chair back and mumbles dreamily, "Imagine, I was only 46 that summer . . ."

On another morning Bergman's cold and mood are improved. Someone tells a story lightly peppered with obscenities. Bergman's roaring laughter echoes across the marshlands and makes the hen yard's only rooster so indignant that he isn't heard for the rest of the day.

Björnstrand and Ullmann talk about a trip they made to the Sorrento Festival together with Vilgot Sjöman, Jörn Donner, Harry Schein, and a few others. They stayed at a labyrinthine hotel where they kept getting lost, particularly Björnstrand, who said he invariably ended up in a cleaning closet or the kitchen.

Bergman announces that next year he will preside over the festival.

Björnstrand: "You? With your sense of direction! You'll get terribly lost. You're going to crawl out a window, fumble along the walls, and scream for help, only to be photographed by *paparazzi.* Then we'll have fine headlines: *Bergman cat burglar in Sorrento."*

Bergman, looking slightly worried, starts to talk about *The Forsythe Saga.* He and Ullmann watch it faithfully every Wednesday night in their house by the sea, the newly constructed abode that has inspired many rumors and that Bergman defends with the same energy as the loyal denizens of Fårö. Wild-eyed summer tourists have come sputtering up in their cars to the vicinity, stopped in front of some local resident, and breathlessly hissed, "Where does Bergman live?"

The resident would respond, "I'm not quite sure." And then, pointing in the wrong direction, "Oh, it's somewhere over towards the lighthouse."

The people who live in the house have quietly been adopted by the inhabitants of the island. Liv is already called "astumor," which in the local dialect is equivalent to "neighbor's wife." And their one-year-old daughter Linn babbles happily and at length while the household's priceless Siri Werkelin keeps her entertained by using the island's unique dialect. As for Bergman, he feels deeply and genuinely anchored in a place whose natural surroundings reflect the same strict simplicity he infuses into his work.

Bergman: "When I am dead, they can stuff me, put me in the cutting room, and stick a mechanism inside me that will make me nod repeatedly over the work table. I'll sit there, and the summer tourists can put a *krona* in the collection box to see this wonder. But until that time I hope I can be left alone in my house!"

*The Forsythe Saga* comes up again in conversation. Bergman finds the male actors extraordinary, but the women . . .

He scratches Ullmann on the back of the neck and adds softly, "Here, the situation is almost completely the reverse!"

Von Sydow and Björnstrand rumble objections and for a long while the men exchange self-satisfied insults which make them all feel comfortable. Bergman and Björnstrand work incredibly well together and are clearly enjoying their duel.

Off at the edge of the woods a group of experts works on what they consider will be the century's greatest explosion.

Explosives expert Rustan Åberg has been called in from Oskarshamn and has together with military advisor Stig Lindberg spent days talking seriously about black powder, explosive paste, and the guarantee that the greenhouse will withstand the blow. In the screenplay a foreign power's airplane explodes near the farm, where former orchestra musicians Jan and Eva Rosenberg have retreated after all normal business has ceased in the country. Enormous scaffolding has been put up in the woods, and trucks and wheelbarrows full of dangerous elements have driven in and out again and again. The moment is approaching.

Rustan Åberg: "This is probably the biggest charge I have ever set. But Bergman isn't content with the ordinary."

When the explosion finally comes, it seems as though all of Gotland has been blown up.

Everyone gasps for breath. Bergman bubbles over with joy, generously passes around Droste's chocolate pastilles, and urges everyone to cheer mightily for Rustan Åberg and Stickan Lindberg. The boys have done well. The dynamite has done well. The day is saved.

Bergman sits in his workshop in the house on Fårö.

This evening he has been the perfect host at the dinner table, sparkling with wit over the meatballs, speaking seriously about theatre over ice cream ("Let them carry on. I sit here like Achilles, sulking in my tent, utterly divorced from reality and tradition.")

Now he is a weary with a long day of takes behind him. And tomorrow in Stockholm, a dentist awaits. It's hard to determine which worry weighs more heavily upon him. Possibly even these concerns pale before the sight of me, a curious and inexperienced interlocutor ensconced in his favorite armchair.

Bergman attempts to direct the questioning according to his own wishes. "Actually, you've already got everything you want about the filming. Right?"

"No."

Bergman glances longingly at the door. He scratches himself below the knee. Some papers on the desk need to be organized. He straightens a framed photograph of himself, Ullmann, and the architect of the house, T. Abrahamsson, all dressed in fur hats. The picture was taken on the primeval beach one winter day when the house was still only a dream. Suddenly he turns around, smiles with all his teeth, and says, "Are you comfortable there?"

I nod.

The atmosphere is still very solemn.

INTERVIEWER:    *"Ingmar, what exactly do you think of popular culture?"*
INGMAR BERGMAN:    "I remember an evening a while back. Liv and I were sitting and watching TV, a satellite broadcast from all over the world, and we felt incredibly excited at the thought that here, on this little island, in the middle of this great ocean, we had the whole world within our reach. It was fantastic. Then, for the program finale, the Beatles came on, wearing wreaths of flowers and pearls, and pounded out 'All You Need Is Love' or whatever it was. No other music would have been appropriate just then!"

INT:    *"Are you aware that you have it pretty good, to say the least? Hardly anyone can tell you what to do."*
IB:    *"No one can!* I depend my being able to shape my life the way I want. For that reason I'd rather do without a number of things that might be advantageous to me."

INT:    *"Lucrative Hollywood offers, for example?"*
IB:    "For example."

INT:    *"Do you notice that people are often afraid of you?"*
IB:    "Nowadays I almost only meet new people through my work. If someone seems afraid, then it's part of my job to free that person from fear; I know all too well what it's like to be afraid of people!"

INT:    *"Are you implying that you were shy as a child?"*
IB:    "Shy? I was paralyzed in other people's company."

INT:    *"Is this why one gets a sense that you're always playing?"*
IB:    "Rather it's that the longer you're involved in this business, the more you dare to view filmmaking as a game. The moment you lose the

sense of play, you should quit. If you forget that it's a game, that as a filmmaker you are *imitating reality*, then you're headed toward a terrible self-deception."

INT:    *"How do you see yourself?"*
IB:    "Not as some uniform, clearly-defined phenomenon. Rather as something in continuous motion. But that's probably a very common feeling with artists."

INT:    *"You are 49, in your 50th year. Are you starting to feel middle-aged?"*
IB:    "Well, I'm experiencing aging in that I can't read the telephone book without glasses."

INT:    *"And you are careful with your health?"*
IB:    "It's a necessity. I have to produce a small bit of quality product every day."

INT:    *"You said once that the hour between night and dawn was your hell, which you visited every morning. Do you still have the same anxiety?"*
IB:    "I made *Hour of the Wolf* and was freed from my own hour of the wolf."

INT:    *"As a private person, as a man, you have led many lives. Do you yourself feel that the women surrounding Bergman have been numerous?"*
IB:    "No, few. But crucial!"

INT:    *"When does a new Bergman film come into being?"*
IB:    "Usually when I'm in the middle of shooting the previous film. When the factory is working full blast, day and night, and the atmosphere is charged, then I'm usually filled with a new idea."

INT:    *"Like now, for instance?"*
IB:    "Like now, for instance."

INT:    *"Isn't it true that you choose the same actors for your roles time and again?"*

IB:    "Almost all continuously working dramatists have written for particular actors. It's a reciprocal stimulation. You see a certain actor in a certain role at the moment you're writing. Then the actor gives it additional dimension. The manuscript is like the melody part. It must be enhanced by the instrumentation. This happens during filming. By making my screenplays less and less detailed I can follow my basic experience more freely."

INT:    *"Liv Ullmann is currently playing her third role under your direction and the lead role in your private life. Would you draw a small portrait of Liv in words?"*
IB:    "Liv is already like a photograph, a complete commentary unto herself! Moreover, I'm in love with her, artistically and humanly."

INT:    *"Do you see your current state as permanent?"*
IB:    "I have built my house, and here I'm planning to stay!"

He starts to talk about fleeting mornings and doesn't like the thought of having to get up so awfully early.

INT:    *"When the snow comes you'll be completely isolated, won't you?"*
IB:    "Yes. Imagine how nice it will be!"

It's clearly time to be going.

As soon as the guests resolve to leave, their host lights up and rushes to the coatroom. We are dressed and embraced, and friendly admonitions are made to the young man who is driving us home, 21-year-old Jan Bergman, Ingmar Bergman's eldest son, who is on Fårö to "get to know his father."

Later, Jan says, "Everyone talks about my dad. I felt a bit envious . . . before. Felt that everyone knew much more about him that I did. But now I think I'm starting to get my own picture of him, and it feels good. One thing's for sure: He's not like anyone else!"

Forgive me if I can't resist crying, "Amen!"

# Interview with Ingmar Bergman

## LARS-OLOF LÖTHWALL/1968

THE SHAME is Ingmar Bergman's 30th film—a film in which improvisation has played a major part. "But improvisation must be prepared for," says Bergman.

A November noon; a small room in the Svensk Filmindustri studios. Ingmar Bergman, ensconced in a beautiful, baroque armchair, talks. He is interviewed by *Take One's* Swedish correspondent, Lars-Olof Löthwall.

Q:    *During production of* The Shame, *you made certain minor alterations from time to time. Previously, the manuscript has been Holy Scripture to you, isn't that so?*

A:    No, actually I worked in this way with *Persona*. With *Persona*, I had ample time, I had an ensemble of virtually two characters, and it cost nothing to begin experimenting, to try improvising.

But the basis for all improvisation must be preparation. If I haven't prepared, I can't improvise. If I've made careful preparations I can always improvise. Then I know I have something to fall back on. What I detest is formlessness. That terrifies me. It is seldom that mere formlessness in a work of art conveys anything vivid. More often it gives an impression of effort. But a combination of improvisation and planning—that's good.

Q:    *You shot quite lengthy sequences in* The Shame *which you didn't at first think were suitable.*

From *Take One*, vol. 2, no. 1 (September–October 1968), 16–18. Reprinted by permission of the Home Entertainment Group.

A:    I've always done so, that has been my practice for the last ten to fifteen years. You see, one has to begin somewhere in a film; when you do, you're likely to be far out from the centre of eventual interest, you find yourself disoriented. No matter how well you prepare, you don't really know how a film's going to look when you've finished it. Above all, you're not sure of the tone, and that's tremendously important . . . for which reason I always have a margin of at least a week for retakes, usually at the tail end of the production . . .

When we begin a film, the actors know as little about it as I do. Usually I overwork them, as well as myself, in the first week. I'm looking for something. All the time, in this first medley of images I'm in search of some strong, key expression. Now, if you try forcing this into existence by an effort of will, your work of art will be dead and thin.

Q:    *When you've written your manuscript and it's ready for you to start shooting, it's pretty well set up as a visual continuity. Do you work in such a way with your imagination that you can then—if one may express this in a banal way—close your eyes and see the film as a sequence of pictures?*

A:    No. Well, bits and pieces of it, yes. But it would be intolerable, for me and for those working with me, if, at every moment, I were to try and shape the film by force, if I insisted on a sequence of detailed, pre-conceived pictures to illustrate the conception I had as I envisioned or wrote the script.

When I write I must try to capture something in words which for all useful purposes, you might say, can't be expressed in words. Later it is necessary to translate the words again so that in quite another context they'll come alive. To be sure, so long as I have a firm grasp on my point of departure, there will always be an inner relationship between the original version I had and the completed, materialised picture-sequence.

While that original conception must always be in the background, I must not let it become too dictatorial, since, for one thing, I must be prepared to modify it when I switch from writing to directing. For another, my actors, too, have a right—to say nothing of an obligation—to draw straws, to choose among alternatives. The whole process is essentially creative. You write down a melodic line and after that, with the orchestra, you work out the instrumentation.

Q:    *In an interview you said that if you once lost your feeling for play you'd be finished. But in* The Shame *you're actually very close to the intense centre, you have got something deep inside, in a grip . . .*

A:    But that's a game, too. I believe that every seriously intended work of art must contain an element of play. If we believe otherwise, we commit ourselves to a colossal exaggeration. I believe that in this feeling of a game we can find a stimulating sense of shaping a universe, shaping people, shaping situations: we experience the passion of holding up a mirror and finding out what that mirror reflects . . .

Look at the great ones, like Churchill, Picasso, Stravinsky. Picasso and Stravinsky, both, have the eyes of a child, they have "humour lines"; they suggest some kind of secret feeling for the game.

Q:    *Games and games! Your script girl claims that when you did* The Silence *and Ingrid Thulin was supposed to be dying, alone in a hotel bed, she spiced up the situation by doing a cha-cha before taking the scene!*

A:    Certainly; I've often noticed this: if you're concentrating on a serious story, a deeply serious, perhaps tragic situation, a desperately painful involvement, you have a bursting need for jumping off into the opposite—into a lively clowning mood.

Perhaps because the moment of pain which was the nucleus of your creation is now far behind you, experienced long before you wrote it down, and even further away from the production of the film. Each and every artist who creates does so by building on his own painful experience, on a moment of agony which does not necessarily exist at the time of his performance. Of this we are reminded—sometimes with a secret smile—behind the mask we are assuming. This doesn't mean that the experience will then seem less genuine. On the contrary.

Q:    *You have often mentioned the moment of pain which is the kernel of a film's inspiration. Can you trace* The Shame *back to such a moment?*

A:    No. That's a long and tangled thread. It's an experience of humiliation. A long, painful experience of man's humiliation.

For some time, since the first moment of recognition, I have wondered how I would have sustained the experience of a concentration camp, of being forced into such a damnable position.

How noble would I have been?

At the bottom of everything there lies this abomination to which man is exposed, the world over: they club his head in, they scream at him, they assault him, they terrorize him.

The older I get the more ghastly it seems to me. And the harder it is for me to live with in my conscience.

This is what we're attempting, modestly, in *The Shame*: to show how humiliation, the rape of human dignity, can lead to the loss of humanity on the part of those subjected to it.

Q:   *You must despise films that glorify war, that interpret war as a manly adventure . . .*
A:   I think they are swinish.

Q:   *You have said that working with actors involves talk. In getting responses from them, isn't it largely a matter of confidence, or what?*
A:   There is nothing more mysterious in it than that they have confidence in my ear and that I have confidence in their "inner hearing."

Q:   *The rumour that you threw a chair through the window, and such-like, has never accurately been established . . .*
A:   I did so. That happens when one is afraid. The more insecure you are, the angrier you get. Or the more afraid. And fear is transformed into anger.

You can't just stay being afraid.

I used to be very dependent on people's opinion of me: I was tyrannically vulnerable to criticism and was unhappy for days if anyone said anything wounding to me or about me. Today I don't care about anything except the life I have with friends and the work I have to do. This is all that's important to me.

I have no need of power.

I have no need to be influential.

I have no need to be a participant in, or a shaper of, Swedish cultural life.

I have no desire to justify myself before criticism.

I have no need at all to be aggressive. I hate that.

I want to look around at the world, above all to read books and fill the gaps in my education which are a result of the uninterrupted work I have pursued since my student days.

Q:   *Do you experience the times when you don't work as empty?*

A:   Not at all. Once I did, but only for short periods. I never had any free time. Spare time is something I experience as an unbelievable delight! To have a good book in my hands and actually immerse myself in it . . .

I have often thought that I should devote myself to Bach's *St. Matthew Passion.* I mean methodically. Actually stay with it. That takes time and patience. I have two kinds of spare time: one kind is only fugitive—attendant on my getting up in the morning and going to bed at night, eating and perhaps taking a walk. The other kind is methodical spare time, when I take a certain time every day to sit down and do something I believe is interesting. But it must be done at a specified time or the day just flies away.

Q:   *You like working by schedule?*

A:   I love to.

Q:   *You have said that it is more important for the public to feel than to understand.*

A:   To feel is primary, to understand is secondary. First feel, experience—and then understand. Self-evidently, the main thing for the public is to have an experience. Later they can bring intellectual processes to bear. That's always a pleasure. And eventually the intellectual process, itself, may elicit a new feeling.

Q:   *When the audience misunderstands a film . . .* The Silence, *for example—it became a great success because people went to see it not for the film's sake, but to see certain parts of it.*

A:   By now, *The Silence* is as innocent as a kindergarten infant by comparison with the films made since. It's no fun to make pornography when everyone else is making it . . .

Q:   *How do you see your future as a film-maker shaping up?*

A:   I know I'll stay with it; if I make my films cheaply enough I can stay with it as long as I have reasons for making films. Nobody, however indirectly, can prevent me. For one reason: I no longer have occasion to be afraid. Of critics, for example: before now they were either sawing off the branch I sat on, or making it stronger for me. I depended on them for my livelihood . . . There were few moments in my life when I wasn't gambling with my existence.

If *Smiles of a Summer Night* hadn't been an international success I would have been virtually finished. I had just had *The Seventh Seal* refused, in manuscript. When *Smiles of a Summer Night* became a success, after its showing at Cannes, I drove to Cannes to see Carl-Anders Dymling and laid that script on the table and told him: "Now or never." Then he accepted it.

Q:    *You have said that among films by others you have especially liked were* Lady with a Dog, Umberto D., Rashomon. *Have you added to that list?*

A:    Yes, with Fellini's *Il Bidone* (*The Swindler*). I have a great admiration for Fellini. I feel a sort of brotherly contact with him, I don't know why exactly. We have written brief, confused letters to each other many times. It's amusing . . . I like him because he is himself, he is who he is and what he is. His temperament is something I have a feeling for, though it's quite different from my own; but I understand it so damn well and I admire it, colossally.

He is said to be enchanted by my films. That experience is mutual.

Q:    *How many times can you see a film? You have a private collection of* 200 *films.*

A:    How many times depends on how much I like them. I have seen *Les Vacances de M. Hulot* (*Mr. Hulot's Holiday*) countless times.

I sit and wait for the parts I enjoy. These can be whole sequences, great moments or just details.

Q:    *You have maintained that you are self-taught, yet surely a number of directors must have had a certain influence on you?*

A:    I have not been subject to influences from another director's artistic style. But influences are not specifically those that come from one's own occupational involvement. You can be influenced by anything around you: modern photography, TV reportage, pop music—which I find fascinating.

The whole life-way influences one.

But film-makers exert the least influence over me. Because I don't see the world the way they do. Formally, I achieve my results by going my own way.

I don't need help from anyone else's means of expression.

Naturally I am influenced, at large, by the new mode of film-making, by the feeling for film as film, where actually you don't need lighting effects, for instance, and in which you can get effective results without complex equipment. By these means we can return, in a sense, to the origins of film, when it was simple: when you set up a camera in a bush. I have always found this congenial. A purely technical extension of territory attracts me.

Q:    *Is* The Shame *to be your last black-and-white film? You have been discussing colour very much lately.*
A:    I don't know. Colour is interesting. I was at home with some friends Sunday afternoon and a young girl, about 15, came to the house. She had been to the movies and seen a film which I admired personally. But she was contemptuous: it wasn't in colour! Then I thought: this is the new thing today; this new generation finds nothing stimulating in a film unless it's in colour.

It has been a long time since I saw a colour film which I found inspiring. Yes, I was very impressed by the colour in Agnes Varda's *Happiness*. There I felt the colour was deeply sensual.

Colour is best when it isn't colour. That may sound banal, but it's a fact.

Q:    *Music is finished, you said.*
A:    In *The Shame* it has come to that point. No music any more.

Q:    *You have seldom made a film with a purely literary foundation; usually it's from your own manuscript. Does this mean that you don't think books should be filmed?*
A:    I think it's hard to film books or short stories. The material is too rich, it often fences in the film. It's hard to create from it. I don't know. I feel no temptation to try.

Q:    *Films which never become films—why can't you make novels out of them?*
A:    I am not a writer, I am a film-maker. I have no need to express myself with words.

Q:    *Yet your scripts are written with such literary pregnancy.*

A:    That's for practical reasons: so that my co-workers will understand what I mean.

Once I had a literary inferiority complex. I haven't any longer. For some time I harboured the illusion that I would write a play or a novel or a collection of short stories, or whatever. I've entirely given up that idea. I am completely satisfied to express myself in my films.

# Conversation with Bergman

## JOHN SIMON/1971

B:   I am always in a very strange mood when people come to do interviews with me, complicated interviews, because I always have the feeling
that I am responsible for some cousin or far-away brother, somebody
whom I don't know very well, but am answerable to. Well, when we discuss this person, this Ingmar Bergman, we have to discuss him carefully
and I will try to be as open as possible, but I never have the feeling that
we are talking about me.

S:   *It must be a great responsibility, I was thinking, just to be you; because
film is probably the most important art today and I think you're the most
important film-maker in the world. To be the most important man in the
most important art is a terrible responsibility. Does it bother you?*
B:   No. I never think along those lines. My thinking does not work
that way, because when I start writing a new picture, or start shooting
or cutting it, or when I release it to the audience, it's always the first
time, and always the last time. It's an isolated event, and I never think
back or forward; it's just that. Of course, I have amassed a lot of experience over twenty-five or twenty-six years and thirty pictures and, of
course, I have a lot of hopes and desires about what I want to do with
what is still far away; but my relation to my work, my film work and
my theatre work, is completely unneurotic. I'm just a professional; I'm
just a man who makes a table or something that is to be used, and the

only thing that interests me is that it be used. Whether it is good or bad, a masterpiece or a mess, has nothing to do with the making, with my creative mind. So, my reply is: I feel responsible only for the crafts-manship being good, for the thing having the moral qualities of my mind, and, if possible, for my not telling any lies. Those are my only demands. When I make my pictures, I never place myself in relation to the New Wave or to my pictures, or to Fellini, or to the cultural situa-tion in the world today, or to television, or anything else. I just make my picture. Because if I started to think this way and that, there would be no picture. So, I have all my difficulties, and get all my joy, just han-dling the material.

s:    *Well, then, is it difficult to talk about your old films, is it something you dislike doing?*
B:    No, it's the past; it's very far away. If it's necessary, we can talk about it; if it's not necessary, better yet.

s:    *You said a minute ago that you were entering the phase when you were beginning to collect your materials. How long does that phase usually last, and is that a difficult period?*
B:    No, the collecting is very nice; the dreaming, the playing with the material, surrounding oneself with a lot of notebooks in which to jot down things. That is a marvelous time, a nice creative time.

s:    *How long do you spend on that?*
B:    Sometimes a few months, sometimes years. But when I have to sit down to write, to start from the beginning and write the script, that is the hateful period—when I have to make up my mind about what I am going to do and actually write it. I don't like to sit still. I don't feel com-fortable when I write, so I have to saddle myself with a lot of discipline day after day.

s:    *How many hours a day?*
B:    Four or five. I start at ten o'clock or thereabouts, and I'm free at three. That's just sitting and writing; it takes me about two and a half months; yet I have to do it.

s:   *But you don't go back to it in the evening, do you?*
B:   No, never. At three o'clock I have my tea and then I'm free. But of course, when I've been going on for a few weeks, I can't let go of it; it comes back at night or in the early morning. It is a bad, painful time, and I don't like it, but I have to do it. Because I can't just write down ten or twenty pages and go out with a crew and improvise. I am no improviser: I must always prepare everything.

s:   *I don't think that improvisation is such a good thing, really.*
B:   It just isn't my way of film-making; my way is selective: a mirroring, reflecting. I put a mirror down; then I select, I take out, I put together.

s:   *Do you enjoy the shooting period?*
B:   Very much indeed. Sometimes it is quite boring and frustrating, to be sure. But when we shoot, we are together; the actors, the crew, and I—we give and take; we are a very small group and we have all worked together from film to film; we know one another, and know what to do and how to do it. Sitting down with the cutting tape and editing is also very nice.

s:   *How long on the average does the shooting period last?*
B:   About fifty shooting days, sometimes fifty-five, but no more than that. I made *A Passion* in exactly forty-five days, but *Shame* took about fifty-five.

s:   *And the editing?*
B:   A very long time. I like the editing very much; I sit down and it takes me a lot of time, as much as three or four months.

s:   *And you work together with your editor?*
B:   Yes. She is a nice girl, with much patience, who is exactly as pedantic as I am, and she knows everything. I sit down with her and we go at it together. I hate to sit alone, because I am a complete idiot with machines. I am very fascinated by them, but I don't like them.

s:   *What about cameras? Do you know very much about photography?*
B:   Yes, I do. And I have learned everything about the laboratory, about mixing, and sound, and lenses, and everything. Because if I didn't, people

would have to tell me things, and I'd be in the hands of those experts. And I don't trust experts. I just trust Sven Nykvist. He is a very fine technician, an aficionado.

s:    *Do you tell him exactly what you want, or can he guess it?*
B:    I don't know how we work because we don't talk very much. We are very fascinated by lighting. We are always studying light. We are always aware of light.

s:    *Do you mean natural light?*
B:    Yes. The light of reality. And the translation of natural light into artificial light and what we can do with it, that is our science.

s:    *Do you feel then that there is quite a difference between working with Hilding Bladh or Gunnar Fischer, your former cinematographers, and working with Sven Nykvist?*
B:    Yes, of course. They were marvelous people, real professionals. But Sven and I have a special relation; I can't explain it. Sometimes we are very, very unhappy together. It's just like an old marriage. We don't talk very much. We never meet privately. But at the job, I think, we have a marvelous rapport.

s:    *Something seemed to happen with the photography in your films. There was a sudden change that came about in* Smiles of a Summer Night. *Perhaps it was a different film stock that you started using.*
B:    No, no.

s:    *But there was a new sharpness, a definition, a chiaroscuro. The blacks were very black and the whites very white. I remember, particularly in the dinner scene, an intensity I had never seen in your films before, and wondered what had happened.*
B:    Yes. I think it has to do with faces. Because I am always interested in faces. I just want you to sit down and look at the human face. But if there is too much going on in the background, if the face moves too

much, if you can't see the eyes, if the lighting is too artistic, the face
is lost.

S:    *I sometimes have the feeling with your films that one of them comes up*
*with one solution to a problem, and the next one with a different solution to*
*the same problem. That's not deliberate, I suppose; it just happens that way?*
B:    It just happens. There is no orderly progression, no logic, and there
are no rigid guidelines. My pictures always come out of tensions, specific situations, changing conditions. It's always like that. And why one
picture appeals and another doesn't, I don't know. People who interview me always try to find a pattern. Of course, it's their profession. It
isn't mine. My creative life is movement. It's like water. I don't want to
be logical or find motives. That is completely uninteresting to me.

S:    *This is perhaps an unfair question; but does a film begin with some kind*
*of a specific idea: what is it like to go mad, or what is it like to stay together*
*with someone you don't love any more? Is there some kind of simple nucleus*
*around which you build up a film?*
B:    No. It always starts very secretly; I don't know exactly what is
going on. It starts with a sort of tension or a specific scene, some lines, a
picture or something, a piece of music. It just starts as a very, very small
scene. And from this little scene comes a trembling. I look at it and try
to pull it out. And sometimes it remains just this little thing. But sometimes it's more; I can't stop and suddenly I have a lot of material. So I
never know exactly.

S:    *When you say "a piece of music," for example, are you listening to a*
*piece of music and it suggests an idea to you?*
B:    Yes, very often.

S:    *It becomes a shape somehow?*
B:    Yes.

S:    *You are very fond of Bach and Mozart?*
B:    I'm very fond of music. I can't say I have a favorite composer
or period.

S:    *Whom are you interested in now?*

B:    I think Monteverdi. His is very strange, very modern.

S:    *Have you ever liked twentieth-century composers?*

B:    Yes. I'm very fond of music. I like all sorts. I like pop and the Beatles and those protest singers.

S:    *Do you care for painting?*

B:    No, not very much.

S:    *Does this mean that you're not even very interested in it, or just that it doesn't affect your work? You don't like to go to museums, for example?*

B:    No. Of course, when I come to Amsterdam, I feel it a duty to go to the Rijksmuseum; or when I come to Paris, I go to see the Impressionists. And here we have the Gauguin exhibition and tomorrow I want, if possible, to see it; but it is not necessary.

S:    *But music is necessary?*

B:    Yes, music is absolutely necessary. It is the same thing with poetry. Poetry is not necessary, but books are.

S:    *What kinds of books?*

B:    All of them. Don't you think that when you are young, you read a lot of books? I have a good example: I like Strindberg very much and he has written a lot of plays but also a lot of prose: novels and short stories, and when I was young I read them all—I had the feeling I had read them. This summer, because of directing *A Dream Play*, I started to read a Strindberg novel and suddenly I realized, yes, I read it when I was twenty-two, but I had not understood it, so I started to reread everything that Strindberg has written, except his plays. It was a fascinating experience. I like enormous books, enormous novels, the Russians.

S:    *Has Strindberg the dramatist been a great influence on you?*

B:    Yes. I have been reading him since I was twelve or thirteen, and he has followed me around all my life.

S:    *How about Proust?*

B:    Yes, I'm just going on with Swann in *A la Recherche du temps perdu.*

S:    *What about Joyce, which must be very difficult, I imagine?*
B:    Yes, that is too much for me. I have read *Ulysses* but it was out of duty more than anything else.

S:    *Was it the language that made it so difficult?*
B:    I read it in a Swedish translation because I read extremely slowly.

S:    *Even in Swedish?*
B:    Yes, when I read, I read as slowly as if I were reading aloud. It takes me a lot of time, but I remember everything. I don't know why the slowness, but perhaps it's my profession: when I read a play I read as if it were being acted.

S:    *In connection with* Hour of the Wolf *and* The Magician, *I noticed a certain indebtedness to E. T. A. Hoffmann. He must be someone you like.*
B:    Yes, very much.

S:    *Was he relevant to* The Magician?
B:    More to the *Hour of the Wolf.* In *Hour of the Wolf* I really played with him.

S:    *Do you have any absolute favorites among your films?*
B:    No. They are old pictures and already far, far away.

S:    *Do you always like the latest one best?*
B:    No, on the contrary; the latest one is like an infant: it protests and it makes difficulties and it is very much alive. Sometimes I like it and sometimes I dislike it, but in a very unneurotic way. No, I think I have made just one picture that I really like, and that is *Winter Light* (*The Communicants*). That is my only picture about which I feel that I have started here and ended there and that everything along the way has obeyed me. Everything is exactly as I wanted to have it, in every second of this picture. I couldn't make this picture today; it's impossible; but I saw it a few weeks ago together with a friend and I was very satisfied. I very much prefer it to, say, *Through a Glass Darkly*, which, socially speaking, I don't like any more. It's an étude, a study, an exercise; it's a beginning, but it's a pudding. It's so far away, I can't be sure, but my

felling is that it's a pudding, a muddle. Some parts of it are no good, some are really cinematographic, but it can't compare with *The Comunicants*.

s:    *One has the feeling that the Ingmar Bergman figure in the films, at least in the chamber-film phase, is usually Max von Sydow.*
B:    No, no, not at all. I say, like Flaubert, "*Madame Bovary, c'est moi.*" I am all of them, I am inside all of them. It's not especially Max von Sydow or Gunnar Björnstrand or Ingrid Thulin.

s:    *Do you, when you write a part, have a specific actor in mind?*
B:    Always, always, yes. It's very important. I always want to know the actor before I write a script. I don't know why, but I hear a voice, and see the behavior. Perhaps it is wrong, I don't know, but we have always worked together.

s:    *It's wonderful to have such good actors as you have.*
B:    I think it is good, this tradition here in Sweden, that all are working in the theatre, that we work together in different media.

s:    *It is interesting to me that some people do not come back in your films, even though I like them. For instance, I like Maud Hansson very much, but I only saw her twice in your films; Margit Carlquist only once. Is there some special reason why they don't reappear?*
B:    Very neurotic girls. I don't like to work with neurotic people; because they have to *play* neurotics, they should not *be* neurotics; but when they are, they are a disturbance to the work. Because the work in itself is so difficult, we must be very calm and very controlled. The work must be nice, like a family, like joy. We must have a feeling of security and loyalty. If people are without contact and completely imprisoned in themselves, I can still use them, but they endanger the whole production and I don't like that.

s:    *The men presumably are less of a problem, because they seem to last longer than the women.*
B:    Yes. We have grown up together and we have worked together.

S:    *I wish I could see that documentary that you did about your island,*
*except that I might not understand any of it.*
B:    It's difficult to understand. It was necessary to make it, to try; you
know I've lived there four years now and I know these people and I
know their difficulties and I wanted to tell about them and let themselves tell about it all.

S:    *Was it fun handling the camera yourself?*
B:    Yet, it's always so; Sven was with me, but I conducted the interviews for the first time in my life. It was a nice experience.

S:    *Tell me, are there any film-makers that influenced you in any way, that*
*you learned something from, or do you feel completely self-made?*
B:    No, no, no, no. I have grown up in a tradition. I don't think somebody just becomes a director, you know. We are like stones in a building, all of us. We all depend on the people coming before; I am just a
part of this. So, I depend very much on a Swedish film tradition.
Sjöstrom and Stiller, and on the Swedish theatre tradition—Sjöberg has
meant a lot to me. He is my neighbor. He is marvelous. And then, you
know, when I was young, nineteen or twenty years old, I saw the
French pictures—*Quai des Brumes* (*Port of shadows*), Duvivier and
Marcel Carné.

S:    *Did you like* Les Enfants du Paradis?
B:    Not very much. It's a bit boring. Of course, I liked parts of it. But
most of all I liked *Quai des Brumes.*

S:    *What about* La Règle du Jeu (The Rules of the Game)?
B:    They told me that *Smiles of a Summer Night* had some similarities;
but I didn't know that, because I hadn't seen it. And then, you know, I
have a collection of sixteen-millimeter films, and now I own it.

S:    *Do you like it?*
B:    Not very much. I don't like Renoir very much. But then, of course,
I always have seen pictures; I like to go to the movies. I'm a moviegoer.

S:    *What about Carl Dreyer?*
B:    Yes, in a protesting way.

S:  *Against it?*

B:  Yes, some of his pictures have infected me. But in a very strange way, he has always been an amateur. Like Antonioni.

S:  *I think in a way, you have done what Dreyer wanted to do.*

B:  Yes.

S:  *But what about Antonioni?*

B:  I have met him once.

S:  *Did you get along with him?*

B:  Yes, we had a wonderful contact. I liked him extremely much. I liked his courage; he is a completely honest man.

S:  *Whereas Fellini, I think, is not so honest a man.*

B:  No, no please! Fellini is Fellini. He is not honest, he is not dishonest, he is just Fellini. And he is not responsible. You cannot put moralistic points of view on Fellini; it is impossible. He is just—I live him.

S:  *Yes, he is very charming.*

B:  No, much more than that. I think he has not made his real pictures yet.

S:  *I think he has made two great films,* The White Sheik *and* I Vitelloni.

B:  Yes, but you know, I am hopelessly in love with this man. Completely. Because, I don't know why, I have met him a few times and . . .

S:  *This joint project of yours with him has been abandoned, hasn't it?*

B:  It collapsed. Of course it collapsed, because I am a pedant and he is not.

S:  *I understand he submitted an outline that was half a page long.*

B:  Yes, yes, exactly, and I was sitting writing my screenplay.

S:  *How was it to be? How were the two parts to connect?*

B:  That was the wrong way from the beginning. That is the damnation of this movie business, in the economical sense. Because, you know, our idea was to choose five or six actors, to have a crew of about six to ten people; to have some money; to have an empty studio and to start and just to make a dialogue and just to invent things, to improvise, to play together.

s:   *So there was not to be one Bergman half and one Fellini half?*
b:   No. And then the economic interests came in and the Americans came in, and we tried to explain what we wanted to do. And they said yes, yes, yes—more or less—but then he had no money and he was in a bad situation and he was tired.

s:   *Fellini?*
b:   Yes, after *Satyricon*, of course. And he was at work on *Satyricon* and I couldn't wait. Then suddenly we said, all right, I make my part and you make your part, and then we meet in the beginning and at the end. The whole project collapsed at that moment and I am sorry for that. I can teach him something, and he can teach me something.

s:   *Maybe in the future.*
b:   Perhaps. When we are older and cleverer. I think it all collapsed because the Americans couldn't understand what we really intended to do. But, really, he was extremely difficult, though that means nothing because I love his work and I love him as a person, if he is a person, which I doubt, because he has no limits; he's just like quicksilver—all over the place. I have never seen anybody like that before.

   He is enormously intuitive. He is intuitive; he is creative; he is an enormous force. He is burning inside with such heat. Collapsing. Do you understand what I mean? The heat from his creative mind, it melts him. He suffers from it; he suffers physically from it. One day when he can manage this heat and can set it free, I think he will make pictures you have never seen in your life. He is rich. As every real artist, he will go back to his sources one day. He will find his way back.

s:   *What I particularly admire in you is that you always change and develop; and as you learn new things you teach them to the world. Very few artists have been able to do that. Stravinsky, Picasso, a few others. But most of them repeat themselves.*

B:    It's my way of living. I am always curious. It has to do only with that. No matter how depressed I am, I always wake up in the morning, in the very early morning, a bit curious: what will happen today? Sometimes I am very afraid. But always, always, even if it is completely black—inside and outside—I always feel something very strange—a curiosity.

And then, to express, to be in touch with other human beings. To mix experiences, to be involved; that's my life. If I am isolated or feel no contact or something like that, it is catastrophic for me. So I always try to be in contact. It is very difficult to tell you, but if you have a completely unneurotic relationship—I don't say I'm unneurotic, because I'm very neurotic—but if you have a non-neurotic relation to your work, it gives you so much joy and helps you such a lot and gives you a form, a discipline, such honest help. So, I just go on.

S:    *I am only interested in this from your own point of view. Tell me more about your feelings about Antonioni, because I think it'll tell more about you in a way.*
B:    The strange thing is that I admire him more now that I have met him than when I only saw his pictures; because I have suddenly understood what he is doing. I understand that everything in his mind, in his point of view, in his personal behavior is against his film-making. And still he makes his pictures.

S:    *How do you mean "against"?*
B:    It all presents obstacles.

S:    *What is your favorite Antonioni film?*
B:    I like most of all *La Notte*, because he had a marvelous actress in it.

S:    *Yes, Jeanne Moreau. But he didn't do very much with her.*
B:    No, he never does, he never comes in contact with actors. They don't know what he wants, and he doesn't know how to talk to them.

S:    *He knew how to talk to Monica Vitti.*
B:    I don't think so. But, you know, I like people who even if everything else is against them, continue, and I like and admire . . . I think it was marvelous that this man, this sleepless, tortured, scared man went

to America to make a picture about Americans. This is a Don Quixote. And I said to him I could never have courage like that, because I haven't even been in America yet. I think even the thought of going to America, even with a return ticket in my hand, scares me, and I think he had such courage to go to America—to disappear into the desert with his crew and to stay there. He is a strange man, he is a marvelous man, and I admire him very, very much.

S:    *Perhaps you like the man better than his films.*
B:    Yes, in a way. Because to me his films always have been a little, little bit boring, and we must be aware that the boring in art is very good in a way, but his is a little bit too boring. But after meeting him, all my reservations are gone.

S:    *When I first saw* L'Avventura, *I was a little bit bored, too, but on each reseeing it gets bigger and better. Have you seen it more than once?*
B:    Yes, I like it very much, too. But to go on about directors or film-makers who have influenced me . . . technically, Cukor, very much.

S:    *In what way technically?*
B:    In the editing. In the beginning we had no schools here for film-making. The only way of learning film-making was to be an assistant to a director—I was an assistant to Sjöberg—and to see pictures. And we had no film library, we had nothing like that when I was learning. Young students didn't get any money to go abroad; we were shut off, we were just sitting here.

S:    *How about Hitchcock? Is he someone you learned from?*
B:    Yes, of course.

S:    *Technically, I suppose. But isn't there a great intellectual emptiness in his work?*
B:    Completely, but I think he's a very good technician. And he has something in *Psycho*, he had some moments. *Psycho* is one of his most interesting pictures because he had to make the picture very fast, with very primitive means. He had little money, and this picture tells very much about him. Not very good things. He is completely infantile, and

I would like to know more—no, I don't want to know—about his behavior with, or, rather, against women. But this picture is very interesting. I learned a lot from all those Americans who knew their profession.

S:    *I find it's a terrible notion in modern film criticism that these people were artists, when they were really technicians. We must distinguish between an artist and a technician.*

B:    Yes, that's important.

S:    *Modern film criticism tends not to distinguish. People like Raoul Walsh or Howard Hawks don't know what art is. They merely have marvelous techniques, some of them.*

B:    They have told their stories and they made their films in a good, effective way. That is a duty: effectiveness in telling a story.

S:    *Yes, that's a very good minimum, but it's only a minimum.*

B:    But it's difficult.

S:    *Are there any young film-makers that you particularly like? I hope you don't like Godard?*

B:    No, no, no.

S:    *I detest him.*

B:    Yes, I do, too. In this profession, I always admire people who are going on, who have a sort of idea and, however crazy it is, are putting it through; they are putting people and things together, and they make something. I always admire this. But I can't see his pictures. I sit for perhaps twenty-five or thirty or fifty minutes and then I have to leave, because his pictures make me so nervous. I have the feeling the whole time that he wants to tell me things, but I don't understand what it is, and sometimes I have the feeling that he's bluffing, double-crossing me. But what about this young Czechoslovakian director, Miloš Forman? Have you seen his work? I like him very, very much.

S:    *There are other Czechs whom I like better. I think Menzel may be more interesting.*

B:    Perhaps more interesting, but not to me. No, because Forman has an approach to human beings.

S:   *There's something a little primitive about him.*
B:   Yes, I like that very much.

S:   *What about Bellocchio? Have you seen* China Is Near*?*
B:   Terrible, *terrible*, very homosexual, very artificial, aggressive in a very empty way.

S:   *What about the early Truffaut? Did you like those first ones?*
B:   Very much; very, very much.

S:   *What's happened to this man?*
B:   He wants to make money; it's a very human desire. He wants a comfortable life. He wants to make money and he wants people to see his pictures.

S:   *Well, don't you think his early films were seen by people?*
B:   But perhaps not by enough, and he didn't make enough money, and he likes the comfortable life of the modern film-maker.

S:   *But the trouble is his new films are not going to make much money.*
B:   Then he made a mistake. Because if you lose both the money and your dignity, then it must be a mistake.

S:   *What about Bresson? How do you feel about him?*
B:   Oh, *Mouchette*! I loved it, I loved it! But *Balthazar* was so boring, I slept through it.

S:   *I liked* Les Dames du Bois de Boulogne *and* A Man Escaped*, but I would say* The Diary of a Country Priest *is the best one.*
B:   I have seen it four or five times and could see it again . . . and *Mouchette* . . . really . . .

S:   *That film doesn't do anything for me.*
B:   No? You see, now I'll tell you something about *Mouchette*. It starts with a friend who sees the girl sitting and crying, and Mouchette says to the camera, how shall people go on living without me, that's all. Then you see the main titles. The whole picture is about that. She's a

saint and she takes everything upon herself, inside her, everything that happens around her. That makes such an enormous difference, that such people live among us. I don't believe in another life, but I do think that some people are more holy than others and make life a little bit easier to endure, more bearable. And she is one, a very, very simple one, and when she has assumed the difficulties of other human beings, she drowns herself in a stream. That is my felling, but this *Balthazar*, I didn't understand a word of it, it was so completely boring.

s:    *You could almost say the same thing about the donkey, that when the donkey has taken on other people's suffering . . .*
B:    A donkey, to me, is completely uninteresting, but a human being is always interesting.

s:    *Do you like animals in general?*
B:    No, not very much. I have a completely natural aversion for them. Have you seen this picture *Il Porcile* (*Pigpen*)?

s:    *Yes, terrible. I think Pasolini is awful altogether.*
B:    Yes, awful, awful. Meaningless. Completely.

s:    *There was a period in your life and work when the question of God was all-important, but not any more, surely?*
B:    No, it's past. Things are difficult enough without God. They were much more difficult when I had to put God into it. But now it's finished, definitely, and I'm happy about it.

s:    *In an interview, discussing* Hour of the Wolf, *you said that you believed in demons; but how can you not believe in God, yet believe in demons? Aren't the two things connected? Can one have the one without the other?*
B:    Well, if I say I believe in demons, of course, it is just a little joke. You sort of want to name things . . .

s:    *Things that bother you?*
B:    Yes, of course. Yet it's not exactly a joke, because when I was younger, not very much younger, say, five, six, ten years ago, and back into my childhood, I was haunted by extremely terrible dreams,

sometimes daydreams; sometimes things happened to me in a very, very strange, mysterious, and dangerous way, and I was very scared, and sometimes my dreams were so real that when I tried to remember something, I didn't know exactly if it had happened in reality or if I had dreamed it. It was very painful; but now it has disappeared—all of those things.

S:   *Why do you think it went away?*
B:   I grew up. I worked a lot; I was director of the Royal Dramatic Theatre for three years. I started in the morning at eight o'clock and was there until eleven at night; then I went home and slept. I was at it ten months a year and there was no place left for demons and dreams. Then I went to my island; I have lived there four years. On the island, reality is so real, it's no place for demons and bad dreams. Instead of bad dreams, I now have very ridiculous ones, comical dreams—I often laugh.

S:   *Can you use those dreams in your work?*
B:   Perhaps, I don't know. It doesn't interest me any more. To me reality is very real now, and other human beings.

S:   *More important than dreams?*
B:   Yes, exactly, and if you have difficulty with your relationships with other people and reality around you, it is a place for demons; but if you are in contact with yourself and other people and reality, there's no room for dreams.

S:   *Would you say there is a central theme now in your work? Robert Graves, the poet, says that the two real themes, the only themes, are love and death. Do you have any such principal themes?*
B:   Yes and no. I want very much to tell, to talk about, the wholeness inside every human being. It's a strange thing that every human being has a sort of dignity or wholeness in him, and out of that develops relationships to other human beings, tensions, misunderstandings, tenderness, coming in contact, touching and being touched, the cutting off of contact and what happens then. That's what is fascinating. I feel that I have come out into an enormous field, and I can now get started.

I'm very curious about the pictures waiting for me around the corner. It's very difficult to explain. Because of that I made *A Passion* and my documentary, and because of that I am writing my new picture (*The Touch*).

s:    *Then your main theme is interpersonal relations?*
B:    Yes, but much more so now than before, because I feel much freer.

s:    *Is it unfair of me to ask about certain episodes in your films that I find difficult to understand?*
B:    No. I will try to be honest.

s:    *For example, in* Hour of the Wolf, *the episode with the child, the fishing and the drowning. What is the relationship of the hero to that boy—is that his son?*
B:    No, I don't know exactly. I think it was based on a dream I had.

s:    *You were saying that in* Persona, *those little scenes between the titles meant the impatience of the film to begin. And you were talking about your sickness, your ear infection—what was it called again?*
B:    Morbus Menieres; sounds like a dish.

s:    *It made you lose your balance. How did that affect* Persona?
B:    I was at the hospital for two months, and I wanted to make a poem of the atmosphere in which *Persona* grew.

s:    *Is that why Elisabet is in the hospital for quite a while?*
B:    No, that has nothing to do with it.

s:    *Those first shots, then, before the titles, that is the poetry?*
B:    That is the poetry, yes.

s:    *And you had that from the beginning?*
B:    Yes.

s:    *You began with that? I thought perhaps it was an afterthought.*
B:    No, but perhaps I elaborated.

S:   *Is there much change between your script and what happens when you start shooting from it, or do you stay fairly close to it? Some little changes?*
B:   Yes, in *A Passion* many, because *A Passion* was written in a very strange way; I just dashed it off—not my usual way of writing. Then, I think, I translated it back when I shot it.

S:   *I find the most difficult part about most of your films is the ending, because the ending always to me is more of a question than an answer. But I'm sure that's what you want it to be. For example, in* Persona *the thing I find very difficult to comprehend is why we only see Alma getting on that bus and why we don't see Elisabet any more. A lot of people have taken this to mean that the whole thing takes place in Alma's mind.*
B:   It does not. You see Elisabet for a very, very short moment. She's in the studio. She's at work.

S:   *But it's the same shot you've used before.*
B:   Yes.

S:   *So one doesn't know whether that's the future or the past.*
B:   She's going on. You know here, in the theatre, we play the same play every night for years. So she's back.

S:   *She's speaking again.*
B:   Yes.

S:   *Because that one word which she says, "nothing," that, I think, she says in one of Alma's dreams. So that's not really Elisabet speaking.*
B:   Elisabet has come back. She has invented a new aspect of her emptiness and she has filled up with Alma, she has fed on Alma a little bit. And she can go on.

S:   *Where does that leave Alma? Is Alma eaten up completely?*
B:   No. She has just provided some blood and meat, some good steak. Then she can go on.

S:   *And there's enough left for Alma.*
B:   Yes, Alma is still alive. You must know, Elisabet is intelligent, she's sensible, she has emotions, she is immoral, she is a gifted woman, but she's a monster, because she has an emptiness in her.

s:    *Do you think most artists have this emptiness?*
B:    No, it has nothing to do with artists; it has just to do with human beings.

s:    *So she does not represent the artist?*
B:    For heaven's sake, no. It was just a way of putting it—it was convenient.

s:    *But surely a character like the Magician does represent the artist in some way.*
B:    He is an artist.

s:    *And Vergérus is the scientist. Was the point there that somehow both of them are struggling for an answer, a different answer, that neither of them can finally come up with—or does somebody come up with an answer?*
B:    I have no answers; I just pose questions. I'm not very gifted at giving answers.

s:    *Was the ending of* The Magician *based on Brecht's* Threepenny Opera *somehow, because of the happy ending out of nowhere?*
B:    No. It just happened. It was the right way of doing it. I just had the feeling that I had to end with some tour de force.

s:    *What about something like the last image of* The Seventh Seal, *the Dance of Death? Was that meant at that time to suggest that there is some kind of life after death? I mean was that a form of life, death leading these people, or was that a form of non-existence?*
B:    When I made *The Seventh Seal*, I was still involved in all these complications. I can't remember exactly.

s:    *It was a very ambiguous image; it could mean that something goes on after death.*
B:    Yes, *The Seventh Seal* is, in a way, very concrete, like a medieval play. Everything is there, you can touch everything. The Virgin Mary is real, with the child. When they are dancing, they are concrete; they are. It is not fantasies or dreams or imaginations. It is always my intention to be

exact, to be precise, to be concrete; and sometimes I succeed, sometimes not. But my intention is always to be very simple.

S:     *That was a very concrete image, visually; but what it meant metaphysically was not quite so clear.*
B:     To me that is not so interesting.

S:     *Well, then, would you say that* Persona *is really about how a person who feels empty, depleted, and sick gets back into life again by using another person?*
B:     I don't want to say anything about that. *Persona* is a tension, a situation, something that has happened and passed, and beyond that I don't know.

S:     *Speaking of tensions—does living on an isolated island minimize them?*
B:     When I write, you know, people say, "Come, come and have dinner with me tomorrow." I say, "No, I can't, because the airplane is booked; it is too complicated to come." so that is that.

S:     *It's a very practical solution.*
B:     And when my girl friend and I quarrel and she wants to go away and she is all packed, everything is always too complicated; first she has to drive by a very complicated way through the woods; then, the ferryboat leaves only on the hour; from there, she has to find a flight. So, she ends up staying.

S:     *At one point it was announced that you would make a film out of* Peer Gynt. *Are you still working on that?*
B:     No.

S:     *What happened there?*
B:     Nothing.

S:     *Then it was not true?*
B:     Yes. They asked me if I wanted to make a film of *Peer Gynt* after I had done it on the stage.

s:    *Yes, in Malmö.*

B:    Yes. I said that could be nice. And they asked how much it would cost, and I said, "A lot of money." "How much?" "Give me five million dollars." Silence!!

s:    *That's too bad, for we have never seen a good production of* Peer Gynt *in America and your film would have explained what the play is all about.*

B:    I think the only way to explain the play is to play it on the stage, because a film must be an adaptation; it is not the same thing; you must translate. It's hard work; I prefer to write my own scripts; not adapt; it is too much of a job.

s:    *My editors, looking at your films on the Movieola, felt that you were fascinated by certain objects, like doors or windows or curtains; do you share that feeling?*

B:    Yes, it's a bit childish. To a child, a window is very interesting; or a door, or a mirror. My attitudes can sometimes be a little bit childish. Infantile. But if an artist loses his joy in playing, I think he is no artist any longer.

s:    *Yes, you know Nietszche, who spoke about the child in man?*

B:    But look at Picasso or Stravinsky. Look at their faces. They are children, grown-up, old, wise children, with wonderful childish eyes. Marvelous!

s:    *In other words, you find no special symbolic significance in doors? You just like doors.*

B:    It's fascinating. A door separates you from other people, or you can open it and come in.

s:    *A mirror probably does have more significance than that. Since you are so interested in faces, a mirror tells you more about a face.*

B:    Look at a woman. Look at a woman looking in a mirror. It is interesting. Especially if she doesn't see you, if she doesn't know that you see her.

s:    *What about growing old? Do you have any feelings about growing old in general? Is that a terrible thing?*

B:    No, no. It's nice. I've got everything; really. I have everything in life that a man can ask for and I am still curious and I am still looking forward to the film around the corner. The only thing that troubles me is that I must use eyeglasses.

S:    *Why does that disturb you?*
B:    I always forget them and that makes for complications. But physically I have no difficulties. I feel well. No, growing old doesn't scare me at all.

S:    *Isn't it infuriating to think that scientists may discover processes by which they can freeze people and bring them back to life, and that we will have lived just a little too early for this?*
B:    To me it would be no privilege; to me it would be terrible.

S:    *Why?*
B:    If you live on an island, at the seaside, with farmers and fishermen, everything has its proportions. Here in the town nothing has proportions. If I am in a bad mood here at the theatre, at a rehearsal, everything grates on my bad mood. Brpphhh. Here in town everything is a little bit perverted. And your reactions seem extremely important to yourself and the contretemps of a spotlight not coming up on this place but on that is an absolute catastrophe. On the island, everything has its proportions; you are a very small part of this island and of the life there. If you scream, it has no effect, nobody hears; or perhaps a bird will fly up. You can make as much noise as you want, you can suffer, and it's only a part of the whole. And it gives to a hysterical mind such as mine—I was born hysterical; it's inherited from my parents— the proportions, the definite proportions of reality, it gives you peace. Because you know you cannot alter anything. That is good and healthy . . .

S:    *Let's put it another way. You were talking about your interest in the picture that's still waiting for you around the corner. Suppose you have to die when you are, let's say, seventy-five or eighty, and there's a picture waiting for you around the corner at eighty, which you can never get to. Isn't that a pity?*
B:    No, it's all right.

S:    *You think the others are enough?*

B:    Yes; some people think they are more than enough.


S:    *Do you feel that your film-making has profited from your work in the theatre, or are they two separate things?*

B:    Sometimes it's the same and sometimes it's quite different. I have done very much in the studio and in the theatre, and I got good experience from both.


S:    *What about film actors? Do you think they profit a lot from acting on the stage or can one be a good movie actor without knowing anything about the theatre?*

B:    Yes, I think you can be a good movie actor without being a good actor on the stage. It is a special talent, being a good movie actor, but I don't know exactly what it is. I think it is a sort of presence, a very strange, creative mind and a very special form of concentration that makes a good movie actor.


S:    *I must confess I have seldom if ever discovered minds in actors, at least as I conceive of the mind.*

B:    That's not my experience. They have another way of expressing themselves than we have, and I understand their way very well because I often have the same way of expressing myself. Not when I talk with you but, I tell you, I always think when I talk and if I don't talk, I am intuitive, I have my radar. But when I have to talk and to explain things, I think that I think. I am most of all intuitive and I have trained my intuition; I trust it and always use it in my profession, but I don't discuss with it. So my intuition is my best weapon and my best tool.


S:    *There is one statement of yours that everybody is always quoting: about your thinking of yourself as a humble, anonymous workman on a Gothic cathedral.*

B:    Very romantic. Forget it. What I meant originally was that anonymous creation in art, in music or painting or sculpture or theatre, was very unneurotic. And that is the best kind of all, creating unneurotically; which is why the nineteenth-century romantic notion of original genius strikes me as very silly, and as having nothing to do with real creation.

s:    *But, then, if you're neither the nineteenth-century original genius nor the medieval workman on the cathedral, what third possibility does that leave— something in between?*

b:    Yes, I am a man making things for use, and highly esteemed as a professional. I am proud of my knowing how to make those things.

s:    *You were telling me that* Shame *was influenced not so much by the Vietnam war as by your recollections of Hitler's Germany.*

b:    Yes, exactly. When I was a boy I was in Germany, as a sort of *Austauschjunge* (exchange student) before the war—1935, 1936—and I had German friends; I was fifteen or sixteen years old and came from Sweden completely ignorant, a political virgin. I stayed with the family of a German minister and his four sons and four daughters and a typical German mother in a little village in the interior. I liked them very much. Later, one of the sons, the same age as I, came to Sweden; we spent much time together and I learned German. We were all very fascinated by the fact that he was in the Hitlerjugend, and I went with him to school and they were reading *Mein Kampf* in his religion class; in Weimar, I was at the tenth anniversary of the *Parteitag*. It all held an enormous fascination, and we were all infected by this. Then the war started and I was in the military service; I was drafted from the University and suddenly we realized in Sweden what had happened in Germany; we finally understood. After the war, so many Swedish, Scandinavian, English, and American heroes told us what the German people should have done under the pressure of the dictatorship, what they really should have done. All these very, very clever people telling us what the German civilians should have been thinking and saying; how they really should have reacted to the concentration camps. All this was terribly painful for me, because I'm not very courageous and I hate physical violence. I don't know how much courage I would have if somebody came to me and said, "Ingmar, you are a very talented man, we like you very much; be the head of the *Schauspielhaus* (National Theatre); if not, you know what will happen to you, your wife, and your children. And, you know, we are having some difficulty with the Jews, and we don't want them in the Theatre; you will fix that for us. If you don't, you know what will happen to you. And I don't know exactly, I don't know at all, how I would have reacted in this situation.

That uncertainty was very painful to me, and that is the main problem in *Shame*—what happens to ordinary people in such a war.

s:   *If I may jump back now to* Persona, *what about those dead bodies in the morgue at the beginning, and the boy who seems to be dead too but then comes to life?*
B:   It's just my poetry. I was in the hospital; the view out of the window was a chapel where they were carrying out the bodies of the dead, and I knew that house was full of dead people. Of course, I felt it inside me somewhere that the whole atmosphere was one of death, and I felt like that little boy. I was lying there, half dead, and suddenly I started to think of two faces, two intermingled faces, and that was the beginning, the place where it started.

s:   *And did those two merging faces have a special meaning for you?*
B:   No, but if I put two faces together, I get this third person.

s:   *But was one the face of innocence and the other the face of experience?*
B:   No, nothing like that.

s:   *Just two faces?*
B:   Yes, Bibi Anderson and Liv Ullmann didn't know that I did this, that I put them together into one face, and I wanted to give them a surprise, so we made this composite in the laboratory and we got it back to the island where we were and then I asked them to come to the editing room. When they saw those two faces together on the Movieola, Bibi said, "What a terrible picture of you, Liv" and Liv said, "No, it's not me; it's you."

s:   *And the scene with Gunnar Björnstrand is purely in Alma's imagination; the actual man isn't there?*
B:   No, it's just a sort of dream.

s:   *Some critics made terrible fools of themselves by analyzing that as if he were actually there, making love to Alma. Speaking of critics, do you have any afterthoughts about your famous incident with Johnson? [Bergman had hit this critic at an open rehearsal.]*
B:   No, the only thing is exactly what I said, I hate physical violence.

S:   *What did this particular critic do to make you so angry?*
B:   He doesn't believe in what he's doing and he's cynical and he plays a game with other human beings, and I hate this way of behaving. Not of humiliating me, because I know who I am and what I am, but he has a way of humiliating, in a terrible way, the actors. I have seen too much of what he has done to people in this theatre and in other houses.

S:   *But you're not against criticism in general?*
B:   No, for heaven's sake, no; we are both acting, don't you think? And, in a way, we are all acting together. Even if we are of different opinions, it doesn't matter. So, in a way, I like to read good criticism, and good criticism is telling me things about . . .

S:   *Yourself?*
B:   No, not me, but things I see.

S:   *Do you read much criticism about your work?*
B:   I read the reviews in the four Swedish papers, just to get the immediate reaction. But the rest—it takes too much time. You must understand, it's not the reading that takes time, but the effect of it that remains inside you in a very strange way. If it's favorable criticism, it leaves you all atwitter; if it's hostile, you feel poisoned. Just for a few hours, but still, it's a silly waste of time.

S:   *Let me ask you just one other thing. In* The Naked Night, *at the beginning, when the wagons are arriving in the rain and mud, and suddenly there is the image of a broken-down windmill which is no longer turning; how does that windmill get in there? Do you feel the deliberate need to symbolize some kind of breakdown in human events, or do you happen to be shooting out there and come upon the windmill, and you say, "OK, I'll put the windmill in"?*
B:   Both. It's always like that when you're creating the right way; you always find things around you that you can use; they seem to be there just for your purpose. It is very strange; suddenly you find things.

# I Live at the Edge of a Very Strange Country

## RICHARD MERYMAN/1971

DURING THE WINTER of 1970, Ingmar Bergman's personal agent, Paul Kohner, met with Martin Baum, president of ABC Pictures, a subsidiary of American Broadcasting Companies. Kohner: "How would you like to have Ingmar Bergman's first film in English?" Baum: "Great! Give me the script!" Kohner: "There is no script." Baum: "Can I read the story?" Kohner: "There is no story in writing." Baum: "Then what do we do?" Kohner: "You've got to come to London where Bergman is directing a play and let him tell you the story. And you've got to be willing to make the commitment then without anything in writing." Baum (gulping): "OK." Kohner: "That's not all. There are people you report to. Bergman says you have to bring everybody who can say yes or no to the commitment." Baum (gulping twice): "OK."

Paul Kohner's proposition involved more than a million dollars—and under most circumstances would simply have provoked a chuckle about directors' egos. But Ingmar Bergman's 32 films include the radically innovative *Persona*, *Wild Strawberries*, *The Silence*, *The Seventh Seal*, *Winter Light*, *Smiles of a Summer Night*. His movies deal with the ultimate themes of living—God, death, love, man, hate, isolation, truth, madness, sex, communication—and they have been a historic force behind today's regard for film as a serious medium for personal expression. Obsessive in his dissection of his own emotional life, Bergman has always explored on film the most private of his agonies and quandaries. But at the same time he has kept the everyday Mr. Bergman so remote that the source of all those remarkable films has remained a tantalizing

From *Life*, October 15, 1971. © 1971 TIME Inc., reprinted by permission.

mystery. Undoubtedly, to the ABC brass, one of the lures of Ingmar
Bergman—beyond his success—was the chance to touch this remote and
illusive genius. So, on May 2, 1970, there assembled for dinner in
a private room of London's Connaught Hotel Ingmar Bergman;
Leonard Goldenson, president of the entire ABC corporation; Sam
Clark, vice-president for nonbroadcast activities; Larry Newton,
vice-president for film distribution; Paul Kohner; Martin Baum—and
Mrs. Baum.

When one first meets Bergman, the very first glance catches quite an
ordinary-looking fellow, medium-sized, hair thinning on top. But then
he moves and speaks—and the vitality pours forth. He is the kind of
man who grabs your heavy suitcase and carries it despite your
protests—and the sort whose words come to you conducted by graceful
hands always in motion. Bergman is a man who, when he says no, can
do it with a crudity that is almost obscene. Or he can say no, and
immediately reach out and touch you—on the back of the hand the
shoulder—to reassure you that all will be well, that you must not be
unhappy, dismayed. Either way, he exudes absolute, total finality.

He is a man who casts spells. When he describes a memory special to
him, his voice takes on a hypnotic note. His gaze turns away from the
listener. His eyes, permanently saddened by slightly drooping eyelids,
seem to fill with a dreamy, mystical distance—the look of worlds and
wisdoms long traveled. When he talks, though his English can be awk-
ward, he achieves with a very uncomplicated vocabulary a special econ-
omy and precision. As one who has endlessly explored the complexities
of life, he makes you feel with his tone of tolerance and sensibleness
that he has found for everything the simple answers.

When Bergman told the story of his film during dinner, he addressed
himself almost entirely to Mrs. Baum, giving the men only peripheral
attention. Describing the moment after Bergman finished, Martin Baum
said, "We were to give our answer to Mr. Kohner in a few days. But I
could see from the faces that he had sold everybody in the room. And
my *wife*! With her he had scored a *bull's-eye*!"

Immediately, the ABC audience began to discuss casting. They talked
about the role of "the outsider," Bergman's name for the English-speaking
archaeologist who was the fulcrum of the plot. This man, a seminomad,

comes to a small Swedish city to excavate near an ancient church. He meets the pretty, devotedly domestic wife of a successful, attractive physician, and has a violent affair with her. In the end, exhausted by the outsider's demanding childishness, she returns to repair the wreckage of her marriage. The assembled ABC officers made up their list of the most important American film actors of the right age: Paul Newman, Robert Redford, Elliott Gould, Dustin Hoffman. Bergman agreed to see sample films of these men and make a decision.

Two days later the deal was made with Kohner. ABC Pictures would pay $1 million on delivery of the film's negative and also pay the salary of "the outsider"—ultimately $200,000. Bergman would have a script in their hands by July 15, and would start shooting on Sept. 15. ABC would have absolutely no control over Bergman or the final cut of the film. That is a freedom commanded regularly only by a super exclusive group: virtually just Federico Fellini, Mike Nichols, Akira Kurosawa—and Bergman.

All of this scheduling conformed to Bergman's minutely timetabled yearly routine. Bergman shoots a film almost every fall. Then, practically the same day film production ends, he begins directing one or more plays at the Royal Dramatic Theater in Stockholm. In the spring he starts writing his next movie. Then without a break he goes back to theater-directing until time to begin the weeks of meticulous preparation for the fall filming. There are no gaps, everything meshes, exquisitely scheduled.

There is very little socializing. Bergman has placed the execution of his art ahead of every other consideration in his life. In nonworking hours he is husbanding and storing up strength for the next day. There are very few friends with whom he can completely relax, and he is currently unmarried—though there have been many alliances and four marriages. He has remained on very good terms with all his former wives and has eight children. Every moment he does not *have* to be in Stockholm, he is at his stone house on the tiny island of Fårö. Just off the large island of Götland, far out in the Baltic Sea, Fårö is a three-hour, auto and ferry trip from the mainland.

It was to Fårö that he retired last May to write his script of *The Touch*, his movie for ABC. As in most areas of his life, his script-writing routines are rigid. Writing *The Touch*, he rose early each morning, made his breakfast, took a walk for an hour. Exactly at half past nine he sat down in his workroom at a plain table facing a windowless wall. He labored until precisely 3:30. He used blocks of lined yellow paper, writing in a very round, very personal, very hard-to-read hand. If he made a mistake, wanted to change something, he would not cross out and scratch in the new words, but instead would recopy the entire page. Once the script is printed up, he writes all over it, makes sketches, even doodles hearts on it.

INGMAR BERGMAN:    Before I start the writing of the final script, I write and write and write books and books of notations. They are very personal: dialogues and discussions and personal expressions and situations, memories, things that have nothing directly to do with the picture or with anybody but myself. It is very boring. I hate it. And afterward I throw everything away.

But I boil all that down in the final script. I put all those things together as in a dream—so you don't recognize anything. It's always thousands of details, and these combinations are emotionally stimulating to my creative mind. From these combinations I build a selective reality, a mirrored reality. Suddenly it's a newer reality.

My whole life I have trained my intuition. It's a sort of rail I travel the whole time. The first moment I meet you, my intuition starts to work inside—a computer that gives me information. I see how you move. I see your eyes, your face. I listen very much on the voice.

I used to have a feeling of mean and bad—a moralistic stomachache about all the time taking pictures in my mind. But you just have to accept that this has nothing to do with coldness or a twisted mind. It is just part of me and I can make something out of it. For example, the opening scene of *The Touch* is built on the death of an actor friend 15 years ago—but I did use one thing from my father's death. I saw my father 15 minutes after he died. The window was open and all the sounds of life—buses, car horns—came from the outside. His head was turned toward the window. The eyes were closed, but not completely. The illusion was that he was looking far away. I found it so extremely strange and beautiful and full of secrets.

The most important thing in the creative job is to let your intuition tell you what to do. I am writing my script and I plan for this man that he will do such and such. I know that if he does not do such and such, all these other things in the plot will fall into pieces. But my intuition tells me suddenly that this man says he will *not* do such and such. So I ask the intuition why. And the intuition says, I never tell you why. You have to find out for yourself.

Then you go on a long, long safari in the jungle to follow where the intuition has directed. But if I refuse the intuition, then I have merely arranged things. So my characters, they don't obey me. They go their own way. If they had to obey me, they would die.

On exactly July 15, the day promised, Bergman's agent placed the script of *The Touch* in the hand of Martin Baum. It was essentially a 56-page novella, not at all in the conventional dialogue form. But every scene and line was there, surrounded by the moods and tones Bergman wanted. By that time the film had been cast. For the Swedish parts, Bergman could draw upon what is virtually his private repertory company, a select elite of actors who have peopled film after film of his, and have become literally extensions of Bergman's imagination. For Andreas, the doctor, he chose Max von Sydow, who had appeared in ten Bergman movies. Karen, the wife, would be Bibi Andersson, one of Bergman's closest friends and veteran of nine films. After seeing *Getting Straight*, Bergman picked Elliott Gould to play David, "the outsider."

INGMAR BERGMAN:   I'll tell you exactly what I found in Elliott. It was the impatience of a soul to find out things about reality and himself, and that is one thing that always makes me touched almost to tears, that impatience of the soul.

You can say it's childish, but then you can say Mozart was childish and Picasso is childish and Stravinsky was childish. As Christ said, if you are not as children, you will never come to heaven. I think all real artists have this childishness—they never feel that "now I am completed." They are always curious and they are always on their way and they are always impatient.

You know, I love actors by nature. Of course, they can bore me extremely—the same as they can be bored by me—but I think they are lovely. You know, if we are real people of the profession, we are related to each other because we have the same difficulties. We have the same longing for contact, for tenderness, for hard work, meaningful work. Actors are very, very delicate—very sensitive—and very tough.

Elliott Gould is one of the absolutely real actors. I think it is a catastrophe for the creative powers of this man just to make pictures, because he is also a Shakespearean actor, an Ibsen actor, a Strindberg actor. A wonderful Molière actor. He has this certain atmosphere, a certain mind, a certain sort of imagination, a certain thing you feel that the body of the actor is an instrument, and that he is conscious enough and talented enough to play on it perfectly—the whole time.

Elliott Gould was sent the script. "I read it," said Gould, "more intently than I've read anything in my life. I probably memorized it in one reading. And I got a migraine headache. It was a classic Bergman thing—so cellular and diagrammed and microscopic and universal. There were certain scenes which were wonderfully erotic, really intimate scenes which frightened me in terms of bringing myself to Bergman and conceivably having intercourse while on camera. It was a very difficult thing for me to consider."

Gould turned down the role, insisting that he was "too ignorant" and could not "put myself into Bergman's hands totally." So a phone call was arranged. "In 90 seconds," said Gould, "he was just so reassuring, so interested, so enthusiastic. I knew that I trusted him. I felt that, regardless of my feelings. You never heard an eagerer man than myself, and on the other end of the phone a man more desirous of making me comfortable. He was just so sensitive, terrific."

Bergman's choice of Gould gives an insight into the director as well as into the actor. While the character of Karen was patterned after an acquaintance of Bergman's, he based David in part on what he regards as the explosive, childish, even boorish side of his own very split nature.

MAX VON SYDOW:    Ingmar has these special characters who are reincarnated from film to film. There is the very sensitive, very emotional person who cannot bear his own feelings. He is usually destroyed by the second type of character, the one who is emotionally inhibited by his intellect, who never has had any real emotional experience and longs to be almost the victim of an emotional explosion just in order to feel something. This shows, I guess, that Bergman is constantly struggling within himself between these two extremes.

INGMAR BERGMAN:    The only thing I care to tell you about my tensions is that much of the eternal dialogue inside me is between the 50% of my mother and the 50% of my father I carry inside. Both were extreme and very strong personalities. They were married 52 years, but they did never understand a word one of them said to the other. They were as water and fire. I was always sensitive and I did not stand any pressure. That I got from my mother. But she had her enormous self-discipline from childhood. Women are always stronger in the way of bearing the pressure of a situation, of going on. My mother had no patience with us children because she educated us the whole time. She was an extremely intelligent, impatient woman, full of temper and extremely bright.

On my father's side, they have always been clergymen and farmers. From my father I think I have got some good red blood and my closeness to the landscape, to the seashore. I don't want to say anything bad about him, but I got from my father the most difficult qualities. He was a very dangerous man because he had a lot inside of him. He was a very good clergyman. I think I am that too, a little.

My education was insane, crazy, completely ridiculous. Here was God, King, Father, Family—this hierarchic construction in that order. Freedom did not exist. So it was necessary that education created not characters, but obeying machines. Brutality and cruelty were inevitable.

In Bergman's films, the characters constantly speak with his voice, articulating both Bergman recollections and philosophy. Their speeches give perhaps the best of all looks past the mystery and into the darkest corners of his mind. In *Hour of the Wolf* there is an artist, Johan—a deliberate self-portrait of Bergman. The film follows his descent into madness. In one scene Johan describes an incident at the hands of his parents, which is a true story from Bergman's own childhood.

"It was a kind of punishment," Johan tells. "They pushed me into the wardrobe and locked the door. It was silent and pitch dark. I was mad with fear and I pounded and kicked. You see, they had told me that a little man lived in there, and he could gnaw the toes off naughty children. When I stopped kicking, I heard something rustling in a corner. I struck out wildly to save myself from that little creature. I howled with terror and asked to be forgiven.

"At last the door was opened and I could step into the daylight. My father said, "Mother tells me that you are sorry.' And I said, 'Yes, please forgive me.' 'Get ready on the sofa,' he said. I went up to the green sofa and arranged a pile of cushions. Then I fetched the cane, took down my pants, and bent over the cushions. Then father said, 'How many strokes do you deserve?' And I said, 'As many as possible.' Then he caned—hard—but not unbearably. When it was over, I turned to mother and asked. 'Can you forgive me now?' She wept—and said, 'Of course I forgive you.' She put out her hand . . . and I kissed it."

INGMAR BERGMAN:    You know *Hour of the Wolf*? It's not a very good picture, but it's a very personal picture. What I talked about was the demons, the friends who become friendly, and started to destroy that man. I think it had very much to do with my own fear of them—but I will never let them do that.

I wrote *Hour of the Wolf* in a very quiet room. I never have any sun in the room where I write. I was sleeping in this room too, and after a few weeks I had to stop. The demons would come to me and wake me up and they would stand there and talk to me. It was very strange.

I live at the edge of a very strange country and I don't know what will happen. There is a real problem in my character which is no secret: I am extremely aggressive. Disciplined aggressivity can be a very good thing in my profession. It's a good horse. And of course that is very much in my films. But I have a fascination to the brutality and cruelty in life because I feel a relation to the power of cruelty. It's a very dangerous thing to carry. It's a sort of dynamite inside.

But I know my neuroses and I can say hello to them and I talk to them and I have them under control. I am extremely healthy. My doctor thinks I will be 110.

I never use drugs or alcohol. The most I drink is a glass of wine and that makes me incredibly happy. Music is always there, every day, every night, and this is absolutely necessary for me. If I had to choose between losing my eyes or ears—I would keep my ears. I can't imagine anything more terrible than to have my music taken away from me. It is my most important stimulation, it gives me impressions. When I am completely sleepless, then I have a very good friend in music. Johann Sebastian Bach gives me a lot always, but I am extremely stimulated by modern music—the Rolling Stones. The most rough, brutal, aggressive pop music I put on so the walls almost shake.

Though he was contractually obliged to spend only four weeks at work on *The Touch*, Elliott Gould went to Stockholm three weeks early so he and Bergman could get acquainted. They were to meet at 8:30 the first night and go to dinner. Gould had been warned that Bergman was such a demon for promptness that he was always five minutes early, a habit ground into him by his father. Precisely at 8:30 Gould and his girl, Jenny Bogart, descended to the lobby of the Grand Hotel.

ELLIOTT GOULD:    We went downstairs and he was there. He must have been pacing—with his little windbreaker and sweater. We just walked toward one another and immediately hugged each other. Then we looked at one another's eyes. I guess we always were brothers. I don't know why. Maybe he recognized an ignorant sensitivity and deep kind of feeling in me that he knows. Perhaps he also recognized an inno- cence which I still don't understand.

Gould and Jenny Bogart spent the weekend at Bergman's house on his island of Fårö. Invited guests, especially foreigners, are extremely rare. Fårö, the last Swedish land before the Soviet Union, is a military reser- vation, and complicated official permission was needed for their visit.
     During the weekend Bergman showed them *The White Sheik*, one of the earliest films of his favorite moviemaker, Fellini. It was part of Bergman's very large private collection of films, including his own, which he reruns to study and learn from. They toured the island, and at one point Bergman asked what was Gould's greatest fear. "Not being what somebody I cared about expected me to be," Gould said. "Mine is to be locked in a tiny space," said Bergman.

BIBI ANDERSSON:    I think Ingmar's island mirrors his own personality. Now this island is extremely poor, so he feels as though he is flowering there because everything is gray—the stones, the crippled little trees that can hardly grow because it's constantly blowing. There are flowers but small, dry flowers. The island is so old, it's ageless. No feeling of time. Nothing has happened there for hundreds of years. The people look the same as they have for centuries. The only animals are sheep. They come and look in through his windows, and on the seashore—there's no sand, just rocks—there are the white bones of dead sheep. I think from this island he can start.

He has built there on this terribly uncomfortable island a cozy little world surrounded by a stone wall. It is very strange because when you come in through these walls, you have a feeling that you have neighbors and people around, because it's very warm—all yellow and wood. He has a swimming pool there. You have a feeling you can pick up a telephone and go to a neighbor. And then you go out and there is empty land all over.

INGMAR BERGMAN:    My island is so good for me. The atmosphere, the people, the landscape, the sea, the rhythm of my life there—life and reality have their right proportions. I will try to explain. If I go to the Royal Dramatic Theater and I start rehearsal and I am very angry on that morning, suddenly the whole theater knows. Four hundred people say Bergman has a bad temper—oh, how terrible. I can suddenly have the feeling that I am somebody and that my mood is very important.

If I have a bad temper on the island and I go to the seashore and perhaps I scream or something, then the only thing that happens is that maybe a bird flies off and says, *Waaa, waaa.* So here is the exact position, Mr. Bergman, of your life, of your importance.

That gives a security, a sort of rest. I think it's very healthy for grown-up people to learn their exact proportions on earth, very good for the creative job. Then that will be more proportional.

Elliott Gould toured Europe for a week and returned to begin the shooting of *The Touch.* He joined an almost impenetrably closed circle—Bergman's film crew, his so-called "18 friends." Almost all of them—the electrician, the clapperboy, the continuity director, costume designer, cinematographer, etc.—have been with Bergman for 15, 18, 20 years and are as reflexive and as sure as the fingers on his hand. At the same time they are expected to have a strong say in the making of the film, especially in the weeks of preparation for every contingency, and in the testing on film of every possible combination of color in costume and props. "A film," says Bergman, "is selected reality." Everything in a Bergman movie is done by conscious, explored decision; nothing left to chance; complete control.

MAX VON SYDOW:    In Ingmar's films there are always moments of subtle humiliation. In *The Passion of Anna*, for example, I as Andreas visit the other man, Ellis, in his studio and he keeps photographing me. The way he does it becomes a strange, terrible torture—again and again, keeps on forever—till there is an eerie quality in it. "Don't move. No. No. Turn your head like that. Look that way. Hold your breath"—and you are kind of hypnotized and humiliated.

What does that tell me about Ingmar? It tells me about a man who is very sensitive and very afraid of being handled by other people. A man who is very anxious to stay in command and who is very good at being in command—who worries terribly beforehand when, for example, he makes a movie; who is so terribly well prepared from every angle about every little detail just in order to avoid every risk of being caught off hand by situations—to keep control of everything.

INGMAR BERGMAN:    I try always to do things that are familiar to me. I always feel scared to death when I have to meet new people. When I travel out of Sweden, I feel exhausted, unhappy, insecure. So the technical solution is to regulate my life just so . . . very orderly . . . ritual. That keeps my tensions in balance, keeps this heavy, difficult thing inside me from starting to roll. It's like a ship in a storm. If the cargo shifts, the ship will drown. I think if I let my routine go, in a few weeks the catastrophe would be complete. I mean some sort of self-destruction.

You know, somebody studying sleep discovered that if they prevent you from dreaming, you go crazy. It is completely the same with me. If I could not create my dreams—my films—that would make me completely crazy.

Dreams are a sort of creative process, don't you think? My films come from the same factory. They are like dreams in my mind before I write, and they are made from the same materials, from everything I have ever seen or heard or felt. I use reality the same way dreams do.

Dreams seem very realistic—and so do my films—and there is a certain security in that reality. And then something happens that disturbs you, that makes you insecure.

All my films are dreams. When I was very little I was happy because I lived in dreams. I was alone and I built puppet theaters and puppets. Sometimes I used to mix up what had happened—what was reality and what had been my dreams—and that would give me trouble with my mother and father. After I saw my first motion picture—it was *Black Beauty*—I was so excited I was in bed three days with a fever.

On the set Elliott Gould fitted right in: each morning he was totally prepared and took everything very seriously. Bergman always had a box of Droste's chocolates, and it was a little bit of an honor when he offered one. It became very special to Gould that after lunch he would get two or three pieces.

They all enjoyed the clown in Gould, who was once a song-and-dance man. He had them all flipping three pennies off their hands and trying to catch them one at a time. A basketball nut, he and the crew and Max von Sydow played half-court games. Gould would sing in his deep basso voice, and sometimes Gould and Bergman would sing and dance together. "Suddenly," says Gould, "it was like we were all kids."

BIBI ANDERSSON:    I love Ingmar. I've known him for 17 years. I admire him for just being alive, because all through these problems he has with himself, he has not grown mentally old and deformed himself. He's marvelous to have to your house because he appreciates everything. And he can be so childlike. For me that is very touching.

We have this loving laugh about Ingmar because he has this silly little private life. He's been wearing the same shoes for 15 years. I think that's very funny. He brushes them so carefully and it doesn't show. Since I know him, he is wearing the same sweater, the same jacket—but they're kept so neat. It's not a gimmick, something he puts on for effect or show. It's that everything should be comfortable.

He constantly eats the same lunch. It doesn't change. It's some kind of whipped sour milk, very fat, and strawberry jam, very sweet—a strange kind of baby food he eats with corn flakes. He says his stomach cannot take any other food, but we all know there's nothing wrong with his stomach and that he just has to make this terror to everyone that he has stomach pain.

It was so funny. He kept talking to Elliott Gould about how healthy this lunch was and he should have it. Poor Elliott, he was so polite and he was eating this stuff, saying, "Oh, I love it." Then Ingmar said, "Now Elliott is going to have this every day for lunch because he loves it." And we all laughed because nobody can eat that except Ingmar.

I can joke about his sour cream and strawberry jam—at the same time he's eating that, he has a film going on in his mind like *The Seventh Seal* or *Persona*—things I admire so much, they're too for beyond me even to talk about. Maybe I can participate in them, but I could never invent them in my whole life. If he was just eating the jam, I wouldn't love him.

To Bergman, the atmosphere on the movie set is crucially important. The actors, a breed regularly haunted by self-doubts and paranoia, must feel completely secure and respected. It is somehow communicated that simply because he, Bergman, has chosen them for the roles, then there is no possibility that they will fail. Therefore, they will trust Bergman completely. All the niggling preparation, the sense that every contingency has been anticipated, surrounds the actor with a security, a good feeling each morning that everything is clean and ready. No outsiders are allowed on the set, so that the actors feel they are watched only by friends. "The actor," says Bergman, "delivers his inner self at all times. If you feel scared, or insecure, or feel there's something wrong with your nose, or with your saying this, or wrong with this gesture, you deliver nothing. But if the actor is in an atmosphere of security, he opens up like a flower." During *The Touch*, Bergman devoted himself constantly to Gould. They spent hours together, mainly Gould talking and Bergman listening.

ELLIOTT GOULD:   Like Bibi said to me when I got to Sweden, Ingmar brings out the best in his actors. He was everything and far more than I had thought—plus dreams I wouldn't dare have. Bergman's universe is so magnificent that to bring my ignorance to him and let him use me while he was loving me . . . I mean, it was an experience that . . . that's sublime. Bergman is sublime.

After one scene where I had to hit Bibi, which was really hard for me, and knock her down and go crazy screaming at her, Bergman asked if sometime I would play Othello—and I thought, Jesus Christ. I said, "Oliver was fantastic as Othello." Bergman said, "Yes, he played Othello fantastically. But you could *be* Othello." I thought, that man, I'd be a snake for him. I would go there and play a box.

He never talks to you about psychology, only specifics. He is never patronizing. When there were really neurotic, complicated things to be done, he would say something. On the next take I would feel almost as if my ribs opened a little bit and something that maybe happened to me when I was 2 would fill in the cracks between the lines. When the take was over, I would get the chills. I would feel very cold and know that I really allowed myself to be touched and that he took that extra thing he felt was there beneath my being a copycat. I'm a brilliant copycat.

Once I went to him for help and I put my arms around him. And he put his arms around me. He said to me, "Don't contract your muscles. Be open even to emptiness because then whatever does come will be real." And it was just so simple and true—I could have cried.

On Monday, May 3, 1971, exactly one year from that dinner at the Connaught Hotel in London, the same cast of ABC officials assembled to see the finished film of *The Touch*. Bergman himself was absent—to spare them embarrassment if they were disappointed. They loved the film and had a big celebration lunch. That afternoon, assured that all was well, Bergman met with them and heard their enthusiasm. In his pleasure and relief, reports Martin Baum, Bergman was positively boyish.

On Friday, May 14, Bergman, Bibi Andersson and Elliott Gould were to be taped with Dick Cavett in Stockholm. Gould had flown to London a week early, expecting to go to Sweden and spend some time with Bergman before the taping.

But to Bergman, *The Touch* was now past history. And he was, by his strict routine, writing his fall film. No invitation was forthcoming. In a final interview given shortly after his return from London, Gould's feelings about Bergman had become suddenly very complicated.

ELLIOTT GOULD:    When I was in London last week I telephoned Bergman. And you know I don't ever call anybody. It was at night and

I woke him up. I said, "Listen, I'm here and I don't want to wait for a week to see you." And he said he couldn't see me—so I said, screw me, and I went home to New York.

It just disappointed me a little because I'm his friend, and he tells me that I'm his favorite little brother in the world, and it was a bit of a lonely time for me. But it's true, like I said from London, any time you want me, just send me a toothpick and I'll be there. What I long for is contact, and he makes movies out of contact.

One of the things that puts me off is the "honor" of acting for Bergman. So an American actor went and worked with this brilliant man! I don't think he's terribly important anymore. As far as young people and the revolution that's going on here, well, I've seen *The Touch* and I told Ingmar it is really quality, but I'm not that impressed.

Sure, he's understanding but it's not good enough just to understand. He's not nice. That's a quote from Ingmar Bergman, and it's true. He's not nice. But he's smart. Bergman is a boy. He's the most brilliant, magnificent, sensitive little boy, and he knows it and he plays it, and God knows I'm a littler boy than he is—but not as mean as him.

I'm just disappointed by perhaps his limitations. I mean, he's been there so long, in his way biting his nails—God knows I respect anxiety—but I think he ought to get out of Sweden. I know I could show him things he never dreamed of. On the other hand, maybe this film with an American actor, in English, with American money is his passport to other things. Don Giovanni! I really would like to do that before I do Othello.

When *The Touch* opened in New York, the major reviews were very evenly distributed between enthusiastic, respectful and disappointed. In some cases Gould's performance was admired, but more frequently it was criticized as not believable. Often it was suggested that Gould was defeated by banal lines written by a Bergman whose Swedish ear was not tuned to detect English clichés. Yet almost every reviewer felt that the film—even if flawed—was still the work of a master.

The day of the opening, Elliott Gould telephoned Bergman to tell him there were lines outside the theater. During a lengthy and warm exchange, Bergman apologized to a very pleased Gould for his brusqueness during their last call.

INGMAR BERGMAN:    The only judge of my work that is interesting to me is what a few friends think and what I think. Sometimes, yes, I am too obscure. But my function is not to explain everything, is not to say every minute to feel this way, that way. I do not imprison emotions, rape them. My job is just to start your emotions and then give them food. But I have no problems with the public. I can assure you that the producers, the people who give the money to buy the picture from me, they don't come to me only for my beautiful eyes.

My main passion—it is a need—is to make contact with people, to influence them, touch them physically and mentally. My pictures are my way of making contact. When you are making a film you are part of a group. If you are a relatively inhibited, shy, timid person like me who has trouble establishing deeper relations, it is wonderful to live in that intimate little world. These are the only reasons for me to go on like this.

Penguins want to be together, to touch each other, to talk together and take walks together. If you have just one penguin, you can feed him and you can talk to him, but he dies because he has nobody else to be in contact with. I feel extremely like a penguin.

I am not interested in making masterpieces of art under the sign of eternity. I and my crew, my 18 friends, we are like one body and all together we make the piece of craftsmanship. We make a thing—like a car or a table or a part of the road—a thing for people to use. It's very simple and very brutal.

Freddy the Great, the Prussian king, his architect built a wonderful castle called Sans Souci. When the king saw it for the first time, the polite men around him said, "Look what you have achieved. Your Majesty." And the king said, "God in Heaven, have I done all this?" I have the same feeling sometimes when I read those people who analyze my films.

Perhaps I should say this about my work. I think we have this dirty, cruel, wonderful, marvelous life—and when it is completed, life is simply switched off and it will not hurt. That is my religion. That makes me secure and happy to know. When I believed in some strange God or a life after this life, I felt anxious and scared and upset.

But there is something wonderful: that for thousands and thousands of years, all our fear, all our hopes, the sighs and longings have crystallized a certain religious feeling inside, an eternal gift from all those generations. So when you hear one of the last symphonies by Mozart or Bach or a play by Strindberg, suddenly the roof opens up to something that is bigger than the limitations of the human being. That makes me very happy. That is a treasure we carry with us. To make a film is to try to open up the roof—so we can breathe.

There is a final piece of Ingmar Bergman which may make it possible for him to survive the inner intensity, the agonizing pace of his work. In a tiny, sunny corner of himself. Bergman is bemused by being Bergman. It is a niche where he does not take himself and his art so very seriously. It is the part which makes him say so often about film-making, "We play the game together."

In *Hour of the Wolf*, speaking through Johan, Bergman sums himself up: "I call myself an artist for lack of a better name. In my creative work, nothing is important except compulsion. Through no fault of mine, I've been pointed out as a freak. I've never fought to attain that position. And I shan't fight to keep it. I felt megalomania waft about my brow, but I think I'm immune. I've only to consider the utter unimportance of art in the world of men—and I come back to earth with a bump. But the compulsion remains."

# A Visit with Ingmar Bergman

## A. ALVAREZ/1975

As A PERSON, INGMAR BERGMAN is not at all what you would expect from his films, with their introspection and penetrating sense of isolation. He is a tall, vigorous man, friendly and effortlessly charming, who has about him a continual buzz of energy—an energy contained and used, not frittered away. He laughs often and easily and possesses what W. B. Yeats called "the terrible gift of intimacy," which means that you find yourself talking to him almost immediately as if you and he had known each other for years. But unlike most possessors of this gift, he is generous with himself and speaks freely of his personal concerns and hesitations. For a man whose art, like Strindberg's, has often been an instrument of despair, he seems astonishingly open and at ease in himself. He has only one nervous tic: As he talks, he turns in his hand a chunk of wood, darkened and grainy from much handling. Years ago, he gave up smoking, after severe nicotine poisoning. The wood, presumably, gives him something to do with his hands.

He is getting bald now, at 57, the dark hair going gray, and the lined, sardonic face of earlier photographs has filled out a little. His mouth is smallish, reddish and very mobile—a witty mouth and exceptionally expressive. Yet your main impression of his face is one of great concentration. Under their bushy brows, his eyes are hooded, the left slightly more closed than the right, so he seems to be taking continual aim at you. And, in truth, he misses nothing, picking up not only the nuances of what you say but also the overtones of what is left unsaid. Late in the

From the *New York Times Magazine*, December 7, 1975, 36, 90–106. Reprinted by permission of Gillon Aitken Associates, Ltd.

interview he remarked, "We have no limits. We go into each other if we get in contact. If we don't, of course, we are very lonely and very far." It is easy to see how he gets those marvelous performances from his actors.

We were supposed to be talking not about his films—even though *The Magic Flute*, his version of the Mozart opera, is currently winning extraordinary acclaim—but about human relations among the Swedes and the enviable social utopia they seem to have achieved. This achievement is partly due to the national sanity which has kept Sweden at peace for over 160 years and neutral in two World Wars. A sudden, spectacular leap in wealth began in 1945 when Swedish industry was ready and eager to supply the vast needs of ravaged Western Europe. But what Bergman calls, "this almost completely unbloody revolution" started earlier, certainly no later than 1932, when the Social Democrats came to power. This party—which is of the left, though not, even by British standards, particularly socialist—is still in power today.

While Bergman discussed Swedish society, our conversation was wider-ranging and more personal because, as he explained, "My view is that of an amateur. And the word is exact, because I love this country and I love its people. But I can't speak authoritatively because I haven't been involved in a scientific way." Because he is the most gifted, as well as the most famous, of living Swedes, his personal reactions have, I think, an interest and authority that those of most social scientists notably lack.

ALVAREZ:    *There seems to be a curious clash between the great social enlightenment of modern Sweden—no poverty, no racial conflicts, universal economic security, political freedom, underpopulation rather than overpopulation—and the apparent growing unease among its people. According to the statistics, between 1966 and 1972 the marriage rate declined and the divorce rate climbed by 50 percent; the remarriage rate has also sunk dramatically and illegitimacy soared. Doesn't that strike you as strange?*
BERGMAN:    I think it's normal. It's like the suicide statistics: in wartime, they go down, in peace they go up. When everything is easy and in balance and suddenly it is not necessary to fight for life, when all the problems seem to be solved, then the difficulties come. I think divorce can be very healthy. Of course, it's painful. But if people take

this step instead of staying together humiliated, then it's an act of courage and mental health.

A:   *It's not only painful, it's also usually expensive. Could it be that the Swedish divorce and illegitimacy rates are up and the marriage rate down for practical reasons—because there are tax advantages in not marrying, or at least none in marrying?*

B:   Certainly, divorce in Sweden isn't so expensive any more. You have to pay for the children but not necessarily for the wife, provided she is not too ill or too old to work. I have the feeling that it is the women in government who have tried to arrange it so that women no longer have any right to live off their husbands. I think this is a very good idea. But it is not new. The relative freedom of women in Sweden now is part of the great freedom they used to have when this was an agrarian country and even earlier, in the 17th century and before, when we were continually involved in aggressive foreign wars. In those days, we had an enormous army and were always running around Europe fighting—in Russia, Germany, Poland. If half a million men from this small nation were away, then the women were left to manage the country. And this gave them enormous self-confidence and freedom. It's an atavistic feeling. Then, when the Industrial Revolution came, it spoiled their self-confidence, their importance as being productive parts of society. But that period was very short and, as a result, the women here are a step forward.

A:   *In Sweden, it seems as if the goals of Women's Lib have been achieved. There are women in government, the professions and every kind of job, even the most manual. But, in the United States, the rhetoric of Women's Lib implies a battle between the sexes. Is there an unusual degree of bad blood between men and women in Sweden?*

B:   I don't know much about other countries, but I have the feeling that here we are at the beginning of an incredible revolution. The women are finally beginning to take over their full burden of responsibility. Of course, they still have so many difficulties that it is impossible to know what will happen. On one side, there is the vocal avant-garde; on the other, a great crowd of women who remain invisible. Yet almost every woman, even in the avant-garde, has some kind of saboteur

inside her. I don't know if it's her mother's voice, or something complicated with her physical construction, or what it is. But they all have a
bad conscience. They feel that something is wrong and they don't
know how to manage it. Even so, something has started which is not to
be stopped, though where it will go and what will happen we don't
know.

A:    *Is this just one aspect of that idea of social perfection that you are working toward in Sweden?*
B:    Probably. But sometimes there's more ambition than wisdom, and
sometimes it's very naive. But you must remember that 50 years ago
Sweden was an extraordinarily poor country—people were starving and
life generally hard. Then this almost completely unbloody revolution
happened in a mere 50 years. This, in my opinion, is remarkable. But,
of course, the more you try to change the conditions, the more you
find out what is wrong: and the more you work with the contemporary
situation, the more you see that there are still wounds from earlier
times and older generations.

A:    *You mean the old moral and emotional Puritanism lingers on?*
B:    Of course. Sweden is a Lutheran, a Calvinistic country, not consciously perhaps, but in a subterranean way. Religion talks about two
things: law and love. The trouble is, everybody has forgotten love but,
inside, everybody remembers the law. That makes for terrible problems.
We try desperately to find solutions, consciously of course. Our politi-
cians have all sorts of visions, or at least ideas. But subconsciously we're
all still in a mess.

A:    *Ilya Ehrenburg once said that "the Swede is the poet of matter." Is it true
that they love materials and things more than they love people?*
B:    In a way. We have a kind of materialism here which we love
because it is new and because we've achieved it under enormous difficulties. So it's very hard for the young men of the radical left to get
through to a worker on, say, a Friday evening in the summer, when he
takes his car and drives his family to his summer house in the country
where he has his boat. He feels free and everything is fine. So how does
the young radical persuade him that he is being manipulated and

exploited, and that revolution would be better for him? Yet the same worker can go on a wildcat strike if he feels that he or his colleagues are being humiliated. That often happens here because the loyalty of the unions is very strong. The problem is that there is now a younger generation, further to the left than the old Social Democrats, which has been educated in a freer way. In this new generation, they ask questions, they don't think it's necessary to obey, and often they intensely dislike agreements made over their heads. So they go on strike. There used to be complete peace when a wage agreement was worked out, but that is not so any more. And that's one of our big problems. But then the gray-suited gentlemen from the Royal Commissions come along, and they sit and sit, and eventually work out a compromise. The reason is, we have no talent for drama.

A:  *It's ironic that you, of all people, should say that.*
B:  It's strange, but although there are very good actors in Scandinavia, we don't have much talent for acting in social life.

A:  *Yet all the world envies Sweden as a kind of social utopia.*
B:  I know. But when people come from abroad and tell us we are living in a social paradise, we are always surprised. Maybe things work well in one or two isolated spots, but in general we have no sense of social perfection. Far from it. But we try. You must remember this is a very small country—only eight million people. What happens here is, to many outsiders, very boring. But we love compromises. People who have absolutely different points of view sit down together in endless conferences, whole days and nights on end, in dusty rooms. Perhaps they hate each other or each other's opinions, but somehow they always work out some sort of compromise. It's not heroic. I think it has to do with our temperament. I must also say that I feel extremely Swedish. I live here and I couldn't live anywhere else for any length of time. I have my roots in this country. We can trace our families back a long way—to the 16th century and beyond. So I live here with my roots. I have no problem in understanding how we react, how things go wrong or right here. And I love it. I also love, in a way, our compromises. I myself am a very impatient man and have great difficulty in compromising. But I know that if you want to do something here, you

can't dictate. You have to sit down and discuss what you want to do with everybody involved. For instance, on the island [Fårö, a remote island in the Baltic, where Bergman now lives and works on his movies], I am reconstructing an old house. The work is being done by the local farmers and fishermen: they are marvelous professionals with their hands. And we have no architect. We just sit down and discuss it together. This is very Swedish. People like to plan together, to discuss, to work things out. It is the same when I make my pictures. I can't say, "Now we are going to do this or that." Instead, all of us who are involved sit down together; we read the script and discuss it. I explain how I would like it and the others say, "Couldn't we do it like this instead?" That's a lovely way of working, and for me it's a way out of very neurotic loneliness.

A:    *Loneliness—ensamhet—is one of the great recurrent themes in your work. I have the impression that this is a characteristically Swedish preoccupation—or is it that I am simply viewing Sweden through your films?*
B:    I don't think loneliness is typically Swedish, any more than it is typically American or English. I think it is typical of all human relationships. My generation was educated in a very bad way, which forced us into this neurotic loneliness. The new generation is more conscious of what it must avoid.

A:    *I wonder if the new social system isn't a way of perpetuating the loneliness? Mothers are now paid by the government to look after their children for seven months and then, if they are to keep their jobs, they must leave their babies in day nurseries and go back to work. It seems to me that to deprive a baby of its mother at such a young age is to lay the foundations of future unhappiness. At seven months, a child is surely too young to be thrust out into society?*
B:    I don't think it's bad for small children to be brought up with other children. What's bad is that it is not 100 percent. It's good and necessary for women to get out of the isolation of their homes into the social life of their work. But, at the same time, perhaps this causes problems for the children who may be hurt by this sudden step. We don't know yet. The day nurseries haven't existed long enough. So we don't know if it's better for children to be with other children all day in the care of women who

have talent for being mothers than to be at home with their own mothers who are terribly neurotic and isolated. My opinion is the absolute opposite of yours. I have the feeling that the family, as it is constructed today, can be very dangerous for children and that the schools and day nurseries must take over some of the responsibility for the next generation. You see, the day nurseries are never big—maybe three or four women to 20 children. These are women who have a vocation, sometimes a genius, for being mothers, and it is they who should educate the children. Other women have no talent for motherhood, but I think it would be very cruel to tell them that they shouldn't have children.

A:    *Yet a hundred years ago that would have been perfectly acceptable, wouldn't it? For women who didn't want to marry and bear children, there was always the church or an honorable spinsterhood of good works.*
B:    A hundred years ago it was very simple because all the generations lived together. When the women had to work with their husbands in the fields, there was always a grandma, an aunt or a cousin to take care of the children. Nowadays, marriage and the social situation are more complicated and, I think, dangerous for the children. The women work all day, then come home, tired out, to the cooking and the chores. They have no time or energy for their children and that's terrible. So we are trying to find a solution.

A:    *I don't agree with the theory but I understand it since, like most English middle-class kids in the 30's, I was brought up by a nanny and hardly saw my parents.*
B:    I was exactly the same. I lived with my parents but had no contact with them. We couldn't talk about anything. Not until after my mother had her third heart attack could we sit down together in peace. She was 74 or 75 by then and I was about 46 or 47. I think if I had been brought up in a day nursery, I would have been much happier today, certainly much happier as a child.

A:    *Could it be that the day nurseries are a first step towards the final dissolution of marriage?*
B:    A country as rich as Sweden is able to give everybody the freedom to choose how they want to live. If they want to work a six-hour day,

give them a six-hour day. If somebody wants to start work at 10 in the morning instead of at 7, it can be arranged. If a woman wants to stay at home with her children for three years, pay her for it. If two people want to divorce, help them to divorce. We have the resources and I think we are on the way. The trouble is, the government of this country is a bit like a nurse; it wants to nanny us. In the enormous ambition that we shall have it very good here, everything is very strict. First, they tell us we must do things in such and such a way because that is the best solution. Then they decide on a compromise, so we have to do things in another way. And we are a little bit too passive, too indolent.

A:   *Isn't it difficult to be anything except passive and indolent when everyone seems to be working for you?*

B:   That is another problem in this paradise: Most people are mentally understimulated. It is going to create great difficulties for the government when the six-hour workday comes in. What are they going to give them to do with all that free time? In a very materialistic country like ours, you have to find ways of educating children to read books instead of comic strips and shock magazines. And this is very difficult. For instance, I have a son of 12. He is a highly intelligent young man, very curious about life and everything, but he never reads a book. Never. He reads Donald Duck and monster comics, but he is absolutely uninterested in reading books. And if people don't read, this creates great problems. As long as words are the chief means of conscious communication, what will they do if they have no words? Where will they find stimulation for their minds? It is a problem of emotional as well as intellectual understimulation. They have feelings but they have no words with which to express them. They lack the ability to put words together to express a complicated experience. So they lose some sort of dimension in their lives and feel very unsatisfied. But if you say, "You are unsatisfied and unhappy because you have no words to express what you feel," they think you are crazy.

A:   *For the foreigner, one of the strangest things about Sweden is the way everyone has a title: Director Bergman, Actor Josephson, Poet Ekelöf, Engineer Martinson, and so on. It is as though the person did not exist apart from his title.*

B:    The big, heavy job for us artists is to tell the state and the citizens of this country that they are not just things that can be put into a box with a title on it. We have to keep repeating, "You are not an object, you are not a box, you are a human being—a difficult, complicated, unlimited individual who suddenly exists here among other living creatures."

A:    *Do they believe you?*
B:    No. But I can go on trying. And if we all keep on saying the same thing—with the help of Shakespeare, Molière, Strindberg, Ibsen, Mozart and all those big boys—perhaps we might gradually give people a sense of the richness and complication of their lives, of the enormous freedom there is in being a human being. But I'm not very optimistic about the result. So if you ask me why I work and why I go on, I must tell you that I do it for myself, not for other people. For me, every drama of any sort—political or religious—is interior drama. It starts inside. If it then works for other people also, so much the better.

A:    *But Scenes From a Marriage got through to a vast, international audience, didn't it?*
B:    Yes, I was very surprised. I wrote it just for fun and didn't know what to do with it. It was like *Winnie the Pooh*. You know, Christopher Robin was ill and, every evening before sleep, A. A. Milne told him one of those little stories. Then he wrote them down and suddenly the whole world bought *Winnie the Pooh*. It was the same with *Scenes From a Marriage*. I wrote it for fun, for myself. I started with the third scene, then I wrote the fourth, then the second. The whole thing took me about four weeks. Remember, it's called *Scenes From a Marriage*, not *the* Marriage. To me, it was very private. Then suddenly it wasn't private any more, suddenly it became a shared experience for a great number of people. In Denmark, for instance, the divorce statistics went up. That's got to be good!

A:    *I think it is a wonderful film, but I have one reservation: The children seem to play no part either in the marriage or in its breakup.*
B:    That's true. But I wanted to focus just on those two people, Marrianne and Johan, and strip away relatives, friends, almost everything extraneous.

If I had involved the children, it would have been too complicated for two reasons. First, because children are so difficult to work with—a horror for the director. Second, because this has been a problem I personally couldn't solve. For me, it has been too bloody, too difficult. You see, I have had six marriages; before I was 30 I had married three times and had five children. The problem was too enormous to face. So I said to myself, as a human being I have made an enormous fiasco, therefore I must try to be a very good director. So I escaped into the theater and the film studio and there I lived happily, more or less. But I ran like a rabbit my whole life until I went to live on the island. That was about 10 years ago. At that point things changed. I stopped running, settled down and tried to find out about myself.

A:   *Was that about the time you made* Persona, *which I think is perhaps the finest of all your films?*
B:   Yes, it was. At that time, I had been head of the National Theater in Stockholm for about two years. In early spring I got a very bad virus infection, some form of pneumonia which also affected my sense of balance. For four months I sat staring at a spot on the wall and, if I moved my head, the whole world seemed to turn upside down. I could hardly even bear to speak. So I began to think how it would be to make a picture with just two people, one talking, the other silent. I wrote the movie in June and we started shooting in August. And I tell you, the shooting of that picture saved my life because, when we started, I was at the end of my tether. Then suddenly everything changed. I realized that I could leave the National Theater, that I was a free man, that I could get a divorce and drop my social life in this city and go to the island. There was also another freedom. My whole life I had fought with religious problems. Then I had this minor operation and for five hours I was away, completely faded out, switched off. After that experience—the five hours that hadn't existed—I was no longer afraid of death. And everything that was outside this world no longer mattered. Since then, I haven't thought about God.

A:   *How strange.*
B:   It is strange. Now I believe that all the qualities I used to associate with God—love, tenderness, grace, all those beautiful things—are created

by human beings themselves, they come from inside us. That, for me, is the big miracle.

A:   *I suppose this explains the change in your work. In your earlier films, the characters had intricate and fascinating souls but no hearts—at least, none they were willing to expose. Now they seem less lonely, more vulnerable, don't they?*

B:   People change, Haven't you, too, tried to find out who you were meant to be when you were a child? Suddenly you discover strange, forgotten feelings—you haven't seen them for 50 years. And this is exactly what happens when you live a calm, regular life on this island, surrounded by people you want to be with. It's a question of finding your own rhythm. I think your pulse, your heart's movements, the movements of your soul, all these things combined, create your own rhythm. This is not superstitious. It is part of my professional thinking. If you live calmly, or just sit down calmly every day for about an hour, gradually you discover your own rhythm. But most of us don't and that's unhealthy, spiritually and physically. The important thing is not to let other people, other situations or conditions or circumstances hurt this rhythm too much. Sometimes, of course, it's healthy to be stressed. Sometimes it is good for me to get away from the island and live a more hurried life. But only sometimes. If you can find your own rhythm, you find a lot of other things at the same time.

A:   *Yet stress and tension are your special themes, like loneliness, and your forthcoming movie,* Face to Face, *is about a suicide attempt, which is the ultimate tension. Is it also very personal, like* Scenes from a Marriage?

B:   Of course. I, too, have felt suicidal, as you have. But it is the creative work that saves us. I have always been at work and you can't commit suicide when you are shooting a picture or directing a play. It can't be done. Or rather, it can be done theoretically, but it's highly unprofessional! I don't envy you because, as a writer, your work is very lonely. But *I* work with people—actors, technicians—and that saves me. You wake up at 4 in the morning with demons on your breast and hell all around. But at 6 o'clock you have to get up and go into the studio or the theater. Immediately you're involved with all sorts of problems—technical problems, other people's catastrophes—and you and the company feel like a single body with many limbs. Then suddenly you think, "Good heavens, this morning I intended to commit suicide. It's ridiculous." So, however depressed I get, I realize I am also the man who tries to overcome difficulties in the studio, who loves to play with the actors and see them laugh. On the island, I haven't had the slightest thought of suicide in all the years I've been there.

A:    *Because it's too beautiful?*
B:    No, because it's too real. Your sense of proportion becomes absolutely exact, your problems exist precisely in relation to their labels—no more, no less. If I am angry and go out onto the beach and scream, perhaps some silly bird flies up from a tree. But if I come into the studio and scream, there will be an enormous explosion and everyone will talk about it. So I can get an absolutely wrong idea of my importance. On the island, nobody cares.

A:    *Do you work harder there?*
B:    No, much less. About four hours a day. I work from 10 to 12 and from 1 to 3, then I sleep for an hour. After that I go across to the bigger island and pick up the newspapers and the mail. In the evening, we read or see friends or watch a movie—I have a big collection of films. It's very regular.

A:    *You may have found solutions for yourself, but are you optimistic about the Swedish experiments in producing a social paradise?*
B:    Not particularly. But you must admit that the trying itself is beautiful. It's like psychoanalysis: It can go on for five or eight or 10 years, it can go on all your life, and sometimes it succeeds. But the idea is beautiful. The trouble is, it has to be confronted with the complication called a human being, and the human being, in my opinion, is a very bad piece of construction. If you were to look from the outside at your own behavior and at the behavior of people everywhere, you would come to the conclusion that it is utterly incomprehensible; it can't be explained religiously or politically. We are simply a strange construction, a strange experiment of life. I think one day we will disappear and the insects will come back, because they are the only perfect constructions. Koestler has a theory that the human brain is like a cancer. Thousands

and thousands of years ago something happened in the head of a monkey. Over his perfect little brain another brain started to produce cells like a cancer. This new brain is a completely crazy construction which has no relation to any other creation in the world. And the contacts between the new brain and the old are very bad. So mankind suffers from this cancer brain, this enormous, impractical thing we have to carry around over the little brain we needed for our primitive, simple functions. I like this theory. It is probably not true, but to me it is very sympathetic because I am terribly pessimistic about the future of mankind. Yet to live, I think, is lovely.

A:    *And think how boring it would be if all we had were those little monkey brains.*
B:    Of course. I don't want to go back to the beginning. I like things as they are. I like waking up at 4 in the morning scared to death. Yes, I like feeling scared to death. I wouldn't want to change.

# Dialogue on Film

QUESTION: *The theory here at the Center is that you can't teach filmmaking, but you can learn it if you come in contact with the right persons. That's why we feel so fortunate you are here, because you are the right person.*
BERGMAN: I am very nervous. I am almost fainting. I always feel very scared when I have to meet so many people, but you look very friendly. I will do my best. Somebody told me the first day I was here that I would come to your lecture, and I fell into pieces. I said, "Lecture, what's that?" Somebody said, "You go to see the students and say hello to them, and it's all over." But I think you make it a job—you ask questions. I don't know what you want from me. I will try to be as honest as possible. It's very difficult because I can't talk my own language.

QUESTION: *Please tell us how you work with actors. For example, the different steps you use to communicate with actors.*
BERGMAN: It can be a very complicated question—we can talk about it for the whole time. And it can be a very simple question, because if you want to know exactly how I work together with my actors, I can tell you in one minute: I just use my intuition. My only instrument in my profession is my intuition. I have the experience that when I work at the theater or in the studio with my actors I just *feel*, and I don't know how to handle the situation, how to collaborate with the actors.

---

From the American Film Institute, October 31, 1975. Reprinted with permission.

One thing is very important to me, one thing. That is, an actor is always a creative human being, and what your intuition has to find out is how to make free—do you understand what I mean?—to make free the power, the creative power, in the actor or the actress. I can't explain how it works. It has nothing to do with magic; it has a lot to do with experience. But I think when I work together with the actors I try to be like a radar. I try to be wide open, because we have to create something together. I give them some stimulations and suggestions, and they give me a lot of stimulations and suggestions. If this fantastic wave of giving and taking is cut off for any reason, I have to feel it, and I have to look for the reason. I know if we try to work with those waves cut off, it is terrifying; it is the hardest, toughest job which exists both for me and the actors.

Some directors work with aggression. The director is aggressive, and the actors are aggressive, and they get marvelous results. But to me it is impossible. I have to be in contact, in touch, with my actors the whole time, because what we first of all create when we start a work together is an atmosphere of security around us. It's not only me who creates this atmosphere; we together create it. But for all those situations, all those decisions, all those very difficult decisions—you have to make hundreds of them every day—I never think. It's never an intellectual process; it's just intuition. I have to go straight into it, and I have to trust my intuition, because if you trust your intuition and train your intuition and not start to make intellectual discussions with your intuition, you make the right thing. Afterwards you can think it over: "What was this? What was that?" You can think over every step you have made.

QUESTION:    *Do you write in the same way, always using your intuition?*
BERGMAN:    Yes, yes, yes. The best time in the writing, I think, is the time when I have no ideas about how to do it. I just play the game. I can lie down on the sofa, and I can look into the fire. I can go to the seaside, and I can just sit down and do nothing. I just play the game, and it's wonderful. I make some notes, and I can go on for a year. When I have made a plan the difficult job starts. I have to sit down on my ass every morning at ten o'clock and write the screenplay. Then something very, very strange happens. Very often the personalities

in my scripts don't want the same thing I want. But I have also the experience that if I try to force them to do what I want them to do, it will always be an artistic catastrophe. But if I let them free to do what they want and what they tell me, it's OK. So I think this is the only way to handle it. All intellectual decisions must come afterwards.

You have seen *Cries and Whispers*? For half a year, I think I went around, and I just had a picture inside about three women walking around in a red room in white clothes, and I didn't know why—I beg your pardon?

QUESTION:    *I was just complaining about the noise from all the cameras.*
BERGMAN:    It doesn't matter. When people sit together and talk, I just want to know what they are talking about. I am terribly curious. It doesn't matter with the cameras. It's just machinery going on, but if people talk with each other, I get terribly curious. I went around with this picture inside, and I couldn't understand why these damned women were there. I tried to throw it away; I tried to write it down; I tried to find out what they said to each other, because they whispered. And suddenly it came out that they were watching another woman who was dying in the next room. Then the screenplay started. But it took about a year. It's very strange. You feel you have a picture. The script always starts with a picture, with some kind of tension in it, and then slowly it comes out.

QUESTION:    *After you have developed a script do you continue to develop the characters through your shooting?*
BERGMAN:    No. I have always worked with actors; I have never worked with amateurs. I made a documentary once, but I have always worked with trained actors. An amateur can be himself always, and you can put him in situations that give the situation a third dimension, as De Sica did in *The Bicycle Thief*. But if you work with trained actors, you must have come to a conclusion, to an idea, about exactly what you are going to do with the parts. We have all the discussions before, and then we work in the studio. We just have the freedom of being together and giving each other suggestions. It's very nice. But the whole time we must have in mind what we meant.

It's very dangerous to go away and suddenly start to improvise. You can improvise, of course, in the studio, but you have to be very prepared before you improvise, because to improvise on an improvisation is always shit. It always goes into a catastrophe. If you are very prepared and know how to do it, you can go back if your improvisation suddenly one day fades away, which of course it does. I think inspiration and enthusiasm and everything like that are beautiful, but I don't like it. I think when we are in the studio we have to be very strict.

QUESTION:    *What do you say to the actors? Do you do exercises with them?*
BERGMAN:    No, no, no, no. Good heavens, no. I say nothing. Before we start the picture we talk a lot. We meet, and we talk a lot. We have some sort of discussions. I don't know how. But when we are in the studio, I think we say strange things to each other. We make some noises, we tell funny stories, we touch each other. We just find the key words, because it's very necessary not to talk too much. Just to hold this intuitive relation is a creative job.

QUESTION:    *Do you tell them the message of the film?*
BERGMAN:    No. Good heavens, no. No, no, no, no. In a way, I don't know anything about messages or symbols or things like that. I am always surprised when people ask me about the message, because I just want to get in touch with other human beings when I make a picture and tell them a story, or just be together with them or touch them and have them feel things. Sometimes when I have the message everything goes wrong. So we don't talk about those things. We just talk professionally: "Be careful. Be slower. Don't be in a hurry." The most important thing of all is the ear—the ear for the director and the ear for the actors—to listen to each other with. Very often when I see a scene I just close my eyes and listen, because if it sounds right it also looks right. It's very strange.

QUESTION:    *In your films you often fuse reality and dreams. Do you feel that reality and dreams are of equal importance?*
BERGMAN:    Yes. To me real cinematography is very, very close to dreaming, as cinematography is when it is at its best. Think only of the

time gap: You can make things as long as you want, exactly as in a dream. You can make things as short as you want, exactly as in a dream. As a director, a creator of the picture, you are like a dreamer. You can make what you want. You can construct everything. I think that is one of the most fascinating things that exists.

QUESTION:    *Have you transferred dreams to film exactly as you dreamed them?*

BERGMAN:    Yes. I have only done it twice. I have written down a dream and filmed it just as I had dreamt it. One is in *Wild Strawberries* with the coffin. Without any translation, it's just put in as it was. The other picture is *The Naked Night*—the first sequence with the clown and his wife. Writing and filmmaking and the creation of pictures are so extremely close to our dreams.

I think also the reception by the audience of a picture is very, very hypnotic. You sit there in a completely dark room, very anonymous, and you look on a spot, on a lighted spot in front of you, and you don't move. You sit, and you don't move, and your eyes are concentrated on that white spot on the wall. I think this is exactly what some hypnotists do. They light a spot on the wall and ask you to follow it with your eyes, and then they talk to you and then they hypnotize you. It's quite different when you watch television. You sit at home, you have light around you, you have people you know around you, the telephone is ringing, you can go out and have a cup of coffee, the children are making noise. The situation is absolutely another situation.

The film medium is some sort of magic. I think also it's a magic that every frame comes and stands still for a fraction of a second and then it darkens. A half part of the time when you see a picture you sit in complete darkness. Isn't that fascinating? That is magic. So we can be as intellectual as we want; we can be as sensible as we want. We are in the position to work with the most fascinating medium which exists in the world, because as in music we go straight to the feelings. Afterwards we can start to work with our intellect. If the picture is good, if the suggestions from the creator of the picture are strong enough, they'll give you thoughts later. You'll start to think. They'll be intellectually stimulating.

QUESTION:    *You speak a lot about music, and we all know that you are very fond of music. We know you use music as part of your plan. What do you feel you can do with music over the sound in general?*

BERGMAN:    I will try to answer the question. I think when the silent picture died and the sound picture came, the silent picture was in a development, in a marvelous development. But now we have sound, and we have to combine the sound and the picture, and they have to work together and live together, and I think that is a marvelous medium. I think we can do a lot with the sound track. I am a little bit worried about music, electronic or conventional music, because I have the feeling that film in a way is rhythm. Music, at the beginning, as Stravinsky said, is also rhythm. They are both unintellectual suggestions. I think it's dangerous to use real music, but to use sounds, different sounds—concrete or synthesized sounds—is very interesting, and I think we have just begun to do what we can do with sound and picture together. And that is fascinating.

QUESTION:    *You have described many of your films as chamber works, as a metaphor to chamber music. What do you mean by that?*

BERGMAN:    It's not my invention. Strindberg, the Swedish writer, had a little theater. It was almost like this room here; I think it was for a hundred people. He arranged, with enormous difficulties, with some friends and some actors a very primitive theater, and for that theater he wrote plays with few actors, with just very simple settings. He called them chamber plays, like chamber music. And I have stolen that from him.

QUESTION:    *Could you have made the kinds of films you make if you were working in America?*

BERGMAN:    Absolutely not. I think it would have been impossible. No, everything is changing now. I came to the business during the war. I came to the business in 1942, and Sweden was isolated completely, and we could only get German pictures. We didn't want them, so we had to make our pictures ourselves. Because this was before the TV, the Swedes were running to the movie theaters very much. This little country with seven million people made about forty or fifty pictures a year. Suddenly everybody who knew the front and back of a camera was a cameraman, and everybody who had ever spoken to an actor was a director. Of course, it was fantastic because in three years I made three pictures, three catastrophes, three flops, and I was still alive. We could just go on and make films, and that was very healthy and unneurotic. It was not a question of making money or making box-office success. But when I made my fifth box-office catastrophe I was kicked out.

It was after a catastrophic opening of a picture of mine. I was in bed, and I was crying, and I said to my girl friend, "Oh, I think they will never let me make a picture again." The telephone rang, and it was a crazy man who said. "Ingmar, I think you are a little bit more modest now, so perhaps we can work together." And I was.

That was the beginning, and I am still grateful to that man. He taught me almost everything about filmmaking because I was a happy amateur, very enthusiastic, and had enormous ideas about making pictures about life and death and everything. Nobody understood my pictures—I don't understand them myself. When I see one of them, I get completely red over my whole body. I think I was a very difficult director. I was very aggressive, and I was absolutely terrifying in the studio because I was insecure, and if you are insecure you get aggressive, of course. But this man taught me a lot about filmmaking.

Do you all know what the most important thing was that he taught me? What I still use? You know how it is when we see our rushes, our dailies. We just ask "God, help me. Help us all." Isn't it so? And then we say, "This is not so bad." And somebody else says, "No, it's pretty good." And then a third says, "It's wonderful." We try to pep ourselves up to have the courage to continue the next day, because very often when you see the rushes you have the feeling that you want to go under the bed and never come out again, like a dog. He said to me, "I hate this pepping up. Sit, be objective, be your own worst critic, be cold. Don't let yourself fall down into a depression or up into a euphoria. Just sit and see it all quietly. Don't blame your crew. All of you have done your best. The only thing you have to do is to estimate: Is this all right? Or may it be so that I have to retake it? Or what can happen? Just be objective.' It's almost impossible, but I think that is one of the best things I have learned in my life, and I still use it, and it's very, very good. And best of all I think is to be alone with your god and the projectionist when you see the rushes. To have nobody there, because it's always so that when people sit there and they are an audience—even if it's a cat—you just sit waiting for something. So it is best just to be completely alone.

QUESTION:    *How have you gone about financing your films and marketing them outside Sweden?*
BERGMAN:    It has never been a problem for me, a real problem. Compared to the American or international productions, my pictures are always low-budget productions. *Cries and Whispers* cost about $450,000. *Scenes From a Marriage* cost us about $200,000. There is always some fool who wants to raise the money. There must be gamblers and optimistic people in the business.

QUESTION:    *What is your relation to the camera? Do you have to buck the technical limitations of the camera?*
BERGMAN:    If intuition is our mental instrument, the camera is our physical instrument. I think the camera is erotic. I think it is the most exciting little machine that exists. To me, just to work together with my cameraman, Sven Nykvist, to see a human face with the camera and with a zoom to come closer, to see the scene, to see the face changing, is the most fascinating thing that exists. I think the choreography of the actors in relation to the camera is very important, because every good actor feels if he is good in the camera sense, he is in a bad position. And if he is in a bad position, he feels stress and is very unhappy. If he is in a good position, in a logical position—he can be with his back to the camera, it doesn't matter—if he feels this is all right, then intuitively he feels secure and he does his best.

So there is always the question about the relation between the actors and the camera in every scene. The camera has to be the best friend of the actors, and the actors have to be secure with our handling of the camera. They must feel that we are taking care of them, because we who are directors must never forget that we are behind the camera and that the actor is in front of the camera. He is nude; his soul is nude. If he has confidence in us, we have enormous responsibility. We have somebody in our hands, and we can destroy him or we can help him in his creative job. To be behind the camera is never difficult, but to be in front of the camera is always a challenge, a difficulty—to be there with your face and your body and all the limitations you have in your soul and all the limitations you feel of the face and your movements. We cannot lie to the actors; we have to be absolutely true to them. And as better actors they like the truth more. Don't you think so, Jeanne?

JEANNE MOREAU:   Yes.

BERGMAN:   That is my feeling.

QUESTION:   *At what point in the planning of a film do you decide on the position of the camera?*

BERGMAN:   The evening before. When I come home in the evening, I just sit down with the script and I read the next day's schedule very carefully. I make up my mind about it, and then I just note the choreography of the actors and the camera. Then in the early morning when I meet Sven—you know, we have worked so many years together—we just very shortly, in five minutes, go through the scene. I tell him about my ideas for different positions of the camera, for the different positions of the actors, and for the atmosphere of the whole scene. And then we can go on the whole day; it is not necessary to have any discussions. He is just fantastic. He is a marvelous man. He is very silent and very shy. Suddenly everything is there, without any complications, and I can look in the camera, and everything I wanted is there.

QUESTION:   *Do you rehearse with the actors on the set before you plan your shots?*

BERGMAN:   No, never. If you rehearse with trained actors, they go form the mood of intuition to what they are trained to do, to acting every evening. It's very difficult. When the atmosphere is created, we come to a sort of intuitive understanding of what the scene means of us. But if you rehearse too much an actor who is trained to play every evening, something new starts to happen, an intellectual process, I think. That process can be very good, but it's very dangerous for filming because you have something in his eyes suddenly, some sort of "Now I do that and I do that and I do that." He's conscious of what he's doing. He has to do it intuitively.

QUESTION:    *Would you talk about some of the similarities and differences in working in the theater and the cinema?*
BERGMAN:    Oh, it's absolutely different. It's absolutely different because filmmaking is a neurotic job. It's un-normal to every creative process I know. It's some sort of craftsmanship. You must have a lot of physical power to make a picture. Perhaps statistically we make three minutes of the picture a day. The terrible thing is they are three minutes of the picture. If you are in the theater you will rehearse—in Sweden we have about ten or twelve weeks of rehearsal. We start slowly at 10:30 in the morning, and then we go on, and it's very lousy, and you can sit down and relax. Everybody feels, "This is not good today but perhaps next Monday or in the middle of next month we will find out." The creative process is natural, is unneurotic.

When you are a film director who has written the script yourself, you have to be some sort of Dr. Jekyll and Mr. Hyde, because if Dr. Jekyll has written the script Mr. Hyde has to direct it, and I tell you they don't like each other that well. I think that is a very schizophrenic situation. In the theater, we are a group of artists who just come together. We come together in a house that is built for us to work in. Everything is very important. We come there like very efficient children with our books. At 10:30 a bell rings, and we all go to rehearsal rooms, and then we are there together with Stringberg or Ibsen or Molière or Shakespeare or any other of those old, marvelous gentlemen, with our thoughts, our emotions. We have the opportunity to go into the drama and live with it and try to understand the wisdom of the drama that we are working with. I think that is a fantastic situation: it's quite another situation. Filmmaking is always an abnormal process.

If I had to make a choice—God save me from that—if somebody came to me and said, "Now, Ingmar, you have long enough made film and theater; you have to make your decision," I am sure I would choose the theater. In the theater if you grow old and stuffy and dusty, you have a lot of experience. If you can just pronounce your experience in some crazy words, the artists will understand you, and you will have a wonderful time with them. My teacher in the theater was a director who was eighty-five years old and he could hardly speak, but still he made wonderful, enormous, incredible performances because his soul was young. But he had no powers; he was absolutely a physical wreck.

You can't be a wreck when you work in the studio—perhaps you are, but it's dangerous.

QUESTION:    *Have your ideas of staging in the theater changed because of film? I remember seeing a production of yours,* Hedda Gabler, *at the National Theater, and I was very impressed by how cinematic the staging was. A lot of things that in the play happened offstage you brought onstage— a lot of long walks where we followed someone uninterrupted by seeing from the side. I was very impressed by the marriage of the two mediums. Was that your intention?*

BERGMAN:    No, it's no marriage. It's a relation. It's just that. When I was a teacher in the dramatic school in Sweden, we always started the first class with a discussion of what you need to make theater. On the blackboard we wrote down about a hundred things: stage, actors, tickets, clothes, money, spotlights, footlights, makeup, theater—more than a hundred different things that we thought we needed. Then I said to them, "Now we take away everything that you think is not necessary." We went on and went on and went on—we even took away the director. Three things remained. What do you think they were?

QUESTION:    *Actors?*
BERGMAN:    An actor, yes. That's true.

QUESTION:    *An empty place, a stage?*
BERGMAN:    It's not necessary.

QUESTION:    *A script?*
BERGMAN:    A manuscript, yes. A message. We could call it a message, don't you think so? Two. And a third?

QUESTION:    *An audience?*
BERGMAN:    An audience, yes. The class wasn't sure that the audience was necessary, but I thought it was absolutely necessary. And that is my theology about theater. What we need are actors, a message, and an audience. If we have those things we have a performance, because the performance is not here on the stage; it is in the hearts of the audience.

It is very important to know that. In filmmaking we can learn a lot from the theater because what we need to make a picture is just that little fantastic machine, the camera, and some film, the negative. That is all.

QUESTION:    *I read once of a famous film director who tried to do a theater production, but he didn't like it because he felt there was only one camera angle. Having seen many of your films, I notice a variance of camera styles from one film to the next. How do you approach a particular film through a camera style?*

BERGMAN:    I have no style—we have no style. We just feel. The director who said that must be a director with an enormous lack of fantasy, because the marvelous thing in the theater is that the theater is unlimited, absolutely unlimited. Do you know the Shakespearean stage? The performance was always in daylight. When Shakespeare wanted people to understand that it was night, do you know what he did? He let the actors come in with torches, burning torches in the daylight, and the woodwinds played a little thing so the people understood it was night. The battles in the Shakespeare plays were made with five or six soldiers, but the audience saw an enormous battle. We have no camera style, Sven and I. What we are interested in is not a style for the camera because the solution of that is in the picture. What we are always interested in is the light or the shadows, the rhythm in the light and the shadows of the picture. These we discuss a lot, and there we have a lot of experiments.

QUESTION:    *But there* is *a difference in style in your films. Sometimes it seems the style is more to accommodate the actors. In* Persona *and* Cries and Whispers *the style seems to be rigorous and disciplined.*

BERGMAN:    Yes, but that is no problem because it's a part of the whole decision. It's not an intellectual decision. It comes out from the whole thing. It's just natural. I think it's difficult to talk about it because you can call it a style if you want, but it's not.

QUESTION:    *Do you ever want to do another film in black-and white?*

BERGMAN:    I hope so, yes, because I think it's tremendously fascinating.

QUESTION:    *Why do you so often have women as your main characters, while your male characters aren't very much in the foreground?*
BERGMAN:    I like more to work with women. I have many good friends who are actors, and I like tremendously to work together with them. But in filmmaking it's job for good nerves, and I think women have much better nerves than men. Women are not, in the first place, women; they are human beings. And God forgive me, but I have the feeling that the prima donnas always are male, and the women aren't like that. It's very difficult to be an actor in our society; it's not so difficult to be an actress.

QUESTION:    *I've heard you say that when you begin to film that you know as little about the film as the actors do. What did you mean by that?*
BERGMAN:    No. Remember I have written the script. I have lived with this script perhaps for one or two years. But the preparation for the next day, in the details—I wait with it as long as possible. Of course, when I made *The Magic Flute* we had to prepare everything before.

QUESTION:    *About* The Magic Flute. *You've talked about rhythm. Did you have a problem in making the film follow the rhythm of the opera?*
BERGMAN:    No. It was wonderful. We had the production time, the enormous time of fifty-five days. It's two-and-a-quarter hours of opera. We have the complete music. We have not changed anything. It was absolutely wonderful. You had to prepare very much before because, of course, every movement, every angle of the camera, everything must be exactly prepared. But to be in the studio and every day to hear this music—I tell you it's the best time of my life. We started at nine o'clock. At four o'clock we felt very tired and very bored and very unhappy. But then we had the music, Mozart's music, the whole time, vitalizing us all and carrying us.

I want to add something. Perhaps it sounds like from an old uncle, but I am so. It doesn't matter. May I give you advice?

RESPONSE:    *Yes, please.*
BERGMAN:    I think it is a relief to me to know that I have an intention, if I have a passion and an obsession, if I want to tell somebody something and if I want to touch somebody, film helps me. But if I have nothing to say and I just want to make a film, I don't make the film.

That is most important of all for me, to have the courage, if I feel I have nothing to come with. The craftsmanship of filmmaking is so stimulating; it's so terribly stimulating, dangerous, and obsessing. You can be very tempted, but if you have nothing to come with, try to be honest with yourself and don't make the picture. But if you have something to come with, if you have emotion and passion, a picture in your head, a tension—you can know that even if you aren't very technical, even if you don't know how to put the camera—the strange thing is that having worked on the script and having worked with the camera for days and days and the whole time thinking of it, suddenly when you see the rushes and when you see the work print and you have cut it together, the thing you wanted to tell is there.

I have a very good example and that is Antonioni's *L'Avventura*. The picture is a mess. He had no idea where to put the camera; he had no money; the actors went away. I think he had enormous problems the whole time. But he wanted to tell us something about the loneliness of the human being. I can see this picture time after time, and I don't know what touches me most—how he succeeds without knowing how to do it or what he wants to say. That is very important, that is the most important of all. You have to have something to come with, to give other people. Picturemaking is some sort of responsibility, that is what I think.

# Ingmar Bergman at Work

JAMES JACOBS/1978

THIS TEXT IS A TRANSCRIPTION of a 45 minute documen-
tary shot by James Jacobs during the making of *The Serpent's Egg*. Jacobs
attended and filmed rehearsals for eight days. He also interviewed Liv
Ullmann about the character she plays as well as her relationship with
Bergman. He then showed the footage he shot to Bergman and interviewed him about it. Their conversation, conducted in the editing room,
renders his perspective on film directing with precision and spontaneity.

INGMAR BERGMAN (to J. J.): The film takes place in 1923 Berlin, during
the week of November 3 to 10. I try to provide the extras with some
background.

BERGMAN (to the extras, in J. J.'s film): The exchange rate of the dollar
is 4.5 trillion Marks. It is a time of confusion, of tension. We try to tell
the stories of some people during that week . . . This scene takes place
in a bar on Kurfürstendam, in which the atmosphere is a bit unusual:
the clientele are wealthy people who come to dance and have fun. The
bar is like a cancerous tumor within this dying city.

BERGMAN (to J. J.): I now try to give them instructions using my rudi-
mentary German.

BERGMAN (to the extras): You all believe that a revolution could break
out at any moment . . . A catastrophe, a holocaust . . . So why not enjoy

---

From *Positif*, no. 204 (March 1978). Reprinted with permission. Translated by Brigitte Sion.

life while there's still time? Why not dance, sing, make love, drink, and forget everything else? I want you to act as if this idea had become your obsession. Do you understand me? One word about the background of the scene. During that week, the weather was ice-cold in Berlin. Snow and rain fell continuously.

All right everyone, take your places and we'll try to shoot!

LIV ULLMANN (to J. J.):    This is the first time Ingmar is shooting abroad. I think it affects him a bit, from within. He's had to adjust. Over the last twenty years, he always worked with the same group of people. Here, in Germany, he has a different team, which has to accept him. Nevertheless, he sticks to proven methods . . . This time, there are other people, producers, above him, whereas until now he has been his own boss.

BERGMAN (to J. J.):    Here is another scene that could be interesting. It is very short. It doesn't last more than 45 seconds. Liv is playing a third-rate cabaret dancer. Her friend Abel, played by David Carradine, goes into her dressing room, but she's not alone. Abel sees a man he hates.

See how I draw the characters' movements before I shoot. I always prepare a scene far in advance. I try to make an ideal diagram. (He shows the storyboard to J. J.) It's not as complicated as it looks . . .

The first question I always ask myself is, "where should I put the camera?" Antonioni once said, "The placing of the camera is an ethical choice." I think so too, because if the camera is at an appropriate place from the start, the rest of the scene will go naturally.

I have simplified the action with these four drawings:

Here is Liv sitting on a stool. At the beginning of the shot, one can see neither her nor her visitor, Hans Vergerus. Only Abel is visible in the shot, as he enters the dressing room.

There is no light backstage, and the dressing room is lit with candles. I've placed the camera in front of the candles in order to provide an atmosphere of insecurity and to play with the shadows.

Here is the dressing room. Over here, a shelf with books, the candles and the camera. Over there, you can see the door through which Abel will enter, and here you can catch a glimpse of Vergerus, his back to the camera. And here is Manuela (Liv Ullmann).

Abel moves like this.

Vergerus goes to the door, stops and caresses Manuela.

BERGMAN (to Heinz Bennent):    You kiss her hand. You stroke her cheek. Gently, very gently.

BERGMAN (to David Carradine):    Now you come here and you ask her, "Do you have a cigarette?"

BERGMAN (to J. J.):    Here I try to show David Carradine how to behave with Heinz Bennent. (Bergman grabs Bennent without warning and pins him violently to the wall of the dressing room. Liv Ullmann steps back and freezes.)

Everybody looks rather surprised. I wanted David to be extremely violent. Liv seems to be a little scared. Her fear is visible. Abel has a fit of rage. He jumps at Vergerus . . . See, he takes him and pins him against the wall. Manuela doesn't react.

Vergerus walks out of the dressing room and Abel paces back and forth. He asks Manuela for a cigarette.

(To Liv Ullmann:) And you reply, "on the shelf."

(To Carradine:) Then you come over here, in the foreground, and you light it up.

Liv, you walk to him and you tell him: "Be nice to me."

That's all.

BERGMAN (to J. J.):    We hold the camera still during the whole scene. The actors move before the camera.

BERGMAN (continuation of rehearsal):    Now they meet for the second time. He instinctively knows that . . .? That's right . . . And all this perfection . . . and suddenly, you feel that . . . You notice that Manuela and . . . Liv! When you enter the shot, we have to feel that his presence bothers you.

BERGMAN (to J. J.):    It's funny . . . When I look at your footage and listen to myself speak to the actors it surprises me that I'm not telling them anything important, just fragmentary sentences through which

I try to convey something in my broken English. But I never stop touching them, watching them. And, instinctively, I try to create a certain atmosphere in which we will all be shrouded.

What is outstanding is the fact that we are able to share a vision of the scene without really discussing it. The work we do in common gives us a real sense of security. We don't communicate verbally but subconsciously.

BERGMAN (continuation of rehearsal):    Stand here so that we see more of him.

BERGMAN (to J. J.):    Here, I put my eye in the viewfinder, as I usually do, in order to frame the scene as precisely as possible. Experienced actors always sense if the camera is well positioned. It is one of their talents.

BERGMAN (to J. J.):    There is now a moment of silence. During the first rehearsal, when we are trying to define the movement within the scene, there is always an infernal racket. Everyone is running around.

But now, it's the actors' turn, and we try to have complete silence and total concentration a few moments before the shooting. I only give them instructions about details.

(The final take of the scene is shown.)

LIV ULLMANN (to J. J.):    Manuela is a former acrobat who has just got a job in a third-rate cabaret. She is neither a good singer, nor a great dancer . . . We had long rehearsals, because even when you play the role of a loser, you have to master completely what you are doing before you bring it down to the level of a failed performance.

BERGMAN (to J. J.):    We used 40 or 50 different sets for the film. The cabaret is one of the most important. We will shoot there for 8 or 10 days.

It was an interesting set to build from an architectural point of view, because we had to create a sense of desolation, misery, and mediocrity. The set designer has an extraordinary and instinctive sense of atmosphere. He knows exactly what kind of emotion is carried by each set. The cabaret will probably be one of his masterpieces.

It may happen that even though the director has prepared everything in great detail, he finds himself on a set that conveys a completely wrong atmosphere. He is then forced to play against the set. With this film, I feel that the sets exactly met my expectations. They even went beyond them and stimulated me.

BERGMAN (to David Carradine):   We are following you all along, until the end, and we end with a close-up of her (a young prostitute with whom Carradine will run off). While the camera follows you, we see the finale taking place on stage. Once here, we move to another shot. You hand her the banknote. You slip it into her blouse and you go out together.

LIV ULLMANN (to J. J.):   This is the ninth film I've made with Bergman, and I've never felt so secure, so free. I know what he wants and why he wishes it.
   The connection we've built over the years of our long collaboration has greatly affected this film, because we are very close. There is a lot of warmth between us, both on and off the set.

BERGMAN (to J. J.):   Abel goes to the cabaret to tell Manuela about her husband's suicide. It is a very difficult scene, and we huddle up against each other. In the middle of all this noise, we create an island of silence and concentration . . . of fraternity.

BERGMAN (to Carradine and Liv Ullmann):   What is important is not the words you exchange, but the atmosphere, the relationship between both of you. Silence will speak on your behalf.
   (To Liv Ullmann:) You're good at silences.

LIV ULLMANN:   David and I are silent actors.

BERGMAN:   And I'm so talkative!

LIV ULLMANN:   No, you are a silent director.

BERGMAN (to J. J.):   Liv is very generous when she calls me a "silent" director.

In 1943, when I met my drama teacher, who had been working in the theater for 50 years, he told me that a director should know two things: shut up, and listen to the actors. One very often forgets that actors are creative people—shy but creative—and that if you exhaust them with advice and explain everything in the greatest detail, they will be afraid to express their own point of view. They will feel that the director knows more than they do, and that it's better to follow orders.

Experience has taught me that if I patiently wait and remain open to their suggestions, a fruitful exchange will follow.

BERGMAN (to J. J., about an excerpt of the "tableau vivant," a scene shot on the cabaret stage): This is a strange scene. We are looking at the "live show" of an erotic scene performed in this shabby cabaret. The sequence created some difficulties, because I didn't want to use expert comedians. The performance had to be grotesque and very tasteless in order to reveal the degree to which love can be degraded and debased.

But how can you show something disgusting without becoming disgusting? I asked this question to the choreographer and he decided to play the part of the woman himself, while one of his friends, who is an excellent dancer, took on the role of the husband.

Here, I am trying to explain to this young dancer how she will have to move. I think I referred to Groucho Marx's walk, to his particular way of moving.

[Shot of a street]

This is our street, a Berlin street in November 1923. We made many trips to Berlin in order to scout locations, but could not find a street we could use. One day, I was flipping through an old issue of the *Berliner Illustrierte*. My eye caught a photograph and I thought right away, "here is our street!" I showed it to Rolph (the set designer). He talked to the producer, who agreed to allow us to build it. I don't think we will regret our decision. This street is a reconstitution of an authentic Berlin street, "Bergmannstrasse."

I never intended to shoot a documentary about 1923 Berlin. I simply tried to capture the spirit of this time, the threatening atmosphere. I don't think that uniformed men raided cabarets at the time, or that such places got ransacked and set into fire. Such things happened ten years later. But if you read newspapers from the 1920s and look at the way they describe the young generation, you can easily imagine such a thing happening.

LIV ULLMANN (to J. J.):    Nobody suspects that the more desperate Ingmar's films seem, the more relaxed he appears during the shooting. He laughs more, he smiles more often . . . And most of the time, we have a lot of fun.

BERGMAN (rehearsal)
    (To Liv Ullmann:) You look for him in the crowd.
    (To Carradine:) And on your end, you try to protect her. It is very difficult because you are surrounded by a very dense crowd, so you try to elbow your way but you can't. You are stuck. You try to get on the stage, but the men in uniform stop you.

BERGMAN (to J. J.):    As you can see in the script, this was a very difficult scene. Crowd scenes are always very delicate, because you must precisely account for the movements of each person. You can see here that the men in uniform are close, that they really form a wall. The camera takes a high angle shot of them. Abel and Manuela are here, with the cabaret owner. Over there is the speaker. I now explain to the actors how to move within the human barricade their bodies have created.

BERGMAN (rehearsal):    Over there, you only move off when I tell you. All the others, you leave right now. Let's go! Action!

BERGMAN (to J. J.):    I have had to express myself in three languages, German, English, and Swedish. Probably the only real difficulty I have had during this shooting is with my inability to give absolutely clear instructions, to express my thoughts fully.
    Scenes like the one we just saw (the cabaret on fire) scare me. If something went wrong, if someone got hurt, the whole film would be jeopardized. The nightmare would become reality. To continue this game—because it's like a game, right? . . . This game is nevertheless a life or death issue for me. This is only an illusion. But when something unexpected happens, one feels suddenly very tired, very sad and without the will to go on.

BERGMAN (to the technicians): Let's have a break until 11:30. Could you please clean that up so that we can change sets? Thanks.

BERGMAN (to J. J.):    It's funny, but sometimes a director feels deeply lonely and sad. The film continues to run in his head, even while he is sleeping. Sometimes, in the middle of shooting, the whole situation seems unreal to him. He asks himself, "What am I doing here?" And also, which is even more comical, "Why are they paying me to do this?"

# Face to Face with Ingmar Bergman

## WILLIAM WOLF / 1980

INGMAR BERGMAN stands outside his ranch house on Fårö, his Swedish island sanctuary, one arm affectionately around his wife, the other waving an enthusiastic welcome. He flashes a broad smile, almost a grin. There is nothing to suggest the brooding genius one might expect from stories about Bergman's anxieties and from his films that have probed despair and isolation.

During the next three hours it would become apparent that there is a new, liberated Ingmar Bergman. At 62, he is as work-obsessed as ever and worried that his filmmaking days may be ending, but the upheaval in his life—set off when he was hauled out of a rehearsal at the Royal Dramatic Theater, in Stockholm, in January 1976 and grilled at police headquarters by overzealous tax inspectors—forced him out of the shadows. Now he not only enjoys traveling and working abroad but has a new interest—playing paterfamilias to the clan resulting from his string of marriages, official and unofficial.

Although publicity-shy, he has even agreed to help promote Scandinavian films. In past visits to New York, Bergman tried to remain incognito. This week, he is due to arrive for the opening of the Museum of Modern Art's "Scandinavia: New Films" program, which begins October 30 and marks a combined effort by Sweden, Denmark, Norway, Iceland, and Finland to crack the American market. He will also be plugging his own new German film, *From the Life of the Marionettes*, another searing dissection of a marital relationship, this one exploding in murder. *Marionettes* won't be shown at MOMA, but

From *New York* Magazine, October 27, 1980. Reprinted with permission of William Wolf.

the series will include his fascinating *Fårö Document 1979*, an update of the film he made ten years earlier, depicting the rigors of life on his cherished island.

En route to the Fårö (pronounced For-EH) rendezvous with the director, I wondered how much more one could expect from a man who has already explored the soul and has analyzed men and women in relation to themselves, to others, and to the profound philosophical questions that have perplexed human beings through the ages.Can he equal or surpass such masterpieces as *The Seventh Seal, Winter Light, Wild Strawberries, The Silence, Persona, The Passion of Anna, Cries and Whispers, Scenes From a Marriage?*

Geographically, Bergman is as remote as some find his films. First there's a chartered plane from Stockholm to the ancient city of Visby, on the Baltic island of Gotland, a 40-minute bouncing ride to a car ferry, a 15-minute chug across the water to bleak-looking Fårö, another 15 minutes past mostly barren land, then along a winding, treelined dirt road leading to fenced-off property with a sign warning, SECURITY ALARM. Plus special permission from the Swedish military authorities, since Fårö, facing the Soviet Union, 100 miles away, is an outpost in Sweden's defense system.

Are there radar installations?

"I'm not allowed to say," Bergman demurs, laughing at the idea of attaching security importance to this tiny isle. Then he leads the way along the stony beach to show off his panoramic sea view. "I first came here to film *Through a Glass Darkly* and fell in love with the island. But I had a lot of trouble getting permission when I decided to build this house. You need permission for everything. It's a simple house." True, the gray wooden structure isn't ostentatious, but it is impressively spacious, with a sizable swimming pool hidden behind it. "Mostly I enjoyed it here because it is so peaceful. When the sea is silent, it is very strange. But it is never frightening."

Suddenly his tone grows somber. He could have been setting the scene for one of his films. "There *was* a time when I was frightened. It happened one night about five years ago, when there was a strange light to the sky. I had this horrible feeling that something was going to happen. And the next morning they found two fishermen had drowned just here." His mellifluous voice is already beginning to have a mesmerizing effect; his manner establishes immediate intimacy, and he laughs easily and frequently.

"Let's talk seriously after lunch," he says pleasantly but decisively. His wife, Ingrid (another Ingrid Bergman), to whom he has been married for ten years, has prepared a smorgasbord that includes gravlax, salad, and a huge bowl of luscious raspberries ("They were picked today by a neighbor") served with fresh cream. Although it is midday, candles illuminate the table in the dining area of their large, knotty-pine-paneled, modern kitchen. Bergman rations himself to a small bowl of raspberries mixed with sour milk. We have coffee in the simply furnished living room, which contains a few paintings and a driftwood sculpture. Near the elevated fireplace, wood is neatly stacked. There is a large television and a videotape machine, with a shelf full of cassettes. In a corner, a handsome grandfather clock ticks away as if auditioning for a Bergman film.

Bergman doesn't recoil at being asked whether he has anything more to say in his films or is in danger of drying up. "I have thousands of ideas. That's not the problem, because I still have an enormous desire to make pictures. I have many things to talk about because of my fascination with the human being, the human face—which fascinates me more and more—all the dimensions of reality, and the conditions of human life, of the human being." But he confesses to the doubts that have been nagging at him in the last decade.

"The problem is that I'm 62 years old. I have been in this business 40 years, and more and more I feel it physically. I get tired. Making a picture is a very tough job. It gets harder and harder, and I can feel that my health isn't what it was five or ten years ago. I don't think that has affected my film-making yet, but there is a risk that one day I'll feel that, no, I don't want any more, I'm too tired. Not bored, but too tired to start a new picture. I have decided that I don't want to wait for somebody to come in and tell me, 'Ingmar, it is better for you not to make this picture because physically you can't take it anymore.' So one day I'll say to myself, 'No, Ingmar, it's over.'

"Sometimes during the last ten years, when I have been shooting a picture, I've been very close to this decision. You know, I'm sleepless—that's my great problem. I sleep no more than four or five hours a night. I can be very tired in the morning when I have to go to the studio, and I think this will be my last picture, because I can't stand it anymore. Then the picture is finished, and I rest a little."

Could he really walk away from it all? "Oh yes, oh yes, oh yes. Because the theater is there, and that's something else. You can come at 10 A.M., go to the rehearsal room, rehearse for four and a half hours, and say, 'Today it was not so very good, but it will be better tomorrow, or Saturday, or Monday,' So, I hope to have the opportunity to work in the theater all my life."

Bergman has been staging plays in Munich, but there has been sporadic talk of his coming to New York to do Ibsen's *Rosmersholm*, with Liv Ullmann. "I would find that fascinating, but the problem in New York is that there is one star. The other actors are good but not excellent. In Munich you can have the best actors for all the parts. And in New York, rehearsal time is so short—about four weeks. In Munich I rehearsed *The Three Sisters* for fifteen weeks. And even if you get bad reviews in four papers, the audiences are so educated that they don't believe what they read and go to see for themselves."

Bergman's film company is based in Munich, where he spends half the year. For tax purposes, he can't spend more than six months a year in Sweden, but Bergman now feels free to return to the homeland he fled in bewilderment and anger. The charges of fraud crushed him and precipitated a nervous break-down. Subsequently, a new Swedish administration exonerated him completely and apologized.

"It was almost five years ago, and it's over, far away. The authorities made a big mistake. It is very seldom that a bureaucracy apologizes. But what happened almost killed me. Of course, it was also stimulating and good for me, because I had once thought it impossible to work abroad. But I had to go away somewhere. I went to New York and Los Angeles and Paris and Berlin and Copenhagen and Paris again, and Munich, and back to Los Angeles. It was fascinating. Anyhow, this fear of traveling, fear of flying—I don't have it anymore. But we don't want to go over everything again. It was part of a political attack. They wanted a scapegoat, but the whole thing is over."

Bergman's wife is more agitated, less forgiving. "My heart starts beating fast when I think of it. They treat people like Ingmar worse than anyone else."

"Please, Ingrid, let's not go into it," he implores.

Mrs. Bergman is known to be extremely devoted to her husband and protective of him. Unlike the actresses who have shared his life (Harriet Andersson, Bibi Andersson, Liv Ullmann, and who knows how many others), she nurtures no desire for an artistic career. Formerly in her family's import-export business, she now manages the details of Bergman's production company. The Bergmans have no household help; Ingrid does everything herself. About to go away for three days, she has prepared all of her husband's food in advance. He won't answer the phone, so she does; she encourages and organizes family reunions, even though it means a staggering workload.

"The first time all of our children ever met was two years ago, for Ingmar's sixtieth birthday," she says. "They liked it tremendously and come back now and again. They really know each other now and like to sit talking night after night, like sisters and brothers. This summer they were all here again."

Bergman is ebullient in describing the summer reunion. A few years ago, Liv Ullmann told me of Bergman's difficulty in relating to their daughter, Linn, but predicted that when Linn grew older, they'd have more in common. "All eight of my children were here, and Ingrid has four children from another marriage. They were here too. We had boyfriends and girl friends, wives and husbands, and grandchildren. Sometimes it's very tiring, so I have to go into the studio to rest. But I like it tremendously."

Bergman's work facilities on Fårö are in another house a few kilometers away. "I bought a farm that's 150 years old, and there I have a screening room, cutting tables, everything I need." His move to Munich posed many problems—adjusting to his self-imposed exile, working in languages other than Swedish. His first expatriate film was *The Serpent's Egg*. "The film was a complete failure, but even failures can be interesting." After his next film, the acclaimed *Autumn Sonata*, made in Norway, Bergman returned to Fårö to make *Fårö Document 1979*. "In a way the film was a medicine, a remedy, coming back here, you know. Here are my sources, my roots. It's the only place in the world where I feel really at home. There are about 500 inhabitants on the island, and I did a lot of interviews. To talk with my friends here, their problems, their lives, to look at them when they are at work—this was extremely personal to me."

Bergman has finished a new script for his next project. He is reluctant to talk about a work in progress, but someone close to him who has read the screenplay says that it again draws upon his childhood experiences. *Fanny and Alexander*, geared for both a television series and for a shorter version for theatrical distribution, is budgeted at $7 million and will star Max von Sydow, Liv Ullmann, and Erland Josephson. Although set in 1910, the analogy is obvious. Von Sydow plays a minister whose rigidity resembles the well-known authoritarianism of Bergman's father, also a minister. He locks his children in a closet for punishment, as Bergman's father did, and comes to a horrendous end. His sister catches fire in her bed, runs to him for help, and they both burn to death.

Bergman has often spoken about the scars left by his childhood. "But my neuroses are not in relation to my work. At least I have the illusion that my work is very unneurotic."

Bergman fled his home and didn't see his parents for four years. Eventually he came to a better understanding with them. He even finds positive results amid the psychic damage. Punctuality is one. "As a child I was a dreamer. Time didn't exist for me, and my father was not very sentimental in that respect, so he educated me in a very tough way. When I went to school I could be one, two, or three hours late when I came home. That was not very good for my backside. Now I hate to steal time from anybody, because I hate when time is stolen from me. If I say to somebody that we will meet at ten o'clock, I will be there five minutes before. So I am grateful to my father."

Talking with Bergman, it is easy to understand how he elicits such magnificent performances. Harriet Andersson says, "When he puts his arm around you, watch out." He looks at you directly, and his gentle, intimate manner suggests how he coaxes actors into doing anything he asks by inspiring their unswerving trust. Gunnel Lindblom, a Bergman actress who now directs her own films, thinks she understands why he is particularly successful directing women: "It isn't just that he likes women—he is interested in learning more about them."

How does Bergman describe his methods?

"It depends on whether you are making a film or directing a play. In the theater you can stop the work and sit down with an actor to discuss the problems. Filming is, of course, a sort of factory. You have to make three

minutes of the picture every day. Everything, every detail, must be absolutely prepared. Everybody, not only the actors, but all my collaborators, must know exactly what to do at every moment. Only then can we
improvise.

"Most important, I think, is to create an atmosphere of security, of
calm, of silence in the studio. It's a very tough job, most tough for the
actors because they are so exposed. They stay there with their voices
and their faces and require a feeling of absolute confidence. They must
be relaxed, and I have to create that atmosphere."

I tell him that actress Ingrid Bergman was surprised at his way of getting
her to express herself in *Autumn Sonata*, when he would tell her to think
of things that had nothing to do with the scene. "Oh, yes," he confirms.
"It is meaningless to talk in an intellectual way when our situation is
completely emotional. The intellectual discussion must have been cleared
out before the start of the picture, because once we are completely in the
middle of the emotional process, you have to talk in emotional terms. You
can say to an actor, 'You feel heavy like a stone,' and an actor knows
exactly what you mean and transforms his body. And when he has the
lines to complete the emotion, then you will have an expression. In the
beginning, Ingrid Bergman was very angry, because when we were shooting I didn't look at her. 'Why do you not look at me?' she asked. I said, 'If I
hear that your voice is correct, I know that you look correct.'"

Hollywood has always been a lure for foreign directors. Now that he
likes to travel, would Bergman venture into Lotusland? He is ambivalent.
"I very much admire the American way of filmmaking. It's very vital, and
extremely stimulating. And American directors have taught me a lot. In
the 1930s, I started my filmgoing with American films. I would see two or
three movies a day. Of course, I had to become good friends with the pro-
jectionists, because I had no money. I learned from the films of Billy
Wilder, Ernst Lubitsch, George Cukor. To go to America, to live there, to
make a picture with American actors and in American studios could be a
marvelous, exciting experience, but just an experience. It could be very
difficult, like going to Japan and trying to make a samurai picture. And if
an American director tries to make a picture in European style—as, for
instance, Woody Allen tried with *Interiors*—he comes into great difficulties. I think the picture is wonderful—I love it. But the critics didn't."
(This critic agrees with Bergman.)

Bergman has a personal collection of some 500 films. "I've concentrated on silent films and early talkies because the other pictures I can get from the companies. In the summer, almost every evening, we went to the movies in the barn. While the children were here, we saw about 40 pictures. Then we sat together and discussed them. It's lots of fun. I like very much to go to the movies. There are not many directors who do. It's from my childhood. Fellini, *fratello mio*, and I feel the same way. He likes to go to the movies more than to the theater. I almost never walk out on a movie. Maybe once or twice."

Is there any new direction that he would like to take in his film-making? A new approach, a new technique perhaps?

"I would like once in my life to make a 120-minute picture with just one close-up. I think it's impossible, but I would love to do it once. To have the right actor and to have the talent to accomplish this. It would be the most fascinating experience of all, just to look with the camera. I am a voyeur. To look at somebody, to find out how the skin changes, the eyes, how all those muscles change the whole time—the lips—to me it's always a drama. Sven [the brilliant cinematographer Sven Nykvist, Bergman's longtime collaborator] and I have been experimenting with how to light close-ups, and perhaps to make that picture, black and white would be better than color, because color is never true. Black and white is, strange to say, more true because then your fantasy is created; you have created it yourself.

"We made *From the Life of the Marionettes* in black and white, the first picture in almost ten years we did that way. We start in color, and then after about three or four minutes go over to black and white, and then the last two or three minutes are in color. Perhaps I'm wrong, but to me the great gift of cinematography is the human face. Don't you think so? With a camera you can go into the stomach of a kangaroo. But to look at the human face, I think, is the most fascinating."

Bergman refused to permit a professional photographer to come to the island to try to capture his face, but he says "of course" when I ask him and his wife to pose for an amateur. While fiddling with the focusing, I suggest, "We should have Sven Nykvist here."

Bergman laughs. "Oh, no. He's a very bad photographer. You can't imagine how bad until you see his private pictures."

# Ingmar Bergman: Summing Up
a Life in Film

M I C H I K O   K A K U T A N I / 1 9 8 3

IT IS A CHILLY, desolate place, this island Fårö. During the summer, tourists come here, bringing with them the laughter of children and the sun, but spring comes late to Fårö, and even in May, reminders of winter remain. A Baltic wind that twists the evergreens into the shape of bonsai trees blows in from the sea, and in the early morning hours, a damp, insidious fog settles over the beaches, draining the landscape of color and turning everything gray.

For Ingmar Bergman, who has lived on Fårö since 1966, the island represents more than the landscape of his imagination, more than a familiar setting for his movies. It represents, he says, the one place where he feels safe and secure, the one place in the world where he actually feels at home.

At 64, Bergman possesses the face of a mandarin. Though his pale gray-green eyes can quickly turn cold and suspicious, there is a childlike brightness to his features and he is capable of expressing a warm bonhomie. These days, in fact, he seems particularly happy to play the role of benevolent paterfamilias—both in the studio and at home on the island. And this new prodigality of spirit is reflected in his latest film, *Fanny and Alexander*—a film that depicts the possibilities and joys of family life as well as its familiar perils. The movie, which opened earlier this month, represents "the sum total of my life as a film maker," says Bergman; he insists it is the last one he intends to make.

From the *New York Times Magazine*, June 28, 1983. Reprinted by permission of the *New York Times*.

"Making *Fanny and Alexander* was such joy that I thought that feeling will never come back," he says. "I will try to explain: When I was at university many years ago, we were all in love with this extremely beautiful girl. She said no to all of us, and we didn't understand. She had had a love affair with a prince from Egypt and, for her, everything after this love affair had to be a failure. So she rejected all our proposals. I would like to say the same thing. The time with *Fanny and Alexander* was so wonderful that I decided it was time to stop. I have had my prince of Egypt.

"To make another picture and have it feel gray and heavy and difficult with lots of problems—that would be very sad. And I have seen many of my colleagues get older and older and more and more dusty until suddenly they are thrown out, and they cannot get money for their next picture and must go around with their hats in their hands. That is something I do not want—better to stop now when everything is perfect."

A testament to the remarkable alchemy of life and art, Bergman's movies form a kind of ongoing autobiography, and *Fanny and Alexander* is at once a nostalgic reinvention of the director's own childhood and a mature summation of his work. All the familiar Bergman themes and motifs are here—the humiliation of the artist, the hell and paradise of marriage, the quest for love and faith—but they are infused, this time, with a new tenderness and compassion.

"It's a big, dark, beautiful, generous family chronicle," writes *The Times's* film critic Vincent Canby, "which touches on many of the themes from earlier films, while introducing something that, in Bergman, might pass for serenity. It moves between the worlds of reality and imagination with the effortlessness characteristic of great fiction."

Indeed, *Fanny and Alexander* possesses a generosity of vision reminiscent of Shakespeare's later comedies, for in summing up his life's work, Bergman seems to have achieved a measure of distance from and acceptance of his own past. "Perhaps it is an illusion, but I have the feeling I can see wider and understand more," he says. "It's like climbing a mountain. The higher you get, the more tired and breathless you become, but your view becomes much more extensive."

For those who have followed the director's career, this movie—so rich in allusions to previous works—provides a kind of index, a Rosetta stone, to his entire oeuvre. And yet the movie is also more accessible, more straightforward in narrative and form, than many of his earlier films, and it also provides the simple delights of a Proustain-flavored fairy tale of good and evil, innocence and knowledge. "The picture," comments the film critic Pauline Kael, "is an almost sustained flight of Victorian fantasy, and it may win Ingmar Bergman his greatest public acceptance."

Since establishing himself in the mid-1950s with *Smiles of a Summer Night*, *The Seventh Seal* and *Wild Strawberries*, Bergman has earned critical acclaim as one of the world's foremost auteurs. Translating the tragic, introspective vision of Strindberg from the theater to the screen, he brought a new seriousness to the form—what was "entertainment" became "art"; the "movies" became "cinema"—and he also demonstrated the medium's ability to probe philosophical issues and interior states of mind.

Though he has been attacked periodically for being willfully obscure, pretentious or irresponsibly apolitical—such films as *All These Women*, *The Touch* and *The Serpent's Egg* have fared particularly poorly—Bergman has managed, time after time, to win back his following with movies like *Fanny and Alexander* and to reinvent his reputation.

During a career that spans some four decades, he has made about 50 movies, and in those movies he has created an immediately recognizable world. Whether it is the distant allegorical realm of *The Seventh Seal* or the banal domestic one of *Scenes From a Marriage*, this world is a place where faith is tenuous; communication, elusive; and self-knowledge, illusory at best. God is either silent (as in *Winter Light*) or malevolent (as in *The Silence*), and Bergman's characters find themselves ruled, instead, by the capricious ghosts and demons of the unconscious.

More persuasively than any other director, Bergman has mapped out the geography of the individual psyche—its secret yearnings and its susceptibility to memory and desire. And in a sense, his determination to focus on existential matters rather than on larger social and political issues mirrors perfectly the nation in which he was born and lives. Neutral in two world wars and virtually free of crime and most other social ills, Sweden lacks the sort of problems that lend themselves to conventional dramatic representation; its dramas are interior ones, hidden deep beneath the bright, clean surface of social engineering.

In chronicling his own anxieties and fears, Bergman has found a parable for both Sweden's peculiar afflictions of the spirit and those of the modern world. The Sweden he has portrayed in such movies as *Face to Face* and *Scenes From a Marriage* is a country where nearly everyone owns a summer house and drives a Volvo, a country where everything, on the surface at least, is orderly and serene.

But Bergman's Sweden is not the paradise envisioned by idealistic social architects. Rather, it is a country given to atavistic rhythms and quickly shifting moods; a country of short, brilliant summers and long winters of despair; a country where even the most sophisti-cated city dwellers live much the way their ancestors did on farms—isolated and trapped within their homes. Here, a Calvinistic sense of fate endures, the one vestige of an age when this most secular of nations still believed. Here, money and technology have wiped out poverty and war, yet have failed to lower the suicide rate or alleviate despair. Here, the meliorative ideal founders on the rock of human nature.

Bergman and Ingrid, his wife of 12 years, live far from the modern planned communities of suburban Sweden, far from the conveniences of mass transportation.

To get to Fårö, one must first fly from Stockholm to Visby, an ancient walled city of medieval churches and ruined choirs. From Visby, there is an hour's drive across Gotland—a rocky island whose flat horizon is broken only by the steeples of abandoned churches, as numerous as telephone poles, stretching to the ocean. A ferry ride across a cold, windy bay follows, and then another drive across the sparsely populated island of Fårö itself, past ramshackle farmhouses and fishermen's shacks, through sheep pastures and pine groves to the director's isolated house—a low frame structure that stands perched like a lighthouse on the very edge of the sea.

The same color as the shale stones that cover the beach, the house seems almost a part of the landscape—gray, stark and inhospitable. Inside, though, the wall-to-wall carpeting and sleek Scandinavian mod-ern furniture lend a sense of happy, if somewhat contrived, normalcy and cheer. There are crayon drawings by Bergman's grandchildren on the study wall, and stacks of family photo albums on the table. The prevailing impression is that of a pleasant, middleclass model home;

only the room of screening equipment and an opulent television set hint that the house belongs to a wealthy movie director.

Dressed in an old flannel shirt, a worn cardigan and a little red woolen ski hat, Bergman, at first glance, might be one of the island's farmers. Alternately animated and introspective, he speaks English slowly, almost cautiously, but becomes enthusiastic when it comes to showing a visitor around his grounds. He prepares his own lunch with aplomb, and drives his green Volvo station wagon along Fårö's narrow gravel roads with careful expertise.

Still, there is a calculated quality to his casualness. Although he says he hates meeting people he doesn't know, he immediately throws an arm over the shoulders of a visiting stranger, and he punctuates his conversation with declaration of his sincerity and good will. One has the sense that this is learned behavior of sorts—the gestures of a lonely and self-preoccupied man who wants very much to be liked, a man who has worked with actors all his life and who is keenly aware of the masks we put on in public life.

Beneath the bluff exterior, in fact, lies a wealth of contradictions. Here is a self-professed agnostic who is deeply superstitious; a puritan who has married five times and carried on highly publicized liaisons with his leading ladies; a stickler for details—he has been known to send a telegram to change an appointment by 10 minutes—who spends hours at a time daydreaming.

"I am very much aware of my own double self," Bergman says. "The well-known one is very under control; everything is planned and very secure. The unknown one can be very unpleasant. I think this side is responsible for all the creative work—he is in touch with the child. He is not rational, he is impulsive and extremely emotional. Perhaps it is not even a 'he,' but a 'she.'"

In his movies, Bergman has frequently taken this double self—the intuitive, feminine side and the masculine, analytic one—and split it into two characters: the worldly squire and the ascetic knight in The Seventh Seal, the artist Vogler and his adversary Vergerus in The Magician, the silent actress and the gregarious nurse in Persona.

In the case of Fanny and Alexander, he has taken the mirror of his personality and broken it into shards, each one reflecting a different facet of his character: the grandmother, "an old professional, who has lived a

lot and is very surprised, though without bitterness, to find that suddenly she is old"; Isak Jacobi, the old Jewish antiques dealer who possesses the powers of magic; Gustav Adolf, the loud, boisterous uncle
who loves the company of women; the dour bishop, who tries to bend
everyone to his will; the mother, Emilie, who as an actress "wears a
thousand masks," and, of course, the movie's 10-year-old hero—
dreamy, secretive Alexander.

In addition to ransacking his own life for ideas and information,
Bergman mines the lives of his colleagues and friends. Just as many of
his artist heroes display certain parasitical tendencies—the novelist in
*Through a Glass Darkly*, for instance, watches his daughter's nervous
breakdown with clinical fascination—he, too, is a voyeur, constantly
watching others and taking mental notes.

Although he declines to talk about his own publicized relationships
with women, Bergman himself often plays the part of reporter.
Introduced to a stranger, he asks all manner of personal questions—a
tactic that reflects both defensiveness and genuine curiosity—and he
evidently does the same with friends. "If I would tell him I have a
cancer and was going to die, he would be extremely sorry, but also
extremely curious," says Harry Schein, the former director of the
Swedish Film Institute and one of Bergman's confidants. "He's interested in the unhappiness of his friends. He dwells on it—he can get
material. We often have long phone calls, and if he asks, 'How are
you?' and I say, 'Fine,' he would be extremely disappointed.
A human being in pain—he can learn much more."

Indeed, Bergman is highly dependent on his observations of others
to give him a sense of ordinary life. Although the theater (which
demands the interpretation of another writer's work) and the island
Fårö (which turns the world-famous director into just another resident)
help reduce his myopia, one suspects that he still shares, with many of
his characters, a difficulty in reaching outside himself.

Preoccupied with his own emotions, he is constantly annotating his
own conversation— "I know this sounds naive," he will say, or, "I'm
trying to be honest"—and from time to time, he will issue public statements about his films, as though he feared being misunderstood. There
are open letters to his cast, subsequently published on op-ed pages, and
there are published versions of his scripts, complete with detailed

descriptions of characters and motivation. Bergman says he has never been in analysis, but he employs the language of psychiatry with ease, and like others employed in the business of self-dissection, he likes to refer to himself in the third person, as "Ingmar."

Bergman has carefully nurtured his intuition, protecting it like a rare plant from the harsh light and noise of the outside world, and the private realm he inhabits resembles the one so often depicted in his movies—a dreamlike place, where fantasy and reality, the conscious and unconscious, overlap and merge.

"It's difficult to explain," he says, "but the other morning I woke up here on the island and came into my study. I was sitting here looking out at the sea, and suddenly I had a very strong feeling that on my left side was my mother. I knew she was there. I was not dreaming. It was just the feeling that she was here, communicating with me. And then the sun came up, and after 10 minutes or 12 minutes, this feeling went away."

Heightened by the intensely personal nature of his movies, Bergman's self-absorption is the consequence of a strangely hermetic life. As a child, brought up by strict Lutheran parents, he felt lonely and inept at communicating with his peers; and since the age of 20, he has lived almost entirely within the self-enclosed world of the theater and film studio.

"My only talent," says a character in *Fanny and Alexander*, echoing the director's own point of view, "is that I love this little world inside the thick walls of this playhouse. . . . Outside is the big world, and sometimes the little world succeeds for a moment in reflecting the big world, so that we understand it better. Or is it perhaps that we give the people who come here the chance of forgetting for a while . . . the harsh world outside. Our theater is a small room of orderliness, routine, conscientiousness and love."

No doubt the decision to live within this little world, safe from the confusions of history, was partly a conscious one—the result of Bergman's one youthful, and devastating, step into politics. Sent abroad for the first time at the age of 16—as an exchange student—he lived with a clergyman's family in Germany. The year was 1934, and he soon found himself swept up in the country's burgeoning enthusiasm for Hitler. He attended a Nazi rally in Weimar and listened to the clergyman deliver sermons based on *Mein Kampf*. "We were absolute virgins politically and we found it marvelous," he recalls now. "We were infected." By the time he returned home to Sweden, he says he had become a "little pro-German fanatic."

Years later, when he saw pictures of the concentration camps, he felt enormous guilt and shame. "I understood I had made a great mistake," he says, "and since then political thinking has scared me to death." For years, he did not read political books or editorials, and he declined to vote. Instead, he told himself that self-knowledge was the most one could hope for, that anything more smacked of hubris and pretension.

It was a position similar to that expressed by Emilie in *Fanny and Alexander*. "All I bother about is myself," she says. "I don't bother about reality either. It is colorless and uninteresting; it doesn't concern me. Wars and revolutions and epidemics and poverty and injustices and volcanic eruptions mean nothing to me unless in one way or another they affect the part I am just playing."

The two Bergman movies that do venture, albeit tentatively, into the realm of politics are actually rooted in his guilt about the war. Set in 1923, *The Serpent's Egg* attempts to examine the seeds of the Nazi evil, and *Shame*, Bergman has said, originated in a question he once asked himself—"How would I have behaved during the Nazi period if Sweden had been occupied and if I'd held some position of responsibility or been connected with some institution?"

It is the politics of relationships and the sociology of the psyche that is really Bergman's concern. Marriage and the perils of domestic life (*Thrist, Scenes From a Marriage, From the Life of the Marionettes, Fanny and Alexander*); the deceptions of love (*Summer With Monika, Smiles of a Summer Night*); the artist and his persecution by society (*The Magician, Sawdust and Tinsel*, the *Hour of the Wolf* trilogy); the difficulties of faith (*The Seventh Seal, Winter Light*) and the psychological complexities of the soul (*Persona, Cries and Whispers*)—these are the preoccupations that animate his work and they all are rooted in intensely personal concerns, in the director's own nightmares and dreams.

Most of his films, Bergman has said, have grown "like a snowball" out of some small flake of experience or memory. He has found that filmmaking has a therapeutic effect and, in many cases, has subjected a particular obsession to this process of analysis and catharsis. "I have been working all the time," he says, "and it's like a flood going through the landscape of your soul. It's good because it takes away a lot. It's cleansing. If I hadn't been at work all the time, I would have been a lunatic."

*The Seventh Seal*, which portrayed a medieval knight's confrontation with death in a plague-ridden land, helped him overcome his own fear of dying. *Wild Strawberries*, which depicted an aging man's reassessment of his barren existence, was made "as a rundown of my earlier life, a searching final test." *Face to Face*, which chronicled a successful woman's descent into madness, helped him give his own Angst "a name and address. In this way it (was) deprived of its nimbus and alarm." And *Fanny and Alexander* has helped him come to terms with the terrors and joys of his own childhood.

For Bergman, that childhood remains curiously palpable and accessible. He thinks of himself as something of a child, and whenever he goes to the studio, he has the sense that he is a little boy again—the same little boy who, after breakfast, would go upstairs to his room, take out his toy theater and put on Strindberg plays.

"I have maintained open channels with my childhood," he says. "I think it may be that way with many artists. Sometimes in the night, when I am on the limit between sleeping and being awake, I can just go through a door into my childhood and everything is as it was—with lights, smells, sounds and people. . . . I remember the silent street where my grandmother lived, the sudden aggressivity of the grown-up world, the terror of the unknown and the fear from the tension between my father and mother."

His childhood, Bergman has said, shaped his imagination and, for him, the past is always present. The world of the church that he grew up in as the son of a minister imprinted his mind with a religious vocabulary and peopled it with images of demons and saints. And his relationship with his parents shaped his view of the sexes with Freudian clarity and force.

While he feared his stern, authoritarian father, he clearly adored his mother ("I was in love with her," he says. "I knew what she liked and disliked and I used to try to find ways to win her love"), and to this day he believes that "women are more intuitive than men—they have their emotional life more intact."

It is an attitude reflected in his films: The female characters are usually endowed with strength, patience and an enduring innate wisdom, while the men tend to be selfish, stupid or somehow incomplete—either self-indulgent artists, eager to sacrifice their loved ones on the altar of their art, or stony intellectuals, intolerant of others' frailties and fears.

Certainly this is true of the men and women in *Fanny and Alexander*. The male characters are all buffoons of sorts: one uncle is a lecher; another, a self-pitying failure, and the stepfather is another of Bergman's obnoxious moralizers, determined to impose his values on everyone else. Most of the women, on the other hand—from the gracious grandmother to the long-suffering mother—represent a panoply of virtues. Sensual, resilient and open to their emotions, they love and humor their men, combining in their passion the devotion of a mother and a mistress.

In *Fanny and Alexander*, Bergman has drawn on memories of his grandmother's house, and he has turned the world of his childhood into a fairy tale set at the turn of the century. The early scenes portray, with almost Dickensian festivity, the daily life of a bourgeois family named Ekdahl who run a theater in a small Swedish town. When their father dies, however, Alexander and his sister, Fanny, find their happy little world shattered from within: their mother remarries, and her new husband, the bishop, institutes an icy, puritanical regime.

Alexander, clearly, is a portrait of the artist as a young boy. Like Alexander, Bergman used to spend hours playing with a magic lantern; like Alexander, he had difficulty distinguishing between fantasy and truth; and like Alexander, he was punished for this "lying." The scene of humiliation in which the bishop whips Alexander and locks him in a closet was based on the director's own experience, and similar confrontations between a young hero and a father figure, between an overly sensitive artist and an unfeeling intellectual, surface again and again in his work.

That repressive atmosphere at home endowed Bergman with both a need to communicate with others and a heightened awareness of how people use power to manipulate one another—emotions that eventually led him to work in theater and film.

"I think I have just one obsession—to touch other human beings," he says. "That desire for contact, I think, was the reason why I came to this profession, because as a child I was very shy and very lonely and very afraid of other people. Of course, it was not only this very beautiful reason, but it was also a longing for power, for manipulating other people. I think that's a disease every director has—a kind of professional illness."

According to his colleagues, that desire to manipulate people often extends beyond the studio. "With his friends, with his actors, he plays the authority figure," observes Jörn Donner, the producer of *Fanny and Alexander*. "In a sense, he has become the father he hated. He can become very jealous, say, if one of the actors in his film works in the theater in the evening. And he tries to influence their professional life. He says, 'You should do that, you should not do this.' In Sweden, he has enormous power—he has made careers and indirectly probably destroyed them—and so people tend to listen."

Insecure and suspicious, Bergman not only values control over others, but over his own life as well. He says that as a young man who already had had three marriages and five children, he realized his "life was a terrible flop," and he decided, then and there, that "if I cannot be perfect in my life, I will be perfect in my profession."

"You can't direct reality," he says, "and that sometimes makes me very insecure and scared. But when you direct a picture, you can decide everything. You can do everything you want, you can control every little detail. It's always handmade."

Acutely aware that this control afforded by art is illusory, Bergman has portrayed the artist in such movies as *The Magician* and the *Hour of the Wolf* trilogy as both charlatan and saint: someone guilty of lies and deceit, but also capable of performing miracles—"the one impossible trick" of making a ball stand still in the air. In *Persona*, the actress Elisabet Vogler chooses to become mute, arguing that her art has no meaning; and Bergman himself believes that the narrative order provided by art is really a placebo taken in lieu of anything better.

For Bergman, faith, like art, offers the consolations of order and redemption, and in a sense, his entire body of work is animated by religious questions. The pastor's son is fond of quoting O'Neill's dictum that all great art deals with man's relation to God; and all his movies are preoccupied with man's spiritual dilemma, his inability to reconcile the importunate demands of the flesh with the immortal longings of the soul. Such titles as *The Seventh Seal* and *Face to Face* come from bibli-cal quotations, and the movies themselves are filled with similar allu-sions. In conversation, the director frequently uses words like "grace" and "salvation," and he remains fascinated by the human capacity for "unmotivated cruelty"—a kind of original sin that cannot be explained by reason.

With *Winter Light*, made in 1963, however, a fundamental change occurs. While such earlier films as *The Seventh Seal* and *The Virgin Spring* were animated by an anguished search for belief, *Winter Light*—which depicts a minister's own loss of faith—implies that whatever answers there are to be found are to be found here on earth.

The philosophical shift, Bergman explains, came during a short hos-pital stay. Coming out of the anesthesia, he realized he was no longer scared of death, and that the question of God had suddenly disap-peared. Since then, his movies have all articulated a wary humanism in which human love holds the one promise of salvation.

In most cases, though, that ideal love eludes Bergman's characters. Instead, love turns out to be a dangerous emotion that either reinforces their loneliness or brings contagion with another's neuroses. It is as though Bergman, in accepting a world bereft of God—a world in which human beings are responsible for everything—had also resigned him-self to a kind of purgatory on earth. Only recently, with such films as *The Magic Flute* and now, *Fanny and Alexander*, does he seem to have embraced the possibility of communion, the possibility of human hap-piness here on a Godforsaken earth.

"When Ingmar was younger, there was a bitterness to his films," says Harry Schein. "With *Fanny and Alexander*, there's a greater sense of har-mony. I think Ingmar has it personally as well. In many ways, I feel he still lives a very difficult life—he talks of Angst, of that anxiety where you wake up in the middle of the night—but superficially he seems more har-monic. On the surface, he is nice and charming and almost civilized."

Certainly, a change in demeanor and in style of life has gradually occurred. The Bergman of the 1950s, who was establishing himself as an auteur, was an angry young man, an inventor of bohemian poses. Having repudiated the bourgeois values of his parents—he left home, after coming to blows with his father—the director reveled in the roles of novice existentialist and temperamental artist. He read Sartre and

Camus and took to signing his letters with the insignia of a little devil. He appeared at rehearsals and filming sessions wearing a beret and scruffy beard, and his cast became accustomed to his fits of melancholy temper: He tore telephones out of walls and on one occasion threw a chair through a studio's glass control booth.

"I was very cruel to actors and to other people," says Bergman now. "I think I was a very, very unpleasant young man. If I met the young Ingmar today, I think I would say, 'You are very talented and I will see if I can help you, but I don't think I want anything else to do with you.' I don't say I'm pleasant now, but I think I changed slowly in my 50's. At least I hope I've changed."

The change, it seems, came partly as an act of self-preservation. As a young man, Bergman notes, "I was a package of emotions on two legs—my life was completely chaotic." Since then, observes Jörn Donner, "Ingmar has been trying to fight the bohemianism in himself by leading a well-ordered life. When you think you are a bohemian or a lazy person, you have to fight that and impose a discipline—it's a little puritanical. He is very much the bourgeois today—he likes to see Ingrid and himself as the proprietors of a small French restaurant—you can't get more bourgeois than that."

His wife, Ingrid—a pleasant, kind-faced woman who bears, Bergman acknowledges, a remarkable resemblance to his own mother—has helped him establish cordial relations with his eight children from previous marriages and liaisons, and every July the children and four grandchildren come to Fårö to celebrate the director's birthday.

Bergman's daily schedule seems equally well ordered, if not a bit fanatical in its precision. He gets up every morning at 8 and writes from 9 until noon. Lunch—which for the last 15 years or so has consisted of berries and sour milk—is followed by two more hours of work and a nap at 3. Before dinner, he takes a walk and after dinner watches television—he is especially fond of *Dallas*—or a movie from his large 16-milllimeter collection.

Like Jenny Isaksson, the psychiatrist in *Face to Face* who suffers a nervous breakdown, Bergman has cultivated neatness and efficiency as a means of containing his anxieties and fears. The surface calm bears a disturbing resemblance to that of Sweden's; beneath it, he says, he remains "extremely neurotic." "Ingmar, at the slightest provocation, will produce a nervous breakdown," says his agent, Paul Kohner. "He has a delicate disposition."

Bergman will always be one of those people who closes doors behind him, who insists on an aisle seat in movie theaters. He will always knock wood when things are going well, and he will always suffer from a delicate stomach and bad dreams. "I have a lot of tics and phobias," he says. "I hate to travel. I hate to go to festivals. I hate it when somebody goes close behind me. I'm scared of the darkness. I hate open doors. It has to do with some primitive feeling of insecurity. I can't control it, but I know where my phobias are and how they work."

Although he maintains that he is unneurotic about his profession ("I look at my pictures and stage productions as furniture, as something for people to use," he says. "I can say, 'This chair is good; this one is very bad' "), Bergman is, nonetheless, compulsive about his work, and he acknowledges that he has frequently used it as a way of escape.

"When I was younger, it was a way of avoiding things," he says. "I would say, 'I have no time now to discuss it.' Or, 'When the picture is concluded, then I will think it over.' Or, 'I will cry when I have had my last shooting day.' Always when a picture opened, I was at work on the next picture, so when something was unsuccessful or a flop, I just had no time to think about it."

Even if *Fanny and Alexander* is his last feature film, Bergman hardly plans to abandon his hectic schedule. He will continue to work for television—the medium, after all, that originally produced *Scenes From a Marriage* and *Face to Face*. His next television project has already been shot and will air next year on Swedish television. Titled *After the Rehearsal*, it involves a dialogue between two actresses and an aging director, who is clearly Bergman himself.

Since the beginning, alongside his more public career in film, Bergman has maintained another one in the theater, and he will continue to stage operas and plays. He has adapted Molière's *School for Wives* for television, and plans to stage *King Lear* for Stockholm's Royal Dramatic Theater.

It was during a rehearsal of Strindberg's *Dance of Death* at the Royal Dramatic Theater in 1976 that Bergman was arrested, in a highly publicized incident, for tax evasion. The charges were later dropped—the

Swedish Government subsequently issued a formal apology—but the director exiled himself from Sweden and moved to Munich.

"It was sad when we went away," he says. "I said to Ingrid, 'There are only two solutions or possibilities. It will kill me or stimulate me.' Looking back now, I think it was, in a way, a very stimulating and fantastic experience." At the time, though, the experience caused Bergman enormous trauma, leading to a nervous breakdown. It not only seemed a fulfillment of all his worst fears of humiliation, but it also meant leaving the country he loved.

"I am so 100 percent Swedish," he explains. "Someone has said a Swede is like a bottle of ketchup—nothing and nothing and then all at once—splat. I think I'm a little like that. And I think I'm Swedish because I like to live here on this island. You can't imagine the loneliness and isolation in this country. In that way, I'm very Swedish—I don't dislike to be alone. Before I married Ingrid, I lived in this house for 16 months. An old woman came three hours a day at 4 and made dinner for me and she cleaned up and at 7 she went away. And that was the only company I had. I lived like that week after week, month after month, and in a way I liked it very much."

Although he had made a pleasant enough life for himself in Munich, Bergman desperately missed his home on Fårö, and one summer day in 1977, he remembered how the lilacs in his garden used to explode into blossom during that one week in June. That evening, he and his wife took a plane to Stockholm. They took another plane to Visby, then drove a car back to their house on Fårö. "The night was clear," he recalls. "And there was no darkness, and we got here at midnight and were sitting outside the old house, looking and smelling the flowers. The next day we went back to Munich. That in a way is very strange, but somehow very Swedish."

Bergman is spending his summers again on Fårö, and after fulfilling some theater commitments in Munich, he says he will return to Sweden for good. "For a long time, I didn't want to come home," he says, "but now in a few years I think I will return. I think it's time for Ingmar to go home."

# For Bergman, a New Twist on an Old Love

STEVE LOHR/1989

WHEN INGMAR BERGMAN completed his Oscar-winning film *Fanny and Alexander* in 1984, he declared it the last of his some 50 movies. But he seems a most reluctant retiree at times. "I dream about doing a film about once a week," he conceded.

The characteristic Bergman confession—a revealing fragment of his own thoughts and fantasies—came Friday during a rare session with the press in Stockholm to announce a new film project. This time, however, the artistic imprint will come from Bergman the writer, not Bergman the director, in a six-hour, two-part feature film entitled *Good Intentions*, which is to focus on a decade in his parents' troubled marriage. Its director, hand-picked by Mr. Bergman, will be Bille August, the Dane who directed *Pelle the Conqueror*, which won this year's Academy Award for best foreign-language film.

*Good Intentions*, budgeted at roughly $9 million, is the most ambitious project of its type ever made in Scandinavia. By way of comparison, *Pelle*, a big-budget film by Nordic standards, cost about $4.5 million. Filming is to begin next year, and the world premiere is to be on Swedish television in 1992, where *Good Intentions* will appear as four 90-minute episodes. The movie, both as a television mini-series and as a two-part film, will then be distributed internationally. Co-producers in some countries, including Britain, West Germany, France and Italy, have already been lined up, while interest elsewhere, such as the United States, is expected but yet to be canvassed.

---

## On Perfection and Temper

Mr. Bergman and Mr. August spent most of the week together, discussing the project at the Bergman summer home on the small Baltic island of Fårö. In the next few weeks, they said, the cast for the Swedish-language film will be selected from a group of favored Swedish and Danish actors. The Danish director, who is 40 years old, and his 71-year-old scriptwriter say they are getting along swimmingly so far. Still, given Mr. Bergman's well-known penchant for perfection and his occasionally volcanic displays to temper ("He used to refer to all those who didn't throw furniture around as inhibited," the actress Gunnel Lindblom said of him), it seems reasonable to wonder how smooth the working relationship will prove to be once filming starts.

When he was just starting out, Mr. Bergman did write works directed by others as a self-styled "script slave" for the Swedish Film Institute. "But this is the first time it was something from my heart," he said. Mr. August has offered to allow Mr. Bergman to look at each day's film takes. "I hope he doesn't regret that," Mr. Bergman noted.

For his part, Mr. August professes not to be intimidated at the prospect of directing a film written by Scandinavia's greatest living cultural personality and, perhaps, having Mr. Bergman look over his shoulder somewhat as well. "I decided to do this not because it was by Ingmar Bergman but because the story was so good—the best story about love I've ever read," Mr. August explained.

## How It Came About

It was a story whose evolution Mr. Bergman described over the course of two hours, during the press conference and in a brief interview afterward. At the end, with just a few people remaining in the Swedish Television studio, Mr. Bergman, who shuns interviews yet fills his films and writing with ruthless self-exposure, maintained that it was the last time he would speak to the press.

*Good Intentions*, he said, is an outgrowth of the family chronicle that began with *Fanny and Alexander*, which drew greatly on his childhood recollections of time spent with his grandmother in Uppsala, the university town north of Stockholm. Next came his autobiography, published last year, *The Magic Lantern*, which roams impressionistically over most of his life but especially his childhood and family strife. Relations with his parents and siblings were stormy and often brutal. Mr. Bergman wrote, for example, that he once tried and failed to kill his sister, and he described disputes with his father that came to blows: "He hit me and I hit him back. He staggered and ended up sitting on the floor."

Still, while going over family records and photographs to research his autobiography and then while writing it, Mr. Bergman said Friday, "I met my parents, not as the people I fought with later in life, but as real people." His autobiography did not provide the vehicle to deal fully with his parents, but he vowed to do it later, and *Good Intentions* is the result.

## "Destined to Catastrophe"

*Good Intentions* is the story of his parents' relationship from 1909 until 1918, the year Ingmar Bergman was born. The picture that emerges, Mr. Bergman suggested, is a far more sympathetic portrait of them than appeared in his autobiography. The marriage of the Lutheran pastor of humble origins and the rather pampered young woman from an upper-class background was opposed by her parents, and their lives were steeped in the social expectations and Lutheran repressions of Sweden at the time.

"Until I wrote this manuscript, I never really knew how complicated their lives were," Mr. Bergman said. "We always regret that we did not ask our parents more, really get to know them while they were alive."

Of his parents, he added, "They went into their marriage with good intentions, but it was destined to catastrophe because of the demands they accepted and placed on themselves."

Those strains, by Mr. Bergman's account, took their toll. At one point in *The Magic Lantern*, Mr. Bergman wrote: "We didn't know that Mother had gone through a passionate love affair or that Father suffered from severe depression. Mother was preparing to break out of her marriage, Father was threatening to take his own life." Neither of them did. Back then, noted Mr. Bergman, who has been married five times, "Divorce was almost unthinkable."

## Mellowing, but Turmoil Intact

Like virtually all Mr. Bergman's films, *Good Intentions* is deeply autobio-graphical, not only in its content but also in its motivation. "When you write a manuscript like this," he said, "it is driven by the urge to seek something in oneself." When asked, he replied that one of the things he learned was that in many ways he resembled his father, whom he openly despised for so long.

If it sounds like a belated reconciliation with his parents, it may be. But Mr. Bergman is at pains to emphasize to anyone listening that he has perhaps mellowed with age, but that the inner turmoil that has been a hallmark of both the man and the artist is still intact. "The anger and the creativity are so closely intertwined with me," he said. "And there's plenty of anger left." A religious reconciliation, for exam-ple, appears unlikely for Mr. Bergman, an agnostic. "I hope I never get so old I get religious," he said.

Mr. Bergman's hair is well thinned and he walks tentatively with a slight limp. Yet despite his self-imposed retirement from film direct-ing—he said he found the cinematic regimen too exhausting—he remains active on the stage. His version of Yukio Mishima's *Mme. de Sade* is playing to packed houses at Stockholm's Royal Dramatic Theater. It started in the spring and has been held over to accommodate demand. Mr. Bergman pointed out that he has stage and opera commit-ments through 1991. "So I'm optimistic about my health," he said. "I plan to keep on going."

# Bergman's Best Intentions

## LASSE BERGSTRÖM/1995

AT SEVENTY-FOUR INGMAR BERGMAN is one of the
world's greatest living filmmakers, a creative genius whose magic touch
also extends to theater, opera, and television. But he is also a most private, even secretive, man and over the years has learned to protect his
privacy. He grants almost no interviews.

My own, exceptional opportunities to speak with him, on the record,
were the result of a long professional relationship and, with time,
friendship. When we first met, nearly forty years ago, it was across
a barricade: he a filmmaker, I a critic. His suspicion was understandable.
He had been so hounded by critics in his native Sweden that, for
a time, he even refused to publish the scripts of his films there. In the
early 1960s I became his publisher; the relationship has endured and
deepened.

A few years ago, we sat down at his home on Fårö, a Baltic island
retreat much favored by the Swedish cultural elite, and the setting for
several of Bergman's films. Altogether, our conversations went on for
more than fifty hours, forming the basis for Bergman's book *Bilder*, published in English as *Images: My Life in Film*. Later, we met again on Fårö.
The following interview is the result of that meeting.

Fårö is Ingmar Bergman's private kingdom, his earthly paradise. He
has lived there in seclusion for nearly a quarter of a century. The house
is shrouded in foliage and nearly invisible, at the edge of a low forest
and above a desolate, stony beach. Even after his arrest and humiliation

From *Ingmar Bergman: An Artist's Journey,* copyright © 1995 by Roger W. Oliver. Published
by Arcade Publishing, New York, New York. Reprinted by permission. Translated by
Richard E. Nord.

at the hands of the Swedish tax authorities, when he left Sweden for voluntary exile in Munich, he was unable to give up Fårö.

"I can understand why people might think it strange for someone to suddenly decide to live on an island he'd never even heard of before," he admitted.

"How did that come about?" I asked him.

"I was about to make *Through a Glass Darkly* in 1960. It is set on an island, with four people who rise up from a twilight sea in the first scene and walk ashore to begin the drama. I had this idea that we would do the film in the Orkney Islands.

"The Orkneys were out of the question, for reasons of cost, and after a few fruitless excursions in the Stockholm archipelago someone asked me if I'd ever seen Fårö."

BERGSTRÖM:    *Was it love at first sight?*

BERGMAN:    I was enthralled, gripped by a strange fascination. Between takes we wandered around the island and when I returned a few years later for *Persona*, I suddenly felt: This is where I want to live!

BERGSTRÖM:    *Can you explain why?*

BERGMAN:    Yes, in part. It's the never-ceasing sounds of the wind, the waves, the gulls. The enormity of the sea creates a sense of timelessness, changelessness, security. But it's also the proportions and ancient character of the landscape. There isn't a whole lot of leafy foliage, not a whole lot of sandy beach, cliffs, and rocks, and not a whole lot of woods. But there is something of it all here in a kind of wonderful balance and harmony—the low stone walls running through the flat landscape, which can appear harsh and drab, only to suddenly blossom after the spring melt in vast carpets of color and life. And then there's the light. I can sit for hours just looking out the window, watching how the light wanders and shifts.

At this time, Bergman was already working hard to prepare *The Bacchae*, his first production at the Stockholm Opera since Stravinsky's *The Rake's Progress* in 1961. He had come to Fårö directly after a big hit with *Peer Gynt*. From Fårö, he kept himself informed about the tour to New York of three other productions he had staged in Stockholm: *Long Day's Journey Into Night*, *A Doll's House*, and *Miss Julie*. Meanwhile, he was also proofreading his latest book, *Den goda viljan* (*The Best Intentions*), a novel based on his parents' youth and early marriage. Bille August's film version of *The Best Intentions*, Swedish television's most ambitious project to that date, was the big hit of the Christmas TV season in Sweden in 1991. A shorter, feature-length version had its international premiere at the 1992 Cannes Film Festival.

BERGSTRÖM:   *For an old man sitting by the sea, you have an unusually heavy work load. Don't you think it will soon be time to take leave of the theater, as you have already done with film?*

BERGMAN:   I will. It's absolutely necessary. I look forward to enjoying what I perceive to be absolute freedom, which is being able to sit here in my chair at any hour of the day and read a book I think is fun to read. Or a heavy tome that is hard work to read, and requires me to think over what I've read, underline, and make notes. And then enjoy a movie, take a walk, read the newspaper, and do some writing. As stimulating and enjoyable as it is to work with theater, there is a demand implied in the work which is beginning to weigh heavily on me.

BERGSTRÖM:   *Recently, you've been involved in very large productions, such as* Peer Gynt, *and now the new opera version of* The Bacchae.

BERGMAN:   That's right. But, nowadays, I only do things I think are fun. I've done far too much theater in my life for rational, logical, or economic reasons. Because it's been important for the Royal Dramatic Theater in Stockholm, or for one actor or another.

BERGSTRÖM:   *Is there any halfway position? You once told me you planned to conclude your theatrical career with some small performances on lesser stages, with a few young, beautiful actresses.*

BERGMAN:   There is a big advantage to having worked so many years in the theater. When I was young, experience was a highly valued commodity. Those who had been in the profession for many years and had much to teach were greatly sought after. This attitude has been absent for many years, since zero value has been attached to tradition, insight, and knowledge. Now, people with knowledge and experience—even though they may be old and tired—are once again sought after to help young actors. People have grown tired of woolly-mindedness.

BERGSTRÖM:    *Is this an area where you feel you have something to give?*

BERGMAN:    I don't mean to set up some kind of program. But I think it's fun to be with young people and see that they are making use of me as a resource.

BERGSTRÖM:    *You're referring primarily to the actors?*

BERGMAN:    I'm talking only about them. No one else.

BERGSTRÖM:    *Isn't there any similar passing-on of experience and tradition from you to young directors in the theater?*

BERGMAN:    No, I don't think so. There are young directors who think it's nice to have me around. They nod politely and look interested, but I don't believe for a moment I can be of any use to them.

BERGSTRÖM:    *When we were working on* Images: My Life in Film, *we talked about how the 1968 student movement, viewed retrospectively, wreaked so much havoc in so many cultural fields. Was this due to woolly-mindedness?*

BERGMAN:    The theater was damaged in a devastating way. With film, market forces were still in control, but in government-subsidized theaters—and schools—there was a kind of cultural revolution that left nothing intact.

BERGSTRÖM:    *In the literary field, it could be said, with some exaggeration, that we lost a whole generation of poets and storytellers.*

BERGMAN:    I think that, today, outside the Royal Dramatic Theater, we have adult actors who could have been great thespians, bearers of tradition, but who suffered greatly due to a lack of instruction, and have, therefore, never come into contact with their true artistic identities.

BERGSTRÖM:    *There was an attempt to suppress the classics, wasn't there?*

BERGMAN:    Above all, the classics weren't to be played as classics. They had to be rewritten or butchered, reduced to public polemics or private confrontations. They were dismantled and disarmed. Instead of showing the unadulterated classics in all their explosive energy, an effort was made to reduce them to something cut and dried, clear and concise, easy to comprehend.

BERGSTRÖM:    *Since you came back from Germany, you have gone in for demonstrating the power in these classics again.*

BERGMAN:    I'm certainly not alone in that. There is a trend now to put on plays the way they are written, without trying to change them beyond recognition. But it took a long time to come around to this. A couple of decades.

BERGSTRÖM:    *The enormous success of* Peer Gynt, *with both critics and audiences, must please your immensely.*
BERGMAN:    Yes, but it isn't quite as fantastic as when, on returning to the Royal Dramatic Theater, I staged a production of Shakespeare's *King Lear* that ran to over a hundred full houses. It has never been a public favorite.

When Bergman did his first *Peer Gynt*, in Malmö in 1957, it was played almost uncut, running to about five hours, but in his latest production of this play he has cut it by about twenty percent.

BERGSTRÖM:    *Now,* Peer Gynt's *been staged with careful judgment, well thought out, not like in Malmö, where you simply did the whole thing as it was written.*
BERGMAN:    I suppose that's a symptom of age. Even playful works like this one have to be well thought out. To keep the rehearsals from getting tedious, it is necessary to give careful thought even to whims, gimmicks, and spectacular scenes.

BERGSTRÖM:    *I imagine it must feel tedious to start work on a production, but that the tedium turns to fun as rehearsals progress.*
BERGMAN:    It's actually the other way around. The fun part is in the conception. The playfulness, the dreaming, the fun and games are in the notebooks—the wonderful feeling of total freedom, that you can do anything you want. Then, when you have to codify this in contact with the script and the actors, that's when it's important to keep the fun from turning to tedium. You have to re-create it with painstaking care and attention to detail. I have to sit at my desk at home and draw scenery and try to transform what I thought was fun and fanciful into boring arrows and figures. Then this, in turn, has to be communicated to the actors and tap into their creativity, so that they, too, feel all the freedom, fun, and joy. For me, theatrical work has always been broken down into a fun period, when the time flies, and a dull, pedantic period.

BERGSTRÖM:    *Does the pedantic period cast its shadow over the fun period and spoil it?*

BERGMAN:    No, they're so divorced from each other. Then, there is a tremendous sense of satisfaction when I see that the actors are enjoying their work. When we get warm contact during the rehearsals, when they look eagerly at me because they sense we're on the same wavelength, on the same track. Then I feel that all the boring, hard work I've put into my direction books has been worthwhile.

In Bergman's production of *The Bacchae*, he has been careful to give members of the chorus individual faces instead of the anonymous masks that are the convention in ancient tragedy. He sees the chorus as a group of terrorists held together by the cult of Dionysus, now assembled in Thebes to take part in the cruel plot.

He has gone so far as to give each of them a name and life history, following in his imagination their journeys to Thebes right across the map of the ancient world, from as far afield as present-day Afghanistan and Pakistan. These stories will play no part in the action, but Bergman's intention is that they should influence the character portrayals.

BERGSTRÖM:    *We spoke earlier of absolute freedom. You have, undeniably, a nice opportunity now to write freely.*

BERGMAN:    I sometimes think of Lampedusa, who wrote *The Leopard*. He was an old Sicilian nobleman who lived in his somewhat dilapidated villa. Every morning, he took his briefcase and plodded down all the stairs to the trattoria on the corner. There he had his table, there he drank his espresso or whatever, and there he sat writing until lunch. Thus he passed the days, producing thousands of pages of manuscript. He apparently had no intention of publishing anything. For me, there is something fascinating about this, since throughout my whole life and career I have always worked with an audience in mind. Now, I'm looking forward to the summer. From May until Christmas I intend to sit here on Fårö and write just for the fun of it. It's a new feeling: I don't have to worry about whether it will be heard, seen, or shown.

BERGSTRÖM:    *But is this just another kind of artistic activity, alone in a room away from the big artistic machineries that otherwise keep you occupied?*

BERGMAN:    I have always envied my writer friends when they say: "I don't think I'll finish my novel this year. I think I'll need another year." What a wonderful sense of timelessness! Lampedusa was undoubtedly a happy man. For me, now able to live here on Fårö like an aging country gentleman, with a somewhat stormy life behind me, it's a delight to settle down to a peaceful existence in which I can write page after page here at my desk, taking pure enjoyment in letting my hand go. My sole audience and reader will be my wife, Ingrid, which is really quite enough for me.

BERGSTRÖM:    *There are many people who say that a text is meaningful as long as it has a single reader.*
BERGMAN:    I already feel great contentment today when I answer all the mail I get as a filmmaker. I can say quite honestly: "I'm sorry, but I've retired. I can't regard myself as being involved. Thank you for the honor, but I don't have time. I don't want to, I'm not playing the game anymore."

BERGSTRÖM:    *There's a curious aspect of* The Best Intentions *in relation to your autobiography,* The Magic Lantern. *You wanted to correct the picture of your parents, understand something that wasn't clear even when you wrote your autobiography.*
BERGMAN:    It's an even longer process than that. I started to come to terms with Mother and Father while they were still alive. For many years, my relationship to my parents had been very neurotic, a terrible business, with a great deal of hate and misunderstanding. My whole lifestyle, my whole way of existing and grabbing what I could in life, frightened both Mother and Father, since they had always lived under strict ethical laws. The only thing we had in common was that, ever since childhood, I had been plagued by a terrible sense of duty. That was one thing they had really succeeded in instilling in me, and it's still solidly in place.

BERGSTRÖM:    *Maybe it's not such a bad legacy?*
BERGMAN:    For someone like me, who has a somewhat hysterical disposition, with a constant need to run away and pull a blanket over my head, the whip in the flesh is undoubtedly a good thing. You must never run away, you must never try to shirk your responsibility. My parents taught me that in blood. But the picture of my parents that

emerged publicly from everything that was written in biographies and articles about my unhappy childhood and my horrible father—it wasn't true. My childhood was difficult in many ways, but it was also colorful and rich. I was never bored.

BERGSTRÖM:    *But it was the dark side that came out in your films?*
BERGMAN:    Yes, that was the visible side, the hellishness of bourgeois life and all that. But then I wrote *The Magic Lantern* and started to get another picture of Mother and Father. One day, while watching a Swedish TV series, I started thinking about a subject for a TV series of my own, encouraged by the fun I had had writing *Scenes from a Marriage*, an earlier series I had done. The first thing that came to mind was this business of Mother and Father, which I had been pondering for a long time. I had looked at photographs from their youth and started to put together what I knew. It was like jumping from one ice floe to the next. Some things Father had told me, some things Mother had told me, and a little I got from the family chronicle. Then when it started to come together it turned into quite a drama. At the end of *The Magic Lantern*, I have a chapter in which I visit Mother after her death. Afterward I didn't think it turned out so well. I just couldn't make it work, simply because I lacked a deep enough understanding. Today, I would be able to write that chapter much more successfully. Now, I have access to my mother's diaries, and, besides, I've written *The Best Intentions*—I know and I feel so much more.

It was truly a pleasure to delve into all of this and write about it. And during the course of the work, I felt I began to get to know my parents, their ambitions and their helplessness, their competence, their kindness, their anger, and their jealousy. I started to see them as two living human beings. It may be because I am very much a half-and-half product of Mother and Father. It's almost absurd how much like both of them I am. And I'm sure you can understand that, after this, every form of reproach, blame, bitterness, or even vague feeling that they have messed up my life is gone forever from my mind.

BERGSTRÖM:    *That must be great relief.*
BERGMAN:    It is a blessing. My brother died unreconciled. My sister is still raging. I am privileged.

# Face to Face with a Life of Creation

## ALAN RIDING/1995

EVEN FOR THE SHORT FLIGHT TO Stockholm from his
home on the island of Fårö, Ingmer Bergman confesses to swallowing
tranquilizers. So it is hardly surprising that he will not be in New York for
the four-month Bergman Festival that opens on Friday and celebrates
his extraordinary life's work as a movie, television and stage director
and as a writer. "I hate to travel," he said. "I don't go anywhere."

Of course, as might be expected of the enigmatic Swedish artist,
it is not quite that simple. Traveling also disturbs the ordered and
introspective life he now leads. Even the "demons" he tried to exorcise
in many of his films seem under control. "They know they can reach
me in the early morning and, if I stay in bed, they invade me from all
sides," he said with a laugh. "But I cheat them because I get up. And
they hate fresh air. I walk quickly in all sorts of weather—and they
hate that."

Now, at the age of 76, he directs two plays every year at the Royal
Dramatic Theater in Stockholm. And at his house on Fårö in the Baltic
Sea, he spends his mornings writing novels, plays and television scripts.
But since he stopped making movies in 1983, he has purposely turned
away from his fame.

He seems relieved to be out of the limelight. His last film, *Fanny and
Alexander*, took seven months to shoot and drained him of the will to
make more movies. Above all, he wanted time to deal with the unfinished business of his life without the disruptions of film making and

---

promotion. "I thought, 'Now it's over,' " he said. "It was a good feeling. And I decided as a principle not to give any more interviews."

On this point, however, he relented. The Bergman Festival, which is being produced by the Brooklyn Academy of Music, will include a near-complete retrospective of his films and his television dramas. It opens simultaneously on Friday at the Walter Reade Theater at Lincoln Center and at the Museum of Television and Radio in Manhattan. Two of his recent productions for the royal Dramatic Theater of Sweden are also part of the festival. And it was thanks to persuasion by Lars Löfgren, the theater's artistic director, that Mr. Bergman found himself one recent afternoon sitting in Mr. Löfgren's office, looking unhappily at a tape recorder.

He was dressed informally, a green cardigan over a brown sweater over a checked shirt. His thinning hair is now white; his hands trembled a little. But, even with a stubbly goatee, his sad, elongated face looked familiar. "I am very shy with people I don't know," he said. He was particularly worried about his English and had asked for an interpreter as security. But he had also made a deal with himself. For what he described softly as "the last interview" of his life, he said, "I will try to be absolutely honest."

What this meant, it transpired, was that a three-hour conversation about his life's work would involve only peripheral discussion of his more than 45 films, his numerous television dramas, the 130 or so plays and the handful of operas that he has produced, and the score of plays, the autobiography and the novels he has written. It was as if all these had by now taken on a life of their own—or had died. What interested him were the memories and feelings that still belong to him and continue to shape his work.

Yet, even for a man who has revealed so much of himself in his films and, more recently, in his 1987 memoir, *The Magic Lantern*, it was not always easy for him to talk. At times, he fell silent or sighed deeply. At other moments, he leaned backward anxiously, lowered his head or covered his face with his hand. Then, just as suddenly, he would break the tension with laughter, cheerfully describing himself as a "pedant" and a "nut case."

"Of course I am autobiographical," he said after one long pause. "I am autobiographical in the way a dream transforms experience and emotions all the time." But it was always like that. Since his childhood, he said, it was always a matter of playing games with fantasy and reality—and it still is today.

"The doors between the old man today and the child are still open, wide open," Mr. Bergman said. "I can stroll through my grandmother's house, and know exactly where the pictures are, the furniture was, how it looked, the voice, the smells. I can move from my bed at night today to my childhood in less than a second. And it has exactly the same reality."

His talent, of course, has always been knowing how to translate his memories, of pain or pleasure, into art. "When I write something horrible or depressing, I am not depressed or horrified," he said. "I am just at work. And what I am writing about is far away. I can stand in the center of a drama, hearing the people around me saying things, I can hear exactly the way they speak, and I look at them and I just write it down because what they do can be very astonishing for me. But I have already passed through it, mostly."

It was this gift that enabled him to step outside his life into his world. From an early age, he would try to escape the harsh discipline and short temper of his father, Erik, a Lutheran minister, and the moodiness of his mother, Karin, by writing, sketching, playing with puppets and magic lanterns and making theater.

Still, he was caught in an emotional helter-skelter. "I was very much in love with my mother," he said, barely minutes into the interview. "She was a very warm and a very cold woman. When she was warm, I tried to come close to her. But she could be very cold and rejecting."

At the age of 19, by now no longer on speaking terms with his parents, young Ingmar left home and, after a brief stint at university, found a menial job in the Stockholm Opera. It drew him into the world of theater. He began writing plays, which he now dismisses as "lousy," and was soon also directing plays in student and local theaters. When he was 24, he was hired as a "script washer"—to polish screenplays—by Svensk Filmindustri, Sweden's main production and distribution company. And movies entered his life.

"It was a good way of learning script-writing because what we saw was American film and what we admired was its dramatic structure, its way of telling stories," he recalled. "That's how I learned the profession.

Then, when I knew how to do it, I could throw it away and I had my own way."

Within a year, one of his screenplays had been turned into a movie, *Torment*, by Alf Sjoberg, Sweden's dominant director of the day and one of Mr. Bergman's subsequent mentors. (The Bergman Festival includes a retrospective of Sjoberg's films at the Museum of Modern Art in June.) Its success gave Mr. Bergman the chance to direct his first movie, *The Crisis*, and others soon followed.

By the mid-50's starting with *The Seventh Seal* and *Wild Strawberries*, the movies that founded the Bergman legend began to flow. Recognition came quickly: *The Virgin Spring* (1960) and *Through a Glass Darkly* (1961) won the Academy Award for best foreign film in successive years. Crucially, in 1960, Mr. Bergman also began working with Sven Nykvist, the Swedish cinematographer who has shot 22 of his films (and who will be the subject of a program in June at the American Museum of the Moving Image in Queens).

Throughout the 1960's, shaped by the bitter memories of his childhood, his movies mirrored his own intense and often gloomy vision of life and death. Then, in the early 1970's, he turned toward another turbulent facet of his life—his five marriages and numerous passionate affairs—and, in such films as *Cries and Whispers* and *Scenes From a Marriage*, both in 1973, he peered deeply into male-female relations.

"Bergman was the first to bring metaphysics—religion, death, existentialism—to the screen," Bertrand Tavernier, the French film director, noted. "But the best of Bergman is the way he speaks of women, of the relationship between men and women. He's like a miner digging in search of purity."

It was with *Scenes from a Marriage* that Mr. Bergman also discovered television. And it reminded him of his mother's bedtime stories. "She would read for an hour, then close the book and you had to go to bed," he said. "But you knew that next Wednesday we would sit there again. And television is to me a wonderful storyteller. The family can come together, discuss what they see. And there's another thing wonderful about it. It's on the air for one or two hours, then it's gone."

When *Scenes*, which was originally shot in installments for the small screen, was first shown on Swedish television, he was surprised by its impact. "I had to change my telephone number because people called me to ask about their marriage problems," he said.

Yet, throughout his career, film making caused him anxiety. It was one reason he liked to work quickly—"30 days yes, 40 days O.K., 50 days already too much." And it was perhaps the main reason he was relieved to give up movies. "You work eight hours and you make three minutes of the film and you know those three minutes have to be absolutely top," he said. "Sometimes, it would drive me crazy."

In contrast, theater brought stability. He was strongly attracted by the classics—Shakespeare, Molière, Ibsen and particularly his countryman August Strinberg—but he also directed plays by Pirandello, Anouilh, Tennessee Williams and Edward Albee. And, between 1952 and 1966, he was successively director of the main repertory theaters in Gothenberg, Malmo and Stockholm.

In fact, it was while rehearsing Strindberg's *Dance of Death* in Stockholm in 1976 that he was briefly detained on charges of tax evasion. It brought on a nervous breakdown and, although the case was dropped, he felt so betrayed by his country that he opted for exile in Munich, Germany.

He resided there for nine years and, in hindsight, believes that he overreacted. "It was silly to stay away that long," he said. "I was so angry when I left Sweden, but the anger went away." Once again, though, he sought refuge in the theater, directing 11 plays in Munich and making just two feature films, including *Fanny and Alexander*, which won four Academy Awards in 1984. When he finally returned, he went "home" to the Royal Dramatic Theater, known locally as the Dramaten, where he had first attended a play at the age of 9. He even remembered the occasion—a Sunday matinee in March 1928—and the place where he sat. "Sometimes in the silent hour of the house, between 4 P.M. and 5 P.M., I go in there and sit in that seat," he confessed. "Sentimental, nostalgic. But then I lived in this house all my life."

As if to anchor himself back in his country—"this country of gray boring compromises that I so love"—he chose works by Strindberg, *A Dream Play* and *Miss Julie*, to be among his first productions. They were followed by *Hamlet*, a sexually charged production that was performed at the Brooklyn Academy of Music in 1988.

In late May and early June, the Dramaten will be taking Mr. Begman's critically acclaimed versions of Shakespeare's *Winter's Tale* and Yukio Mishima's *Madame de Sade* to Brooklyn, while his newest production, Molière's *Misanthrope*, will probably travel to BAM next year. (The troupe performed *Madame De Sade* there in 1993.)

Mr. Bergman clearly relishes working with the Dramaten's 80-member permanent company. As a movie director, he liked to use the same actors and actresses (and, in the cases of Max von Sydow and Liv Ullmann, with whom Mr. Bergman has a daughter, launched their international careers). And many of the actors who now appear in his stage productions (like Bibi Andersson in *The Winter's Tale*) were previously in his films. Somehow, all those who work with him become part of his broad family. "He takes great care of his actors," said Donya Feuer, the Dramaten's American-born choreographer. "He listens to them and looks after them."

But whether it is theater, film or television, it is all, as Mr. Bergman puts it, "playing games." And in the end he said, what counts is the audience: "One task is to make people laugh and be happy and forget themselves. But another is to show them what is unbearable and terrifying in a way that they can bear it and learn from it."

Certainly, Mr. Bergman himself can now face things that once haunted him. "When I was young, I was extremely scared of dying," he said. "But now I think it a very, very wise arrangement. It's like a light that is extinguished. Not very much to make a fuss about."

He remains a pessimist: how can one not be, he asked, surrounded by such "horrifying and unbearable" reality? But "if I am in a good mood, I am a pessimist in a good mood. I won't allow myself my depressions."

Only occasionally does the dark Bergman resurface. "Is suffering a part of your education as a human being?" he wondered aloud at one point. "Is there a pattern that you can't see, is suffering a part of that pattern, is there a real grace, or is it a coincidence?" He sighed. "I'm not ready to discuss this."

Old age has clearly mellowed him, however. He has found contentment in his long partnership with Ingrid Karlebo, a well-to-do woman then in her early 40's who left her husband in 1971 to marry the director. The womanizing of his early years Mr. Bergman now views as "a big mistake." Years of estrangement from several of his nine children are also over.

Most crucially perhaps, through the books he has written in recent years, Mr. Bergman has made peace with his parents. The fiercely confessional tone of *The Magic Lantern* set the stage. Three novels followed, one about his parents (*The Best Intentions*, which became an award-winning movie directed by Bille August), one about his father (*Sunday's Children*, which was made into a film, directed by his son Daniel) and one about his mother (*Private Confessions*, for which he was written a television version).

The last proved the hardest because it involved discovering a different mother, a woman whose most intimate feelings were reserved for a secret diary that she kept until two days before her death in 1966. Mr. Bergman remembers his father reading the diary through a magnifying glass and slowly realizing that "he did not know the woman he was married to." It is with an episode from this diary that Mr. Bergman has completed the trilogy. "I have the feeling that I was so unfair to my parents when I was young," he said. "Now I feel very satisfied and happy that I have done this."

He nodded toward the clock in Mr. Löfgren's office and warned he would soon have to leave. There was one final question: Had he become such an acute analyst of human behavior by undergoing therapy? "No, never," he said quickly. "If I didn't have my profession, I think I would be sitting in a nut house. But I have been unceasingly at work, and this has been very healthy for me. So I had no need for therapy."

He rose slowly to his feet. The director who always meticulously prepared every film or play now seemed also to have brought order to his life. "I will make some productions here in this theater," he said of his immediate plans, "and I will go to my island and read books I did not have the patience to read or the patience to understand. And I will listen to music." He seemed pleased by the way he had finally staged things. "It will be a very good life, I think."

# Encounter with Ingmar Bergman

JAN AGHED/2002

INGMAR BERGMAN will turn 84 this summer, but he shows no signs that his creativity or energy is flagging. After a successful staging of Henrik Ibsen's *Ghosts* at the Royal Dramatic Theater of Stockholm, he turned to the other icon of Scandinavian theater, August Strindberg. In an experimental radio adaptation of *The Pelican*, he included fragments of an unfinished play by Strindberg inspired by Arnold Böcklin's painting *Der Toteninsel*. Now, Bergman is preparing to write and direct an important television project in which he will return to the protagonists of *Scenes from a Marriage*, the acclaimed television series he made thirty years ago. Erland Josephson (79) and Liv Ullmann (63) will again play the roles of Johan and Marianne. When, on the telephone, he agreed to meet me and be interviewed for *Positif*, he talked with evident enthusiasm about the opportunity to shoot the sequel with a new digital video camera. Filming is scheduled to start this fall and to last eight weeks.

He meets me in the lobby of the *Dramaten*, the Royal Dramatic Theater. He ran this venerable institution from 1963 to 1966 and returned many times in subsequent years to direct celebrated productions. As he guides me along the hallways and the stairs to the rehearsal room and the office he still maintains on the third floor of this impressive building, he asks if I have read *Doktor Romand*, the Swedish translation of Emmanuel Carrère's short novel *The Adversary*. When I tell him it was one of the most unpleasant reading experiences I have ever had, he laughs and says: "Yes, it creeps under your skin in a very disagreeable way, but it is awfully well written!"

From *Positif*, no. 497 (July–August 2002). Reprinted by permission. Translated by Brigitte Sion.

It turns out that while rehearsing Ibsen's play, Bergman gave a copy of Carrère's book to every actor. They discussed the book during rehearsals. Bergman's idea was that the story of the criminal Dr. Romand had significant similarities to *Ghosts;* Ibsen's characters also live a destructive lie. "Ibsen describes an intense deception that lasts a lifetime. Façade, disguise, and lies consume a human being from the inside. That's why Romand's story was so useful to us. It's a great book, fantastic and fascinating, and at the same time horrible and unpleasant. After I read it, I thought that it could be transformed into a film as is, that it had to be made into a film." Bergman was not aware of the films based on Romand's tragedy and directed by Laurent Cantet and Nicole Garcia. When I mention them to him, he shows great interest and says he is impatient to see them.

Strikingly, even today, in conversation, Bergman reveals that he has lost none of his passion for or fascination with the cinema. He talks with youthful enthusiasm of his films, old films, new films, old and young directors, his favorite directors and, last but not least, of his own collection of videos and 35 mm prints. His curiosity about and love for the cinema have remained intact since he started to go to the movies as a youth. Personally, I have never met a film director, particularly of Bergman's age, with such an insatiable hunger to see films.

He tells me that the governing board of the Swedish Film Institute, the equivalent of the French Cinemathèque, has made a special decision for his benefit. Every spring, he requests 150 films from the Institute's archive. In June, all these films are delivered by truck to his house on Fårö Island, where he can view them in the ultra-modern screening room that he has built. All summer long he sees a movie at three in the afternoon, five days a week, often in the company of his children and vacationing grandchildren. Each Monday, he gives them a program which lists the films that will be screened that week.

Besides these 150 titles, there is another list consisting of the most interesting or most talked about films that have been shown to the public the previous season. Their distributors kindly make them available for Bergman. With only a slight delay, he can thus follow recent production, not only in Sweden but all over the world. If you mention François Ozon's *Under the Sand,* he will tell you it is a superb work that impressed him so much he watched it many times.

Additionally, Bergman lovingly cares for a private collection consisting of 400 titles on celluloid and a video library of 4,500 films compiled by a London-based company that has specialized in videos since that format was born. He projects the videos on a giant television screen.

It is therefore not surprising that Bergman has an encyclopedic knowledge of cinema history, from an artistic as well as a technical perspective. It matters little that his opinions about certain directors and their works seem unorthodox or opposed to the general view.

Take, for example, his assessment of Orson Welles. "To me, Welles is a phony. He is greatly overrated, empty, and uninteresting. *Citizen Kane*, which I have in my collection, for example, is of course cherished by all critics, always topping their lists of the best all-time films. To me, this is incomprehensible. Look at Welles's performance. It's cheap. Welles wears a mask, playing a potentate who is meant to be William Randolph Hearst, but we see the seams of his mask and his own skin all the time. Terrible! No, it's a bad movie, deathly boring in my opinion. *The Magnificent Ambersons*? Oh no! Very boring as well. I never liked Welles as an actor either. In Hollywood, there are two categories of people: actors and personalities. I find this distinction very useful. Welles was a unique personality. But as Othello . . . I will not even tell you what I think, it couldn't be published."

Though there are two exceptions, Bergman has nothing positive to say about Michelangelo Antonioni. "I was never enthusiastic about Antonioni, except for two films that are completely different from the others: *La Notte* and *Blow Up*. I have *Il Grido* on video: my God, what a bore! Desperately dull. You see, Antonioni never completely learned his job. In fact, he is an aesthete. If, for example, he found a certain street for *The Red Desert*, he would have the houses of the damned street repainted. This is the shortcoming of the aesthete. He concentrated on the individual shot, but couldn't understand that a film is a rhythmic flow of images, a breathing, a moving process. To him, by contrast, everything depended upon this shot, and then that one, and then another one. To be sure, his films have brilliant details.

"By contrast, *Blow Up* is incomparably well assembled. The same with *La Notte*, which I also have, and to which I return sometimes with great admiration and great pleasure. It's a wonderful film partly due to the young [Jeanne] Moreau. But this *Avventura* that was so celebrated! No, thanks! I feel nothing for it. Only indifference. All in all, I can't fathom why Antonioni was so highly regarded. As for Monica Vitti, I've always thought she was a bad actress.

"I have a very different feeling for Federico Fellini and his films. He used to call me '*fratello mio.*' At one point, the two of us and another of my favorites, Akira Kurosawa, were each supposed to make a segment of a film produced by Dino De Laurentiis. The idea was that we would each do a love story. I wrote my scenario and flew to Rome where Fellini was finishing *Satyricon*. We enjoyed our time together for three weeks while waiting for Kurosawa, who was suffering from a severe pneumonia attack. Eventually, De Laurentiis gave up and said there would be no film.

"Very frankly, it was difficult for Federico to decide which story he was going to tell. I had written and brought a very precise and organized script, while Fellini had a three-page outline that he intended to develop into a script with one of his writing partners. They did manage to write something, if I remember correctly, but everything fell through because Kurosawa's frail health prevented him from traveling. In Rome, I spent time with Fellini in the studio. I watched him work on *Satyricon*. I very much regret that this film by the three of us never got made. I liked Fellini's persona. I visited him and Giulietta Masina on the coast for a memorable Easter dinner. We were very fond of each other. And of course, I continue to watch his films. I like *La Strada* and *Amacord* most.

"If we talk about film directors whose work has meant the most to me at a basic level, we must begin, first and foremost, with Victor Sjöström. Then comes Marcel Carné, and Kurosawa, and Fellini. I name these in no specific order. I just have a very special relationship to them. I try to see Sjöström's *The Phantom Carriage* [1921] at least once a year. It has become a tradition to begin my movie season with *The Phantom Carriage* and end with *The Girl from Stormy Croft* [1917]. I am very attached to these two pictures. Seeing them again and again has become a kind of tradition. It's an addiction. Or, if you prefer, a vice. When Victor's Hollywood movies are discussed, one mentions *The Wind* [1928] first, which is indeed a remarkable work. But personally, I find *He Who Gets Slapped* [1924] even more remarkable. It's unbelievable that he adjusted to Hollywood and managed to be innovative at the same time."

Later in his life, Sjöström [whose career as a director ended in the 1930s] was an artistic consultant for Svensk Filmindustri (or SF, the large production company behind most of Bergman's features until *A Passion* in 1969). It was during this period when Sjöström's 28-year-old admirer directed his first film, *Crisis* [1946], in the company's studio at Rasunda, in the Stockholm area.

"He was such a lovely old man," continues Bergman, "generous in advice, simple, but very wise. 'Don't make a fuss when you direct,' he would tell me. 'Don't create difficulties for you and your team. Don't worry about making sophisticated camera movements. You don't know how to control them yet, so don't concern yourself with them. Don't make the actors' work complicated. Stick to simple, bare sets.' Invaluable advice for a young iconoclast excited to be experimental!

"I guess I have a certain weakness for silent films from the second half of the 1920s, before cinema became infected by sound. At this time, cinema was creating its own language. There was Murnau and *The Last Laugh* [1924], with [Emil] Jannings, a film told exclusively with images, with extraordinary dynamism and fantastic sensuality in its visual choices, superbly directed. Then Murnau made *Faust* [1926] and eventually his masterpiece *Sunrise* [1928]. Three astonishing works, which tell us that Murnau—at the same time as [Erich von] Stroheim in Hollywood—was well engaged in the process of creating a largely original and autonomous language. I have many favorites among German movies of this period.

"To be honest, I must confess that I have a weak spot for post–World War I UFA films. But when I started to work for SF as an assistant in the script department (this was in 1942; I was 24), my main task, along with my five or six co-workers, was to apply principals of American drama to the material we had. On floor below us, there were three screening rooms for the distribution department. They showed films constantly. As soon as I had a moment, I would go downstairs to watch some. We had unlimited access to American films and the American methods got so much under our skin that it became impossible to write or revise a script without applying Hollywood rules. When I directed my first films, I was so happy to have these solid foundations to rely upon. Later, I got rid of them, of course; but in the beginning, it was a firm and vigorous support.

"As for American dramaturgy, none of it touches me more than the films of that old Viennese Billy Wilder. I can see the greatness of John Ford as a director, but his films don't speak to me. With Wilder, it is the opposite. He is a virtuoso with the actors. He always casts them with perfection, even Marilyn Monroe. I met him when he was shooting *Fedora* in the Bavaria studios. I was in Germany preparing *From the Life of the Marionettes*. I've always loved his films."

As a child and teenager, Bergman would go to the movies every time he could, especially to Sunday matinees. He often watched two screenings in the afternoon, the first at one p.m., the second at three.

"When, after a time, the price of a movie ticket rose way above my weekly allowance, I tried every means to find the money. But children at the time had an even tougher problem. On Sundays, after having listened to our father, minister Eric Bergman, preach, there was another ritual called 'church coffee.' We were required to attend and be on our best behavior. The trick was to disappear discretely in order to be on time for the first matinee. If the second show went on too long, I also risked being late for the other mandatory family ritual, Sunday dinner, which took place at 5 p.m. Thus, as a young movie fan, I was always running. Fortunately, our Stockholm neighborhood at the time had a number of small movie theaters, so I managed."

Were your parents shocked by your mania for film? "Not at all. Both went to the movies and loved them. I remember only one instance when my mother got terribly angry with me. I must have been 18 at the time: I had seen the latest film by Julien Duvivier. I said to her, "You have to see it." My parents took my enthusiasm seriously and went to see *Pépé le Moko* [1937]. My mother was furious. Duvivier's film was not acceptable entertainment for Minister Eric Bergman and his wife. How could you like such horrible, immoral filth? After that, I stopped recommending films to my parents.

"My memory of this incident is still very vivid. It reminds me of another episode that took place at a festival in France at the end of the 1960s. I can't remember why I was there. I was before an audience of reporters and someone asked what films had most influenced me. I candidly answered that Carné and Duvivier had a decisive impact on my desire to become a film director. Between 1936 and 1939, I was deeply affected by *Quai des brumes*, *Hôtel du Nord*, and *Le Jour se lève* by

Carné, as well as by Duvivier's *Pépé le Moko* and *Carnet de Bal*. I thought that if I became a director, I'd like to make films à la Carné! His pictures touched me powerfully. But when I mentioned Carné and Duvivier at the French festival, the audience reacted collectively with a derisive and scornful giggle. I could see the expression on their faces: this Bergman is so stupid, such an idiot! Had I said Jean Renoir, everything would have been fine. But how could someone in their heart of hearts believe that Carné and Duvivier were any good?

"If I am not mistaken, the so-called *'politique des auteurs'* was very popular at the time. Under François Truffaut's pointing finger, most influential French critics had repudiated what they called 'le cinéma de papa.' Jean-Luc Godard was praised as the new cinema idol, and so on. Hence, it was a terrible *faux pas* on my part to pay tribute to two old farts! But I still enjoy watching their films. I do so joyfully; I think they are very good. They convey a distinctive sadness, tenderness, and sensuality that I find absolutely superb."

Truffaut and Godard, like a number of other critics who wrote for *Cahiers du Cinéma*, found Bergman's *Monika* to be a revelation when they saw it a few years after its famously harsh reception in 1953. Afterwards, as Antoine de Baecque notes in his book *La Nouvelle vague: portrait d'une jeunesse* (1998), *Monika* became a model for the *nouvelle vague* as the movement's young writers advanced towards careers in directing. Godard wrote about *Monika* with great admiration. Now, years later, *Monika*'s director notes that "there is a symbolic scene in *The 400 Blows* [1959] when the kids steal Harriet [Andersson, the star of *Monika*]'s picture from the window of a movie theater. I liked Truffaut very much. I admired him. His way of addressing an audience, of telling a story is fascinating and moving. It's not my way of telling stories, but his films reveal a wonderful relationship to the cinematographic medium. *Day for Night* is a magical film. I can see some of Truffaut's films again and again without growing tired of them. *The Wild Child*, for example. Its humanism made a great impression on me."

Nevertheless, Bergman expresses fierce and unfaltering resistance to Godard and his avant-garde impulses. "I have never been able to connect with any of his films. I have never understood them either. Truffaut and I met many times at film festivals. We had an instant understanding, which extended to his films. But I find Godard's films affected, intellectual, full of themselves, and, from a cinematographic point of view, pointless and frankly tedious. Endless, dull, Godard is desperately boring. I've always thought that he made films for the critics. He made a movie here in Sweden, *Masculin-Féminin*, that was so boring it made my hair stand on end. No, I'd rather speak about Claude Chabrol, the third chief director of the *Nouvelle vague*, who specialized in criminal dramas. He is a great storyteller in a very specific field. I always had a weakness for his thrillers. I feel similarly about Jean-Pierre Melville, whose stylized aesthetics of criminal drama is accompanied by an excellent sense of lighting. I very much enjoy watching his films. Moreover, he was one of the first directors really to understand how to use Cinemascope in a sensible and sensitive way.

"A French critic, writing about my film *Autumn Sonata,* said that 'Monsieur Bergman has started to make Bergman films.' He didn't mean it as a compliment. On the contrary! However, I think he made a smart and incisive remark that really cut me to the quick, because I knew exactly what he meant. He was absolutely right. This is what a director has to avoid at all cost. Fellini made some Fellini movies, not many actually. He didn't live long enough to make more. But look at Andreï Tarkovski. For him, leaving the Soviet Union was a complete artistic disaster. Take *The Sacrifice.* This film is a hopeless waste. Erland Josephson, his main actor, wrote a wonderfully funny and revealing radio piece about a summer night when Tarkovski and his team were shooting outdoors. It eventually became a theater play.

"And yet Tarkovski gave me one of the best and most unforgettable experiences in my life and in cinema. Late in the day, in 1971, I was watching a film with Kjell Grede (a Swedish filmmaker) in a screening room from SF. Afterwards we took a look at the screening booth where a number of film cases were lying. 'What's that?' I asked the projectionist. 'Some fucking Russian film.' And then I saw Tarkovski's name and told Grede: 'Listen, I read something about this picture. We have to watch it and see what it's all about.' We then bribed the projectionist so that he would show it to us . . . And it was *Andrei Rublev.* And so, at about 2:30 a.m., we both came out of the screening room with gaunt eyes, wobbly, completely moved, enthusiastic, and shaken. I will never forget it. What was remarkable is that there were no Swedish subtitles! We didn't understand one word of the dialogue, but we were nonetheless overwhelmed. Tarkovski made another film that I like a lot, *The Mirror*.

"Erland Josephson played in two of his films, and he used to talk a lot with Tarkovski. Erland told me that Tarkovski had an unusual idea about his performers. He didn't want them to act at all. Anyway, I still think he was a fantastic human being. But let me tell you about the strange relationship I had with him. One day, he was in Gotland (a large island off the eastern coast of Sweden, separated by a thin strait from Bergman's famous Fårö) to shoot outdoors scenes for *The Sacrifice*. It would have taken me twenty minutes to get there but I didn't go. I thought about it a number of times. Here is someone who meant so much to me, who influenced me decisively—perhaps more because of his attitude about life than as a film director. So why didn't I visit him when he was so close? I think it was the issue of language. He spoke neither English nor German, two foreign languages in which I feel reasonably comfortable. He spoke a bit of French, a bit of Italian, and we would have had to communicate through an interpreter. But for the matters I wanted to discuss with him, I could not use an interpreter. It would have been impossible. Thus, we never met. I regret it now, especially because he had so little time left to live."

When he was still making films, did Bergman take into account what the critics were writing? Did he ever worry about the way his works were received? At one point, he interrupts our conversation by waving a finger at me and saying, "You attacked me more than once! I considered you one of my enemies!" He then bursts into laughter. "Not to worry. You observed me for years. It's good." But Bergman mentions other critics less cheerfully and tolerantly, critics who have left painful scars.

"At the beginning, I had a difficult time of it. Nobody remembers this now. I can still recite some of my early reviews. About *Sawdust and Tinsel*, a prominent critic from an evening paper wrote, 'I will not stoop to consider Mr. Bergman's latest stream of vomit.' And then there was an influential literary critic, a big name in cultural circles, who deigned to see *Smiles of a Summer Night* and then warned his readers that it was the 'dirty fantasy of a pimply young man. I am ashamed to have seen this film.' To see such reactions in print was neither encouraging nor entertaining. I had to face much similar opposition."

Critics from other countries seem to be wiser than their Swedish colleagues in evaluating your films. "That may be true. But at the same time, you have to understand something. This so-called fame that is attached to my name as a film director is completely and fundamentally foreign to me. It is as if people were writing or talking about a remote cousin, someone distant from me. In fact, I almost never watch my old films."

Because you don't like them? "No, that's not the reason. It is because they overwhelm me, they shake me. I am swept by a surge of memories—often very painful—that relate to the shooting. There is something wonderful in staging for the theater. You direct a play, it is shown to the audience a number of times, and then it's gone. But films remain. And their existence can be agonizing. Sometimes, you discover that they have been manipulated by insensitive hands and that they were massacred. As you know, each print of a film begins with a leader for the projectionist. For the leader of *Persona*, I put in a shot of an erect penis. It was just three or four frames. Since film runs in the projector at 24 frames per second, you can imagine how long the image of the penis was visible on screen . . . one sixth of a second. It was a subliminal image. Yet it was discovered. This film triggered great interest outside Sweden and was shown pretty much everywhere, but the erect penis was always cut! So I checked the Swedish negative and, believe it or not, the penis wasn't there either! Fortunately, I was able to find a print of the film where the leader was untouched, including these four frames, and I had a copy of the negative made as a basis for new prints. But this discovery really shook me.

"When people attend a theatrical performance, at the Dramaten for example, it is important to me that they be completely aware that they are seated in a theater. The same should be true when watching a film. It is essential that audiences recognize the miracle of cinema, its unique ability to capture the human face. A director must work very hard to build a scene to maximum effect so that it functions in an absolutely perfect way. Cinema is a marvelous medium because just like music, it transcends the intellect and directly touches the emotions. A good close-up at the right moment can have an enormous effect. If a close-up is shot wisely, composed well, correctly lit, concentrated upon a good actor or actress, you can allow it to continue on screen as long as you want! When I was still active as a film director, my great dream was to make a feature film that consisted of a single close-up.

"To get back to the distant cousin I told you about earlier, I never considered myself anything more than as a craftsman, a hell of a skilled craftsman, if I may say so myself, but nothing more. I create things that are meant to be useful, films or theatrical productions. I've never felt the need for . . . what's the word? . . . *sub specie aeternitatis*. I have never created for the sake of eternity. I was only interested in producing the good work of a fine craftsman. Yes, I am proud to call myself a crafts-man who makes chairs and tables that are useful to people."

# INDEX

CONVERSATIONS WITH FILMMAKERS SERIES
PETER BRUNETTE, GENERAL EDITOR

*The collected interviews with notable modern directors, including*

Robert Aldrich • Woody Allen • Pedro Almodóvar • Robert Altman • Theo Angelopolous • Bernardo Bertolucci • Tim Burton • Jane Campion • Frank Capra • Charlie Chaplin • The Coen Brothers • Francis Ford Coppola • George Cukor • Brian De Palma • Clint Eastwood • Federico Fellini • John Ford • Terry Gilliam • Jean-Luc Godard • Peter Greenaway • Howard Hawks • Alfred Hitchcock • John Huston • Jim Jarmusch • Elia Kazan • Buster Keaton • Stanley Kubrick • Fritz Lang • Spike Lee • Mike Leigh • George Lucas • Sidney Lumet • Roman Polanski • Michael Powell • Satyajit Ray • Jean Renoir • Martin Ritt • Carlos Saura • John Sayles • Martin Scorsese • Ridley Scott • Steven Soderbergh • Steven Spielberg • George Stevens • Oliver Stone • Quentin Tarantino • Andrei Tarkovsky • Lars von Trier • Liv Ullmann • Orson Welles • Billy Wilder • John Woo • Zhang Yimou • Fred Zinnemann

CPSIA information can be obtained
at www.ICGtesting.com
Printed in the USA
BVHW081310300119
539043BV00003B/200/P

9 781578 062188